OCLC# 38732215

H37
1998

D0592366

The Other Feminists

SUSAN M. HARTMANN

The Other Feminists
Activists in the Liberal Establishment

Yale University Press   New Haven and London

Printed in the United States of America.

Library of Congress Cataloging-in-Publication Data
Hartmann, Susan M.
The other feminists : activists in the liberal establishment / Susan M.
Hartmann.
p. cm.
Includes bibliographical references and index.
ISBN 0-300-07464-6 (alk. paper)
1. Women in public life—United States.   2. Feminism—United States.
3. Women's rights—United States.   4. Liberalism—United States.
I. Title.
HQ1391.U5H37   1998
305.42′0973—dc21   98-15218
                                                                  CIP

A catalogue record for this book is available from the British Library.

The paper in this book meets the guidelines for permanence and durability
of the Committee on Production Guidelines for Book Longevity of the
Council on Library Resources.

10 9 8 7 6 5 4 3 2 1

CONTENTS

ACKNOWLEDGMENTS

Thinking about the debts that I have accumulated in the research and writing of this study makes me aware of how poorly the image of the solitary writer reflects the actual creation of a book. Many individuals who are or were associated with the organizations that I write about encouraged me with their enthusiasm for the project and helped me find sources. Gloria Johnson not only gave me photographs and access to International Union of Electrical Workers records at union headquarters but also commented on the draft of my chapter about the IUE. Ruth Weyand and the late Winn Newman also read an early draft of the IUE chapter and shared their own copies of key documents. Thanks also to Jim Quigel, IUE project archivist, who assisted me as I worked my way through the collection at Rutgers University.

Hilah F. Thomas shared her knowledge of Church Women United and the National Council of Churches and put me in contact with other helpful individuals. Margaret Clark, Dorothy Galbraith, Nancy Nicalo, and Olive Tiller made records available that were still in the NCC headquarters, and Sarah Vilankulu located photographs. I am grateful to the archivists who expedited my research in NCC records at the Presbyterian Historical Society and to Kristin Turner, who helped with documents and photographs from the CWU collection at the

General Commission on Archives and History of the United Methodist Church at Drew University.

I thank the staff at the Ford Foundation Archives, especially Nancy Weltchek, who facilitated my research there, and Jonathan Green who found photographs for me. Susan Berresford, Gail Spangenberg, and Mariam Chamberlain kindly commented on early drafts of the Ford Foundation chapter. For his help with ACLU archives, I am grateful to Thomas J. Rosko at the Seeley G. Mudd Manuscript Library at Princeton University. I also thank archival experts at the Library of Congress, the Sophia Smith Collection at Smith College, and the National Archives for Black Women's History in Washington, D.C. Eva Moseley and her staff at the Schlesinger Library of Radcliffe College have made me look forward to every visit there, and Marie-Hélène Gould helped me locate photographs. For permitting me to use their records at the Schlesinger Library, I am grateful to the officers of the National Organization for Women and the Women's Equity Action League.

Interviews with individuals who participated in the feminist activity described here enabled me to fill in gaps in the written record, test my early interpretations, and—not least—enjoy the company of some very dynamic people. For talking to me about their own pasts and the histories of these organizations, I am deeply grateful to Susan Berresford, Mariam Chamberlain, Chris Cowap, Myra Dinnerstein, Gloria Johnson, Ruth Mandel, the late Pauli Murray, the late Winn Newman, Suzanne Post, Alan Reitman, Faith Seidenberg, Gail Spangenberg, Sheila Tobias, and Ruth Weyand.

The women's studies and history departments at the University of Missouri—St. Louis and Ohio State University have furnished supportive and stimulating environments for my scholarly work. Although the time and energy devoted to building women's studies programs at two universities delayed completion of this study, I benefited tremendously from the support and friendship at the heart of those enterprises. I especially thank Marcia Dalbey, Mary Margaret Fonow, Judith Mayne, Terry Moore, Suzanna Rose, and Victoria Sork. Particular thanks go to Leila Rupp, my ever-generous sounding board.

I am grateful to my graduate assistants in the departments of women's studies and history at Ohio State who often went beyond the assignments I gave to provide new insights for my work: Julia Applegate, Hong Cao, Palahvi Das, Xioahong Hu, Eric Karolak, Christina Lane, Kathleen Laughlin, Lisa Maatz, Caryn Neuman, Kim Sanders, and Kate Wiegand.

This book has been greatly improved by the generosity of many individuals who read and commented on portions of it: Mary H. Blewett, John C. Burnham, Joan Cashin, Dorothy Sue Cobble, Mary Margaret Fonow, Nancy F. Gabin, Joyce Gelb, Cynthia Harrison, Lisa Kannenberg, Caryn Neuman, Rosalind Rosenberg, Leila Rupp, Stephanie Shaw, Birgitte Soland, Verta Taylor, Warren Van Tine, and Robert Zangrando.

A number of friends put me up when I was doing research and entertained me when I was not. I cherish the friendship of Nicki Nichols and Richard Gamble, Linda Henry, Jean and Gregg Johnson, Kay and Robert Montagné, and Ann Sheffield.

Both the University of Missouri—St. Louis and Ohio State University provided sabbatical leave and research support that, in conjunction with fellowships from the National Endowment for the Humanities and the American Council of Learned Societies, gave me the time necessary to research and write this book. Susan Laity and Gladys Topkis at the Yale University Press made the final product as fine as it could be.

The Other Feminists

Officers and staff of the International Union of Electrical Workers at a rally in Washington, D.C., August 1977. Left to right: Mary Callahan, Paul Jennings, Nora Clark Davis, Gloria Johnson, Ruth Weyand, and William Gary (Courtesy of the IUE).

CHAPTER ONE

Introduction

Feminist Footholds Everywhere

In this struggle we need women with footholds everywhere.

—Suzanne Post

I n the late 1960s and early 1970s, when a new wave of feminism swept across the United States, Susan Berresford, a 1965 Vassar College graduate, was a researcher at the Ford Foundation. Winn Newman, in the middle years of a legal career devoted to organized labor, served as chief counsel for the International Union of Electrical Workers (IUE). Joan Martin, a recently ordained African American Presbyterian minister, worked at the National Council of Churches (NCC). Dorothy Kenyon, a lawyer who had been born in the nineteenth century, helped make policy for the American Civil Liberties Union (ACLU) as a member of its executive board.[1]

None of these individuals played major roles in the National Organization for Women (NOW) or in any other independent feminist group. Yet they and others associated with the male-dominated liberal organizations in which they worked or held active membership made critical contributions to feminist change in the late 1960s and 1970s. They established the "footholds" whose importance Suzanne Post, chair of the Kentucky Civil Liberties Union, recognized in 1973 as she strategized with her ACLU colleague Pauli Murray over affirmative action. In fact, the actions of individuals and groups outside of organized feminism help explain how a sea change in attitudes, practices, and policies regarding gender roles could occur throughout the social and structural fabric of the United States, despite the relatively limited personnel and resources of the formal organizations of the women's movement. Moreover, the cultivation of feminism in major American institutions helps explain its continued power at a time when other social movements of the 1960s have languished.

In exploring the development of feminism in male-controlled liberal organizations, I here challenge both popular and scholarly conceptions of the women's movement. When did the resurgence of feminism begin? Who started it? What kinds of women and men took part in feminist activism? What issues comprised the feminist agenda? How did feminist change take place at a time when men monopolized power and authority? Scholars who have looked *inside* the women's movement at explicitly and exclusively feminist organizations and individuals locate its development in two parallel movements of white middle-class women that culminated in the founding of NOW and in the rise of the radical women's liberation movement. Different narratives emerge, however, when we look at a broader landscape.[2]

Not all of the women and men doing the work of feminism in these organizations in the 1960s and 1970s would have called themselves feminists. Some may have been indifferent to the label, and some may have recoiled from it. Alice Walker did not coin the term "womanist" until 1983, but it is likely that many of the black women considered here would have worn it easily. I use the term "feminist" in this book because all of the individuals I discuss worked toward goals that have been embraced by self-identified feminists and because all of them fit a definition of feminists that historians have found workable: these women and men recognized that women as a group occupied a disadvantaged position; they believed that position to be humanmade and thus alterable; and they worked collectively and politically to oppose various manifestations of male supremacy that limited women's lives and opportunities.[3]

Specifically, these individuals compelled their organizations to eliminate sex discrimination from their own policies and practices and to advocate feminist goals in the policy arena. Consequently, the organizations contributed to an increased awareness of gender stratification both among their own members and in society at large. They also supplied the women's movement with funds, expertise, and legitimacy. Because of their multifaceted agendas and diverse constituencies, they helped to make feminism a broad-based movement. And they addressed a wide number of issues that ranged far beyond those that directly concerned white middle-class women. Indeed, it is hard to identify a group of women whose interests were not addressed by at least one of these groups.

Scholars have located the sources of 1960s feminism in broad economic and demographic developments of the post–World War II era. In the 1950s increasing numbers of women went to college; growing numbers of married women worked outside the home; there was a rise in divorce and single-motherhood; and, beginning in 1957, the birth rate declined. Changing behavior led women to think about their lives differently. A majority of women bore their last child at age thirty-two, while ahead lay decades of their lives devoid of childrearing responsibilities. More women had the increased expectations that usually accompany a college education. More women saw themselves not just in maternal and domestic roles but as workers outside the home. And fewer women could count on men to support them and their children.[4]

These changes fueled the feminist consciousness that turned to activism in the 1960s. Studies of this development have focused on mainstream feminism as manifested in such groups as the national and state commissions on the status of women, the National Organization for Women, and the Women's Equity Action League; and they have analyzed radical feminism as expressed in local women's liberation groups. In most portrayals, mainstream feminism developed in a fairly straight line from the President's Commission on the Status of Women (appointed by John F. Kennedy to examine the condition of women) in 1961 and the publication of *The Feminine Mystique* in 1963, through passage of Title VII of the Civil Rights Act of 1964, to the founding of NOW in 1966. And radical feminism emerged first in the black freedom struggle and then in the New Left between 1965 and 1967.[5] A view that takes in the terrain beyond organized feminism, however, enlarges and deepens such accounts.

Not all women affected by the postwar economic and demographic changes joined either the mainstream or radical wing of the women's movement. As a number of studies have demonstrated, the feminists who founded NOW or who launched radical women's liberation groups were not starting from scratch. In their examinations of working women in the 1940s and 1950s, for example, Dorothy Sue Cobble, Nancy Gabin, and Ruth Milkman all recount challenges to sex discrimination by women in labor unions. Such scholars as Susan Lynn, Cynthia Harrison, and Leila Rupp and Verta Taylor have likewise described activism on behalf of gender equity in other locations during the 1950s.[6] Building on such work, I have unearthed an even broader range of early activities that contributed to the feminist revival and demonstrate continuities in reform. In addition, I show that the embrace of feminist goals in mixed-sex liberal organizations was not simply a response to the actions of NOW and the radical feminist movement. Rather, those feminist expressions sometimes moved parallel with or even ahead of organized feminism.

Women in the International Union of Electrical Workers raised the issue of sex discrimination in the 1950s, seeking to implement in practice the gender equity promised by their union's constitution. The IUE campaigned vigorously for the Equal Pay Act of 1963, and when the act and, a year later, Title VII went into effect, the leadership called upon local unions to exhibit "militant watchfulness" in detecting and acting against sex discrimination.

One of the links connecting the old feminism of the suffrage era with the new can be found in the American Civil Liberties Union. Dorothy Kenyon, a foot soldier in the suffrage campaign of the teens, pressed the ACLU to support abortion rights in the 1950s, and she and her colleague Pauli Murray pushed for greater efforts on behalf of sex equity in 1965. That same year women in the National Council of Churches issued a "radical challenge to the Church," criticizing those male leaders who interpreted Christ's message "in such a way as to minimize the personhood of women." Several years before "consciousness-raising" swept through radical feminist groups and into mainstream feminism, NCC women spoke of the need to "help women validate their interior feelings" and gain confidence in themselves.

Scholars of mainstream feminism have acknowledged the presence of African American women, including the ACLU's Murray (a founder of NOW), Aileen Hernandez, the second president of NOW, and Shirley Chisholm, a founder of the National Women's Political Caucus. Key union women like Caroline Davis and Dorothy Haener of the United Auto Workers also appear in accounts of the women's movement. And studies of radical feminism have documented the considerable attention radical groups paid to racial issues and to concerns of poor and working-class women. Nonetheless, relatively well-educated, relatively privileged white women continue to emerge as the primary actors in contemporary feminism.[7] Moving beyond these groups and into male-dominated liberal groups, however, this book brings into view the critical action undertaken by African American as well as white women, by working-class as well as middle-class women, and by men as well as women.

Just because minority women did not flock to explicitly feminist organizations does not mean that they lacked feminist instincts. On the contrary, Murray and Eleanor Holmes Norton in the ACLU, Joan Martin and Emily Gibbes in the NCC, Gloria Johnson, Doris Austin, and Mae Massie Eberhardt in the IUE, and thirty-seven Concerned Minority Women at Ford all prodded their organizations to challenge the gender status quo. A number of these black feminists did more: they stressed to their colleagues and supervisors that race shaped gender, and they focused attention on the particular needs and concerns of women of color. At the Ford Foundation and the NCC, for example, African American women compelled officials to recognize the routine disregard of the needs of minority *women* in programs designed to promote racial justice.

Such actions underscore the critical relationship between the civil rights movement and the women's movement. That link has been amply documented by Sara Evans with regard to the impact of the black freedom struggle on the development of radical feminism, but scholars have not fully captured its influence on the mainstream wing of the women's movement. In this book I examine a number of elements that influenced how these mixed-sex organizations dealt with women's issues. But no factor carried as much force in shaping an organization's feminist agenda as a prior commitment to civil rights. Such a commitment heightened awareness of injustice in general, set precedents to which feminist goals could be attached, and—equally important—encouraged black women to raise feminist issues. These African American women, in turn, called upon the authority of their identities as black women to translate their organizations' position on civil rights into support for women's rights.

This study demonstrates further that some individuals found their way to women's rights issues via an earlier commitment to racial justice. Both Winn Newman and Ruth Weyand, IUE attorneys who helped shape the union's antidiscrimination program, had histories with the civil rights struggle that stretched back to the 1940s. Faith Seidenberg was a lawyer for the Congress on

Racial Equality (CORE) when she began to challenge male dominance in the ACLU. And a number of white feminists associated with the NCC had engaged in antiracist activities as members of Church Women United since the 1940s and 1950s. The majority of individuals, black or white, promoting feminist projects in these groups were middle-class professionals, but by no means all. Among the groups I study, the IUE naturally housed the largest number of non–middle-class advocates for women. Mary Callahan, an IUE executive board member, preferred to promote feminism with other working-class women and men, rather than with middle-class feminists, whom she considered "snobbish," self-promoting, and unappreciative of the benefits of unionism.[8] Feminist demands also emanated from clerical staff at the Ford Foundation. And these blue- and pink-collar women put their particular class-based stamp on the feminism they practiced.

Men in these organizations also pushed for feminist change. Male advocates of gender equity in the IUE included not only Winn Newman, the middle-class professional, but also local union officers like business agent Bob Wire at the General Electric plant in Fort Wayne, Indiana, and chief steward Robert Delano at General Electric's factory in Salem, Virginia, who zealously contested discrimination against their women union members. Harold Howe II, an executive at the Ford Foundation, moved along a different path to feminism, but he too came to champion the cause of gender equity within and outside of the foundation.

The diversity that characterized the men and women who promoted women's concerns outside the movement gave feminism a much broader agenda than can be discerned from the goals emphasized by NOW and other mainstream feminist groups. Over the years, ratification of the Equal Rights Amendment and the right to abortion have stood out as the primary goals of feminists for a number of reasons. Because these were the issues that powered a wave of antifeminist backlash, they compelled NOW to focus most of its attention on them. The media, their antennae tuned to drama and controversy, have likewise focused their coverage of the women's movement on these two issues. And these were issues that white mainstream feminists believed could unite women across a broad spectrum.

To be sure, the mixed-sex liberal groups of this study also supported ratification of the ERA and reproductive freedom and, in fact, contributed considerable resources to the key aims of organized feminism. But these groups gave as much if not more attention to a wide range of issues that included equal pay for work of comparable worth, sterilization abuse of poor and minority women, access to traditionally male blue-collar jobs and to the ministry, lesbian rights, nonsexist language, women's studies, and violence against women.

What issues each organization took up depended on its historical purpose, the nature of its constituencies, the particular demands of the feminist advocates within it, and the particular pressures of feminists outside it. Because of black women's advocacy, for example, the Ford Foundation and the NCC showed particular concern for the needs of poor women and women of color. Harriet Pilpel's commitment to the right of privacy in matters of sexuality, along with the ACLU's historical attention to the disadvantaged, made that organization an early and consistent advocate for the reproductive rights of poor women. And the Ford Foundation's longstanding internationalism meant that it would attend to the interests of women in development projects abroad. Combined, these organizations acted on behalf of professional women and blue- and pink-collar workers, welfare mothers, lesbians, students, women of color in the United States, and women worldwide.

Studies centered on explicitly feminist groups also omit the story of how feminist ideas and practices were disseminated into society at large. In the mid-1970s, only about 300,000 individuals belonged to independent feminist organizations. Even in 1978, a decade after the reemergence of a women's movement, NOW had just 125,000 members, the National Abortion Rights Action League 90,000, the National Women's Political Caucus 50,000, and the Women's Equity Action League 3,500. Surveying feminism in 1977, Maren Lockwood Carden concluded that "if the movement had not found many sympathetic listeners and workers within the institutionalized segments of society, it probably would have disintegrated during the early 1970s."[9]

This study both draws upon and challenges social-science theory about the birth, development, and outcomes of social movements. The ecumenical affiliations among religious women that helped spark feminism in the NCC illustrate the importance of preexisting networks, ties that "resource mobilization" theory posits as important to the development of movements. The money, credibility, publicity, and other assets that the groups in this study provided typify the forms of assistance that "allies" lend to insurgent groups. These organizations similarly exemplify the establishment organizations or "polity members" that scholars employing "political process" or "political opportunity structure" frameworks consider important factors in determining the success of social movements.

Sociologists have noted that social movements can co-opt "civic infrastructures," such as professional organizations, religious groups, and labor unions, but these scholars have not examined or explained how particular organizations actually become allies. Overall, social-science theory tends to identify movement activists and organizational allies as two separate phenomena. Such a theory cannot account for the actions of individuals unconnected to social-movement organizations who nonetheless promote movement goals within an established organization and thereby turn it into a movement ally.[10]

By examining the workings of feminist change at the micro level, this study helps us explain how establishment organizations came to apply some of their resources to the women's movement and to institutionalize feminism within their structures. These organizations were, after all, dominated by men, and incorporating feminist goals into their agendas would not directly or materially benefit the majority of leaders and members. To use the language of sociologists, these were "conscience" constituencies rather than "beneficiary" constituencies. The question becomes, then, what influenced the consciences of the men who had the power to change the organization's agenda?

It would be difficult to exaggerate the critical importance of previous civil rights activism in turning these groups to feminist advocacy. In addition, each organization had been founded with a broad enough purpose that individuals could expand and reinterpret it to encompass women's rights. External pressures promoted that reinterpretation in various ways. Federal bans against sex discrimination in employment exerted a complex influence in the IUE: on the one hand, the union needed to protect itself from liability for sex discrimination; on the other, feminist men and women in the IUE used the law to turn recalcitrant unionists into supporters of equity. External pressures on the Ford Foundation took the form of grant applications from feminist groups.

Regardless of the extent of outside prodding, women—and some men—within the organizations held the key to each group's becoming a feminist foothold. This book examines how individuals exploited the particular histories and structures of their organizations and the multifaceted strategies employed in different groups. Newman, for example, continually referred to the IUE's historical commitment to represent *all* workers and framed the interests of women as an integral part of the class interests of all workers. Feminists at the Ford Foundation and the IUE educated others about women's issues by getting authority figures from the outside to speak to their organizations. Activists promoted female solidarity by establishing internal networks at the Ford Foundation as well as at women's caucuses in the NCC and ACLU. They also forged ties with women outside their group: women at Ford helped establish Women and Foundations, and the IUE's Gloria Johnson was among the founders of the Coalition of Labor Union Women.

Feminists in the National Council of Churches capitalized on its particular organizational structure, which incorporated relatively autonomous divisions. Instead of taking a proposal to the NCC governing board, where conservative as well as liberal denominations formed the power structure, a division could act by securing agreement of its own committees and obtaining funding from supportive denominations. In this way the Division of Education and Ministry and the Division of Church and Society, with the leadership of black feminists, established projects for which they could not have obtained organization-wide support. That distinction, however, was often lost on the public as the media reported actions conducted by a division as if they represented the council as a whole.

The organizations considered here stood between feminism as a social movement and the formal political system. All fell within the liberal wing of the American political order in the 1960s, but they represented quite different areas of civil society. All had substantial resources but in varying kind and degree; their resources and status as polity members equipped them with the ability both to promote feminist policy and to assist in its implementation. The Ford Foundation, by far the largest philanthropic organization in the nation, possessed abundant financial resources, and moreover, its endorsement in the form of a grant could prove as important as the cash itself. The IUE had access not only to the national policy process (at a time when organized labor still wielded considerable muscle in the Democratic Party) but also to the shop floor, a major site of policy implementation. The ACLU's incomparable legal expertise helped feminist suits make it through the judicial system. And the NCC claimed moral authority as well as the attention of millions of Americans through its constituent denominations.

Occupying a position between organized feminism and the state, these groups lent their respectability to feminist policy demands, often through congressional testimony. Harold Howe II, who had been commissioner of education in the Johnson administration before joining the Ford Foundation, testified on behalf of gender equity in education. At hearings on proposed legislation, IUE president William Fitzmaurice urged members of the House Committee on Education and Labor to protect pregnant women from employment discrimination. And Jane Campbell, a member of the NCC's Justice for Women working group, provided testimony on behalf of the organization for a federal domestic violence prevention program.

Examining these particular groups extends our understanding of feminism because together they worked toward a strikingly broad range of feminist goals. The IUE concentrated on economic equity, the Ford Foundation devoted considerable attention to education, the ACLU occupied the vanguard of reproductive rights, and the NCC promoted ordination of women. In addition, in these organizations we can observe feminist advocacy both by employees operating in their workplaces and by members and leaders operating in voluntary organizations. In the Ford Foundation, promoters of feminism occupied jobs in professional *and* support-staff positions. Activists in the IUE included professional staff, elected leaders, and the rank and file, as was true for the NCC as well. In the ACLU, feminist activism took place initially and primarily among volunteers.

Each of these groups has extensive organizational records that document their histories. These, along with the papers of key individuals like Dorothy Kenyon and Pauli Murray, provided most of the material for the book. In addition, I interviewed central players in the feminist development of each of these organizations, a process that further enhanced my understanding of the progress of feminism in mainstream liberalism.

In order to capture the details and analyze the complexities of feminist change at the micro level, each chapter tells the story of a single organization, in roughly chronological order from the time in which the group began to address feminist issues. Both the IUE and the ACLU paid some attention to gender equity as early as the 1940s; the NCC began to take moderate feminist stands in the early 1960s; and the Ford Foundation, although it funded a few women-specific projects in the 1960s, joined the feminist bandwagon last, in 1970.

These chapters highlight a particular function each organization performed for feminism, even while they engaged a broad ranges of issues. The IUE helped to implement feminist policy; the ACLU became feminism's premier litigator; the National Council of Churches undergirded feminist claims with moral authority; and the Ford Foundation enriched the treasuries of the movement.

The participation and leadership of African American women was evident in the records of every organization; this participation is an important thread running through the book. Yet because African American contributions have so often been overlooked in histories of mainstream feminism—and were so significant—I discuss them as a whole in a separate chapter.

My concern in this book is primarily to explain the initiation of feminist change and the implementation of feminist principles and practice in large, male-dominated organizations. To ascertain these organizations' impact on the society at large is beyond my scope here. Nonetheless, I conclude with a brief discussion of how these organizations assisted feminism in the United States, along with reflections on the processes of feminist change.

CHAPTER TWO

Implementing Feminist Policy

The International Union of Electrical Workers

To me, women's lib is when men and women can work together.

—Laurie O'Gara

Laurie O'Gara's high-skilled job at the General Electric plant in Cincinnati, Ohio, had not come easily. Even though she had extensive training and experience in welding, General Electric originally classified her as a "helper." To move up to the classification of welder, she reported, "I fought for my job." She credited her union for supporting her, even though many of the men were uneasy when women began to work at what had always been considered "male" jobs.

In conceiving of "women's lib" as "when men and women can work together," O'Gara referred most directly to her own advancement, which depended on support from male unionists, who helped win her a skilled job in which she worked side by side with men. But her definition of feminism serves also to highlight the distinct principles from which the IUE's actions on behalf of gender equity derived as well as the distinct ways in which the union fostered feminist goals. The unity of *all* workers as a class and the obligation of a union to provide fair representation for *all* workers—men and women working together—constituted the imperative and rationale for the

IUE members and leaders who promoted women's rights and gender equity.

Leaders and experts within and outside of organized labor recognized the union's contributions to feminist change. Eleanor Smeal, president of the National Organization for Women, embraced the IUE as a "valiant ally" in the fight for women's rights. Joyce Miller, head of the Coalition of Labor Union Women (CLUW), asserted in 1980 that the union "stands second to no other Union in the AFL-CIO" in addressing women's concerns. The AFL-CIO president Lane Kirkland gave the IUE equally high marks when he identified it and CLUW as "the two organizations that have been at the very forefront of pushing the issue of wage discrimination to the center of our consciousness." And representatives of both the Equal Employment Opportunities Commission and the U.S. Civil Rights Commission held up the IUE as a model of union antidiscrimination activity.[1]

With 113,500 women comprising one-third of its membership in the late 1960s, the IUE pursued a multifaceted offensive against gender discrimination in the 1960s and 1970s. It educated its members concerning women's issues, began an antidiscrimination program, lobbied for laws on women's behalf, brought lawsuits on behalf of members that resulted in court decisions that benefited all working women, and initiated the fight for equal pay for work of comparable worth. The IUE played a prominent role in passage of the Equal Pay Act of 1963, spearheaded efforts for a national ban against pregnancy discrimination, and provided bodies and dollars for the Equal Rights Amendment ratification campaign.

Making Feminist Policy Work

None of the IUE's initiatives was more critical to bringing feminist change into women's lives than its efforts to ensure enforcement of antidiscrimination policy at the workplace. Achieving a favorable policy was one thing. Enforcing it was another matter altogether—a lesson middle-class feminists learned in their struggles to get the Equal Employment Opportunity Commission (EEOC) to enforce the ban against sex discrimination contained in Title VII of the Civil Rights Act of 1964. Channeling their anger into political organizing, these women founded NOW to serve as a pressure group on women's issues. But although NOW membership surged and new feminist organizations sprang up, these mainstream feminists lacked resources that organized labor was uniquely equipped to furnish.

Even after the EEOC acceded to feminist pressure and began to pay serious attention to sex discrimination, it did not have strong enforcement powers. It could issue guidelines for compliance with the law; but, unlike other government agencies, such as the Internal Revenue Service, which could initiate investigations

International Union of Electrical Workers legal counsel Winn Newman and IUE members at the Coalition of Labor Union Women convention in 1977. Clockwise from Newman's right: Gloria Johnson (with NOW button), Marian Cook, Elizabeth Taylor, Marge Wonderling, Robie Cagnina, Doris Austin, and Marjorie Bush (Courtesy of the IUE).

independently, the EEOC's authority was limited to responding to complaints. Within these confines, it could investigate claims of discrimination and issue findings, seek voluntary settlements with employers, and ask the attorney general to prosecute offenders. But until the March 1972 amendments to Title VII empowered the commission to file suits, as Donald Allen Robinson asserts: "Redemption would depend on the persistence of black and female individuals and on the nature of the organizations that would support them." Even with this persistence, the agency necessarily had to concentrate on relatively few cases. Thus, most victims of discrimination could not count on the government to force an end to unfair practices or to compensate their casualties.[2]

The direct access to workers and the workplace held by labor unions uniquely situated them to become key players in the implementation of antidiscrimination laws—if they so chose. First, unions could inform workers about their rights under the law and educate them on the nature of sex discrimination. The need for such education was not confined to rank-and-file women. Shop steward Mary Callahan helped organize her electrical parts–manufacturing shop in Philadelphia for the United Electrical Workers (a precursor of the IUE) in 1935 and subsequently served in local, district, and national offices. But her interests did not include sex discrimination; as she recalled: "The postings on the board would say female or male. And we never questioned it; either as a union or I, as a person, never questioned it. . . . And it wasn't until the fifties and early sixties that this whole movement [against sex discrimination] got started." Although a few union women did challenge sex discrimination in the 1940s and 1950s, many more shared Callahan's view of the situation as normal. Thus, enforcement of new antidiscrimination legislation depended on the unions' using local meetings and publications to tell members about the new policies and heighten awareness about sex discrimination.[3]

Labor unions could also influence implementation of antidiscrimination policy at the collective-bargaining table; and if that failed they could challenge sex discrimination directly by processing grievances and filing lawsuits. Individuals considering whether to file EEOC charges or lawsuits faced odds stacked heavily against them. Women earning $3.50 or $4.00 an hour would have to confront employers who retained in-house counsel skilled in defending against discrimination suits and practiced in the art of delay. For such individuals, financial and legal assistance from their unions became critical.[4]

If their access to workers and the workplace gave unions the *capacity* to implement antidiscrimination policy, the law itself gave them a strong *incentive* to do so. Because Title VII banned discrimination by labor unions as well as by employers, women and racial minorities could file charges against their unions, which in turn could face stiff fines. Yet even the threat of legal culpability did not prompt all unions to fight discrimination. How assiduously unions responded to their obligations under the Equal Pay Act and Title VII and the degree to which they worked for feminist goals varied tremendously. No union can boast a perfect record in fighting discrimination, but the IUE stands out as one of the most progressive unions in representing women's interests. Contrasting the lip service paid by other unions to antidiscrimination efforts, IUE's Mary Callahan observed: "Well our union says it has to work; and if it doesn't work, somebody's going to move in and make it work."[5]

No single factor can explain why the IUE took the vanguard among unions on women's issues. New federal laws against sex discrimination combined with women's determination to press grievances generated powerful leverage, but why did the IUE pursue gender equity far beyond what the law required? To be sure, it was trying to survive—even grow—in an industry that employed large numbers of women, but so were other unions. Like other unions organized by the Congress of Industrial Organizations (CIO) in the 1930s, the IUE grew out of a radical movement dedicated to unifying and representing all workers—a commitment that was exemplified in the union's support for civil rights in the 1950s and 1960s. A unique group of individuals—rank-and-file and leaders, black and white, men and women—built on and expanded the older commitments. With few ties to either the liberal or the radical women's groups emerging in the mid-1960s, these women and men pursued feminist agendas parallel with and even in advance of the independent women's movement.

The IUE and Gender Before the 1960s

Mary Callahan's recollection of how normal sex segregation and discrimination seemed to men and women alike in the 1940s indicates the immense reorientation of assumptions and priorities that was necessary for the IUE to represent the interests of its female members. The union's acquiescence in management policies that confined women to particular jobs and then assigned them the lowest rates of pay directly harmed women's interests. But at the time, the IUE followed a variety of practices that belittled women and underrated their place in the union. As late as 1960, for example, its monthly publication, *IUE News,* featured photographs of movie actresses and dancers seductively posing in bathing suits or other scanty attire.[6]

Yet alongside this tradition of sexism ran a tradition of union democracy and a commitment to gender equity that was expressed long before the new wave of feminist activism emerged in the 1960s. Like Callahan, most of the IUE's leaders and many of its members had begun their union affiliation in the United Electrical, Radio and Machine Workers (U.E.). During World War II, the U.E. stood out as one of the most vigorous unions addressing women's concerns, thanks to the large number of women workers in the industry and also to the strong left-wing and communist presence in the union. Along with the United Auto Workers (UAW), the U.E. hauled the two industry giants, General Electric and Westinghouse, before the National War Labor Board for sex discrimination. The unions won a favorable ruling, but the war ended and the board disbanded before the employers could be forced to implement the principle of equal pay. The U.E.'s national strike in 1946 forced some concessions narrowing the wage gap between men and women; but attention to women's issues disappeared as the fierce struggle over communism ripped through organized labor in the postwar years.[7]

In 1949, the CIO expelled the U.E. and immediately chartered the IUE under the leadership of James B. Carey, a founder and former president of the U.E. and secretary-treasurer of the CIO. Carey was both a militant anticommunist who did not hesitate to use McCarthyish tactics against his enemies and a passionate liberal who shared a personal and political friendship with Eleanor Roosevelt. When Carey left the U.E., he took into the IUE the commitment of industrial unionism to represent the interests of *all* workers. A strong advocate for racial justice — "the CIO's point man in public civil rights matters," according to historian Robert Zieger — Carey served on the advisory board of the Congress on Racial Equality (CORE) and led 3,000 IUE members in the March on Washington in 1963. As early as 1957, when most liberals who thought about civil rights at all defined it as the South's problem and before a mass movement had emerged, Carey talked about racism as a national problem and pointed specifically to discrimination in housing and education in the North.[8]

The egalitarian and inclusive principles of industrial unionism accommodated concern for women's rights as well as civil rights, and the IUE incorporated the U.E.'s commitment to gender equity in its constitution. In the 1950s, IUE leaders focused that commitment on the issue of equal pay and played key roles in the fight for national legislation. David Lasser, who had worked with radical unemployed workers' councils in the 1930s, used his position as the new union's research director to focus attention on women's concerns. In 1954 he brought onto his staff Gloria Johnson, an African American with an M.A. in economics from

Howard University; Johnson quickly became the union spokes-person for women's issues and remained so for the next four de-cades. Lasser and Johnson represented the IUE on the National Committee for Equal Pay, while Carey labored to convince the AFL-CIO to support the bill.[9]

Male unionists, of course, had a direct self-interest in equal pay. Requiring employers to pay men and women the same wages would discourage them from replacing men with lower-paid women and thus protect men from female competition. Lasser's arguments mentioned the "lure to employers to gain an extra cheap dollar by substituting women for men at lower wages," but he posed equal pay as a class issue, emphasizing women's *need* for adequate income and the "enormous profits" employers gained from the exploitation of women workers. Carey did not even men-tion men's self-interest in his pleas to the male leadership of the AFL-CIO. Rather, he emphasized the injustice of wage discrimi-nation and framed equal pay legislation as a weapon against em-ployers in collective bargaining and as a necessity for unorganized women. To legislators, Carey mentioned the threat of "a low-wage economy geared to the rising female labor supply"; but he highlighted the vital contributions employed women made to the economy and to the international reputation of the United States, and he presented sex discrimination as a "grave and continuing civil rights issue . . . even though women are no longer a minority in this country." Whatever hidden motivations lay behind Carey's public rationale Carey linked women's rights to civil rights and stressed "the equality of *all* workers" as "a fundamental principle of our union." In rhetoric at least, the IUE made women's inter-ests as women an integral part of all workers' interests as a class.[10]

What male leaders might understand in their minds, women workers felt in their bones. In the 1950s, the leadership was not alone in posing women's rights as integral to the egalitarian prin-ciples of industrial unionism. Nancy Gabin has shown that rank-and-file women in the United Auto Workers were also complaining about gender inequity. In the IUE, a few grassroots women also gave voice to those feelings. In the supportive setting of the first IUE-sponsored national women's conference in 1957, women rose one after another to testify to the wage inequities they suffered. "The men are nowhere near as skilled as the women operators, but our base rate is lower than that of the common laborer," reported a woman from the Westinghouse plant in Trenton, New Jersey. "Women earn less than the lowest male rate of sweeper," echoed a union woman from Sandusky, Ohio. A worker with seventeen years' experience at the General Electric factory in Lynn, Massachusetts, protested that men doing the same work earned five cents an hour more than women and that the company was training only men for the new computers being installed.[11]

Even in less hospitable circumstances—at the union's national conventions, where women found themselves vastly outnumbered —a few women raised their voices in the 1950s. In 1956 delegate Mary Klaric reported that despite the two rate increases won for women by her lamp industry local, women's wages still lagged behind those of the lowest-paid men. Pointing out that the national practice of bargaining for percentage increases only widened the gap between men and women, she implored the union to pay more attention to the concerns of women workers, because "the union is about the only source we have to look forward to in this fight." Some women stood up for their rights on the shop floor as well, struggling to upgrade wage rates on "women's" jobs, for example, at a G.E. plant in Warren Ohio, and a Westinghouse factory in West Virginia.[12]

But the most important source of pressure on IUE leaders to take initiatives on behalf of women workers in the 1950s was its ferocious battle with the U.E. for the allegiance of locals. With women comprising one-third of electrical industry workers, it is not surprising that both sides seized on women's issues in the struggle that lasted through the decade. In 1950, U.E. president Albert Fitzgerald told convention delegates that their union had lost to the new IUE in locals where "leaders pursued this policy of discrimination against women workers" but that the U.E. had won "where women were encouraged to come forward in union leadership." Thereafter, the U.E. vigorously encouraged union women's activism and fought against discrimination on the job. And at least in Westinghouse plants, the U.E. proved more ambitious and successful than the IUE in defending married women against layoffs and ensuring women's seniority rights.[13]

If the IUE's record suffered in comparison with that of the U.E., it nonetheless stepped up its actions on behalf of women members as a result of the bitter competition. Like its rival, the IUE targeted women in organizing materials, with brochures boasting "IUE-CIO Leads the Fight for Women Workers" and "IUE-CIO's Fight for Women Workers Pays Off." The U.E. attracted four hundred delegates to a national women's conference in 1953, and the IUE followed suit with its own national women's conference in 1957. Both organizations made sex discrimination an issue in collective bargaining—though with little success—and both lobbied for national equal pay legislation.[14]

Although the U.E.-IUE split increased concern for women's issues, it also fractured worker unity. By 1960, the IUE had established itself as the dominant union, but the battle had weakened both unions at the collective-bargaining table. There they confronted the tactic of "Boulwarism" (named for its creator, G.E. executive Lemuel Boulware), practiced by General Electric, pacesetter for the industry. This strategy, throughout the 1950s and early 1960s, was to announce a "take-it-or-leave-it" package with an aggressive public-relations campaign, thus in effect negating the principle of collective bargaining. Not until 1964 did the National Labor Relations Board rule that these were unfair labor practices.

Until the 1960s, the union effected few actual changes in the workplace, where gender segregation and low wages in women's occupations remained firmly entrenched. The IUE placed discrimination issues on the bargaining table but proved unwilling to go on strike for them. In 1960, for example, the IUE identified elimination of sex-based wage differentials as a major bargaining goal, but its national contracts with General Electric and Westinghouse carried no such provisions. Although the IUE-Westinghouse national contract did not allow discrimination against married women or in seniority provisions, many local agreements did. Leaders of Local 711 at Westinghouse's Mansfield, Ohio, plant signed an agreement providing that "male and female employees shall be considered as separate groups except in such cases when female employees are engaged in male jobs." Local 202 officials in Springfield, Massachusetts, agreed to a clause denying jobs to married women if their husbands were able to work.[15]

Moreover, local union-management contracts were replete with anomalies, guaranteeing sex equity in one sentence and then proceeding to specify a range of disparate treatments. The agreement between Local 701 of Sandusky, Ohio, and Philco Corporation guaranteed "the rate for the job classification regardless of sex, color, or creed." But it went on to establish lower rates for female operators, sex-segregated seniority lists, and discriminatory treatment of pregnant workers. That three of the eight local representatives signing the agreement were women suggests how much gender stratification seemed the natural order to men and women alike. By 1960, the IUE had established a strong verbal commitment to gender equity but a chasm separated its words from deeds.[16]

IUE Leaders and the Resurgence of Feminism

The Equal Pay Act of 1963 and Title VII of the Civil Rights Act of 1964 served as key catalysts in pushing the IUE to match its principles with meaningful action. These laws made the union vulnerable to liability for sex discrimination, and Title VII forced organized labor to abandon its support for protective labor laws, with their discriminatory effects. Yet the union's transformation of feminist principles into actual practices was more complex than a simple response to new laws. The new legislation affected an organization that was already interested in addressing women's concerns. The laws gave ammunition to women who were already disposed to claim equality, provided IUE leaders who were already sympathetic to gender equity with leverage, and armed the union with a new weapon to brandish at the bargaining table on behalf of demands it had sought since its inception.

Moreover, as we have seen, IUE leaders played a direct role in gaining support for the equal pay measure. In a lobbying sweep by forty labor women through every congressional representative's office in 1962, nine represented the IUE. Once Congress passed the Equal Pay Act, the union leadership went out of its way to inform members of their rights under the new legislation. While noting that Congress had weakened the original bill by substituting "equal" work for "comparable" work, the *IUE News* gave prominent coverage to the bill's passage and explained to members how the law would operate. President Carey called for "militant watchfulness" by local unions; it was up to them, he said, to detect and act upon violations. In accord with most labor and liberal organizations, the IUE did not take a stand on the amendment that added sex discrimination to Title VII of the Civil Rights Act of 1964. Nonetheless, when Title VII went into effect in 1965, the IUE undertook an educational effort similar to the one it had launched for the equal pay legislation.[17]

Union efforts to educate members on and attack sex discrimination moved beyond relaying information about new federal policies. In 1966, while both NOW and the radical women's liberation movement were in their infancy, the IUE formally recognized gender issues by renaming its Department of Civil Rights, headed by African American William Gary, the Department of Social Action; the new division launched a program for women workers that was headed by Gloria Johnson. As one of the department's first actions, in 1967 it conducted a survey to determine the roles women were playing in local unions and held a

Mary Callahan, Gloria Johnson, and Elizabeth Taylor at an IUE women's conference, 1970 (Courtesy of the IUE).

national women's conference in which the issue of sex discrimination took center stage. In 1968, for the first time, the union's "President's Report" contained a specific section on "women's activities." These actions in turn helped to awaken rank-and-file members to the existence of gender discrimination and to encourage women to press claims for equity.[18]

As Nancy Gabin and Dorothy Sue Cobble have demonstrated for other unions, IUE initiatives up through 1967 indicate that the union was moving parallel to and sometimes in advance of mainstream feminism. In part, the development of gender consciousness in the IUE proceeded from the same source as the one that launched the formal women's movement. Key union leaders were associated with the President's Commission on the Status of Women, created by John F. Kennedy in 1961. Mary Callahan, who in 1959 had become the second female member of the IUE executive board, served as one of two labor representatives on the commission. Both James Carey and Gloria Johnson served on subcommittees of the commission. Experience with the commission introduced these union leaders to a wider range of issues and individuals than were present in the equal pay network and heightened their awareness of gender issues just as it did for the women who would subsequently found independent feminist organizations. Gloria Johnson's non-union affiliations continued to broaden when she was appointed to the Maryland Commission on the Status of Women, modeled after the national commission.[19]

Local and Grassroots Pressures for Gender Equity

A handful of local union members responded immediately to the new climate created by the federal antidiscrimination legislation and the IUE's spotlight on gender issues. In some cases, men took the initiative. Just a month after the Equal Pay Act went into effect, Joseph T. Hawkins, who headed Local 711 at Westinghouse's Mansfield, Ohio, plant, seized on the legislation as an opportunity to demand meetings with management. Noting that local officers had tried to discuss sex discrimination with management several times since the law took effect, he insisted that Westinghouse "cease its evasion of this Law of Equal Pay." In 1967 his successor got advice from IUE's Legal Department and then helped women who had been laid off on the basis of a sex-segregated seniority list file charges with the Equal Employment Opportunity Commission. Don Rock, president of Local 761 at G.E.'s Louisville plant, filed another early EEOC charge. Supporting the complaint of seven women who had been refused jobs, he pointed out that the company had hired five thousand men in the previous ten years but not a single woman.[20]

More typically, rank-and-file women took the initiative. Shortly after Title VII went into effect, Mary Owens from the predominantly female local at Ingraham Company in Bristol, Connecticut, filed a sex-discrimination complaint with the EEOC. Her charge resulted in a new contract that eliminated separate seniority lists for men and women, adjusted job rates and classifications to reflect actual skill and effort required, and provided women and men with equal opportunities to bid on job openings. Subsequently, coworkers elected Owens president of her nine hundred–member local.[21]

In 1965, women at the General Electric plant in Fort Wayne, Indiana, filed grievances that led to one of the IUE's earliest lawsuits against sex discrimination. Some of these women in Local 901 had been assigned to formerly "male" work at reduced wages. Sharon Drake, for example, replaced a man who was classified at grade R-17 and earning $2.86 an hour; her grade was R-9, at $2.21 an hour. Other women had watched men with less seniority pass them in the competition for better jobs. Helen Avery had worked at the plant since 1942, but when she sought promotion to the male equivalent of her inspection job, she lost out to a man with fewer than three years' seniority. Other grievants included Margaret Louise Burry and Rita Cook, who earned thirty-five cents less an hour than men who did the same janitorial work.[22]

No women sat on the grievance committee at the Fort Wayne plant, although they constituted around 40 percent of Local 901's five thousand members. But the male leadership, particularly business agent Bob Wire, took women's claims seriously and pushed them energetically. He called management's attention to its obligations under Title VII shortly after the law went into effect. As he began handling more grievances, he came to understand the pervasiveness of discrimination and the need for thoroughgoing changes in job assignment, posting, and bidding. The energetic Wire, along with local president Tom Willhelm, also pressured the IUE's Legal Department to act more vigorously. Protesting a decision between General Electric and union officials to seek resolution of EEOC charges through grievance procedures, he complained that the local was "completely out-manned and out-gunned" by the company's staff of experts. Affirming that "our resolve and determination to get a just and equitable settlement is higher than ever," he urged the leadership to take G.E. to court.[23]

The determination of Bob Wire and other male union leaders was all the more important because many women hesitated to join the suit filed by the IUE against the Fort Wayne plant in 1972. Although the union urged women to participate, only eighty of the two thousand female workers signed on to the suit. According to IUE associate counsel Ruth Weyand, who worked directly with the women at Fort Wayne and other plants, this response was typical. Usually only a handful of women in each local stepped forward to fight discrimination in pay and job assignment. Women based their decisions on individual conceptions of what was just and on what they perceived as good working conditions. Like Mary Callahan had in the 1940s, many women accepted the job segregation and pay differentials that pervaded the industry; they felt that men had a right to higher wages. Weyand believed that these women were reasonably satisfied with their work environment and enjoyed the sociability with other women with whom they had worked for years. These women were reluctant to anger foremen by filing discrimination charges; they feared retaliation, including assignment to dirty or arduous jobs. Even as late as 1978, when jobs no longer carried "male" and "female" labels, Callahan noted that women "rarely bid for jobs which will put them as a minority within a work group of males." As we shall see, these considerations did not limit women's participation in the fight against pregnancy discrimination. But at least through the early 1970s, it was largely owing to the IUE's vigorous publicity and litigation efforts that women recognized that job segregation constituted discrimination and that they were entitled to equal pay and opportunity with men.[24]

Those women bold enough to press discrimination charges seized on the new laws and used them to demand action at the national level when local officers resisted their claims. "What has happened to Paragraph 7 of the Civil Rights Bill?" demanded several women at General Motors' Frigidaire division in Dayton, Ohio (Local 801), protesting unequal access to overtime work in August 1965, shortly after the law went into effect. Failing to get satisfaction from their local officials, they did not hesitate to go to the union leadership. "Are we second class citizens? We are union members also," wrote Margaret Call to the international's president, Paul Jennings. Delores Fickert, another Local 801 member, had worked in the plant since 1938. Complaining about the overtime inequities as well as the promotion of a man with less seniority to a job she wanted, she too went all the way to the top. "If this goes to the Civil Rights Commission it will be proven that the female employees are being discriminated against by both the Union and the Company," she warned, and set a deadline ten days hence for action by the international. In December 1965, Fickert and twenty-eight of her female coworkers took their charges of sex discrimination to the EEOC.[25]

Another IUE member with more than two decades of seniority, Julia Kuc, worked at the Westinghouse factory in East Pittsburgh. "I bid on a male job SUPPLYMAN," she charged, but "I wasn't even given an interview." Kuc, too, recognized the importance of the new legislation. "Under the Civil Rights Law," she declared, "men and Women [sic] are equal if they are capable of doing the job." In November 1965, after her union representative claimed that there was nothing he could do, she filed an EEOC charge against the IUE and Westinghouse.[26]

In addition to pursuing sex-discrimination grievances, women members also grew more assertive on the floor at union conventions. Evelyn McGarr's fight went back to the 1930s, when she worked in an RCA plant in Montreal. She managed to get herself hired at the customarily male job of engraver in the tool room; she then persuaded her male coworkers to support her demand for an equal wage. Her election as secretary-treasurer of the IUE's

Canadian District in 1954 won her a seat on the union's international executive board. At the Canadian IUE conference in 1969, she exhorted women workers, "You don't get the right money if you don't have long pants or you don't fight for it." Doris Austin, who joined McGarr and Callahan on the IUE executive board in 1966, complained at the 1970 international convention that most of the men had left before consideration of a resolution on women workers. At the 1972 convention, delegate Barbara Bonenfant made a similar observation, asserting that "this shows discrimination against women right here." When the union leadership presented a resolution in 1970 calling for each local to establish a social action committee, Austin and Mae Massie Eberhardt objected to the proposed structure of the committees. While specifying that there be representatives for five areas of union concern, the resolution called for a women's activities representative only "when possible."[27]

The willingness of these women to challenge male delegates reflected both the importance of civil rights precedents for gender-based activism and the growing influence of the independent women's movement. Both Austin and Eberhardt, who held leadership positions in their districts, were African Americans with experience in the civil rights movement. Eberhardt had helped organize her electronics-production shop for the IUE in the 1950s. Subsequently her local, which was 75 percent white and 60 percent male, elected her president. Austin's specific commendation at the 1970 convention of a "women's liberation" group that had supported IUE women in a strike against RCA indicated the growing linkages between feminist activists and union women.[28]

From Protective Legislation to the ERA

By speaking out about women's concerns at union meetings and by filing discrimination charges, IUE women pushed their union to a historic break with tradition—a change that eventually aligned the union behind mainstream feminists' top priority, the

Equal Rights Amendment. But first the IUE had to shed its defense of protective legislation for women workers, a policy that unions had endorsed since the early 1900s. In the cases filed by Julia Kuc and Dolores Fickert—and in many other cases—both the union and the companies argued that state protective laws, rather than their own discrimination, kept women from job assignments and equitable overtime. To the charges of Fickert and her coworkers, they cited Ohio laws prohibiting women from working more than nine hours a day, from lifting more than twenty-five pounds of weight, and from working more than five hours without a half-hour break. Similarly, Julia Kuc's steward told her that the "male" job she wanted involved a straight-through shift; Pennsylvania law required that women take a half-hour break after five hours of work.[29]

The plaintiffs won in both these cases, with the EEOC ruling that the IUE and the companies had not explored all the possibilities within the federal and state laws for providing equal opportunity for women. Pennsylvania did, in fact, allow employers to file for exceptions to protective laws where necessary for gender equity; but women's increasing demands for equal treatment on the shop floor made the incompatibility between the equal opportunity guaranteed by federal law and the differential treatment of women workers under state law ever more obvious. The EEOC moved toward that conclusion at a measured pace until 1971, when several federal courts finally established that protective laws violated Title VII.[30]

The IUE had always stood with organized labor in general, defending protective legislation and consequently opposing the Equal Rights Amendment on the grounds that it would undermine these laws. But as protection faced challenges from women workers, government agencies, and feminist groups, the IUE reconsidered its position. Union leaders put the issue on the agendas of national women's conferences in 1967 and 1969 and at other union meetings. In 1967 delegates heard Dorothy Haener from the UAW and Pauli Murray, a feminist lawyer and NOW board member, call for full enforcement of Title VII even if doing so meant abandoning protective laws. Rank-and-file women seized the opportunity to demonstrate how they suffered under these laws. Creola Reese, who chaired her district's civil rights committee, charged, "We are held back by overtime bans on women. Many women need the work. . . . Many are head-of-household." [31]

Still, the union held to its opposition to the Equal Rights Amendment, testifying against it before the Senate Judiciary Committee in the spring of 1971. At the same time, however, the IUE narrowed its support for protective legislation to include only what could be considered beneficial and nondiscriminatory laws. Moreover, the union joined legal challenges to particular measures, participating in suits that struck down Kentucky's maximum-hours law for women and Ohio's law restricting the amount of weight they could lift. In 1971 the union's Legal Department instructed locals to assume that protective laws were invalid and warned that relying on such laws to deny equal rights to women workers could result in heavy damages against the union. [32]

The decisive push for the IUE's turnabout on the Equal Rights Amendment came from the national office. General counsel Winn Newman, with the help of Gloria Johnson and the Social Action Department, managed the delicate task of reversing the union's position on a policy it had held from its birth. In a speech at the 1972 convention, Newman pointed out that protective laws were now illegal. His report for the Legal Department discussed the status and expected effects of the ERA, which Congress had passed earlier that year. Gloria Johnson also included an extensive and positive account of the amendment in her report on women's activities. [33]

With this preparation, the 1972 convention adopted a resolution calling for reconsideration of the IUE's historical opposition to the ERA. It took the executive board just three months to study analyses of the amendment prepared by the Legal and Social

Action departments and come to a decision. At its December 1972 meeting, the board voted to endorse the ERA. The third major union to support the ERA (following the UAW in April 1970 and the Communication Workers of America in June 1972), the IUE paid more than lip service to ratification. Delegates from the IUE to the national AFL-CIO convention in October 1973 pushed for that body's endorsement; and the union continued its pressure in subsequent years, urging the AFL-CIO to stronger ratification efforts.[34]

Although its financial support was not as great as that of unions with larger treasuries, the IUE contributed funds and staff time to the ERA Ratification Council and its successor ER-America. Forming yet another link with the independent women's movement, Gloria Johnson served on the corporate board of ER-America and as its liaison with all labor organizations. The IUE urged local unions to join ERA coalitions and resolved to make a political candidate's stand on the amendment "a principal criterion" for union endorsement and support. Union members marched in demonstrations for the ERA, and leaders and staff, including President Jennings, Secretary-Treasurer George Hutchins, and Johnson, addressed ERA rallies. News of ratification efforts occupied prominent space in the *IUE News;* the union paid for radio announcements during the Florida campaign; and it joined the NOW-led boycott of unratified states and endorsed extension of the deadline for ratification.[35]

The Law and Lawyers as Engines of Change

If the Legal Department played an influential role in the IUE's shift to support of the ERA, it occupied center stage in the union's fight against sex discrimination in the electrical industry by pushing for vigorous and comprehensive implementation of the Equal Pay Act and Title VII on the shop floor. The two key figures were white lawyers Newman and Weyand, both with long-standing commitments to civil rights. Newman had fought racial discrimination as far back as his student days at the University of Wisconsin Law School in the late 1940s. He had hoped to put his skills to work for civil rights, but on the assumption that the movement would prefer black lawyers, he cast his lot with organized labor. Newman represented a number of unions, serving as associate general counsel at IUE from 1961 to 1965. Afterward, he worked for the EEOC, where he saw dramatic evidence of the systematic sex discrimination women faced in the workplace. Back at the IUE in June 1971, he resolved to be not simply a technician but an active shaper of union policy. Callahan captured Newman's energetic antidiscrimination efforts when in the mid-1970s she remarked that he was "really up to his neck in this thing." [36]

Newman's associate counsel, Ruth Weyand, also had a long history with civil rights issues, having been named in 1948 to the honor roll of the National Council of Negro Women for her work. She had represented stewardesses and railroad, garment, and packinghouse workers and had worked at the National Labor Relations Board (NLRB) before coming to the IUE in 1965. With feminist principles instilled in her by her parents, she also knew firsthand the problems faced by women workers who were wives and mothers. Although she had little contact with organized feminism initially, through her IUE work Weyand came into association with other feminist litigators, formed coalitions with feminist organizations, and eventually took a leadership role in the Women's Equity Action League. On her retirement in 1977, the president of the IUE praised her work against sex discrimination: "You have brought to our union your special concerns. And we thank you for it." [37]

While Weyand played a key role in developing and pursuing sex-discrimination charges and spearheaded the IUE's attack against pregnancy discrimination, Newman designed overall strategy and persuaded the union leadership to give priority to sex discrimination. The Legal Department expanded its informational role, sponsoring workshops for local representatives and initiating discussions of discrimination issues at union meetings. The department also published accounts of its activities in the union's biennial "Officers' Report" and kept local officers abreast of legal developments through its monthly publication, *Keeping up with the Law*. In addition, Newman helped shape the IUE's contract-negotiation demands regarding discrimination.

The heart of the Legal Department's antidiscrimination strategy was a comprehensive three-step procedure instituted in 1973 for identifying and correcting discrimination against women and minorities. As the first step, each local was to gather data on wage rates, job assignments, classifications, promotions, and pension plans and other benefit programs, in addition to examining the positions held by and benefits available to women and minorities. The second step required union locals to seek remedies for discrimination through grievances and collective bargaining. If this failed, as a third step the union would file NLRB and EEOC charges and lawsuits.[38]

Newman prodded the IUE leadership, and it in turn pressured district presidents, staff representatives, and local officers to implement the compliance program, with repeated letters and instructions from IUE president Paul Jennings. When locals proved sluggish, Jennings followed up with strong warnings. In July 1974, for example, he told field representatives that they were "required to implement the program . . . regardless of personal feelings . . . [and] even if such policies may not be popular with certain members." In addition, he instructed staff representatives to include the status of compliance programs in their semi-monthly reports and to submit written summaries of discussions of the program at local union meetings. Local officials felt the strong arm of the union hierarchy, but they could use that same bureaucracy as a scapegoat if they met with resistance from their constituents.[39]

If management refused to hand over data on employment and wages for women and minority men, Newman would file charges of unfair labor practices with the NLRB, insisting that such information was essential for monitoring antidiscrimination clauses in union contracts. In 1978 and 1979 the NLRB ruled that Westinghouse and General Motors must provide unions with data on the race and sex of job applicants, the numbers of women and minorities hired and promoted, their placement in jobs, and wage rates. The federal appeals court for the District of Columbia upheld the ruling in 1980, representing a victory for all unions and ensuring their access to a critical means of identifying and combating discrimination.[40]

The IUE implemented the second step in its antidiscrimination program during national contract negotiations in 1973, when for the first time the union gave serious attention to bargaining for gender equity provisions. Newman persuaded union officials that the IUE must fight for contract changes or risk liability for discrimination. Thus the union identified treatment of pregnant workers and plant-wide seniority and posting of job openings as two issues that required "special emphasis" at the bargaining table. Although General Electric refused to change its pregnancy policies, its concession to plant-wide seniority nationally and job-posting procedures subject to local bargaining marked a crucial victory. These reforms struck at the heart of the system of stratification by sex and race entrenched in the electrical industry. Plant-wide posting and seniority proved especially critical to women as the industrial sector of the American economy declined in the 1970s. When management confined women to a limited set of jobs, they were much more likely to suffer layoffs; plant-wide seniority and posting, however, greatly expanded the number of jobs women could "bump" into if their former jobs were eliminated.[41]

Although women were able to make some progress through contract negotiations, discriminatory practices were more typically eliminated only in cases where the IUE filed EEOC charges or took management to court. Its first lawsuit under the Equal Pay Act and Title VII, filed in 1970 on behalf of the women at Westinghouse's Mansfield, Ohio plant, won a settlement that awarded back pay to more than a hundred women, increasing the wage rates for nine traditionally female job classifications, and requiring plant-wide posting of and bidding for vacancies. Settlement of a similar suit against General Electric on behalf of IUE women at its Fort Wayne, Indiana, plant provided for more than $1 million in back pay and wage increases and the upgrading of nineteen job classifications. Charges and suits against a host of other companies followed. By 1974 the IUE had filed EEOC charges against General Electric and Westinghouse involving 170 plants, as well as six lawsuits against G.E. and three against Westinghouse. By 1981 the IUE had filed more than five hundred EEOC charges and more than fifty lawsuits on behalf of women and minorities, severely weakening the industry's system of racial and gender stratification.[42]

Though not given that name, the issue of equal pay for work of comparable worth, or pay equity, was embedded in the IUE's earliest sex-discrimination cases. In negotiations on the Fort Wayne case, for example, the union argued that women were entitled to equal wage rates not just for doing the same work that men did but also for jobs that were "comparable and equivalent" to those of men. Settlements in more than a dozen cases, including those at Fort Wayne and Mansfield, raised wage rates in predominantly female jobs. And in 1980 the IUE won a landmark decision from the Third Circuit Court of Appeals, which ruled that Title VII applied to wage discrimination even when the jobs were not identical.[43]

Activists in the pay equity movement regarded Newman as its "virtual founder." Throughout the 1970s he spotlighted the issue of pay equity in speeches to IUE members, scholars, congressional committees, and the EEOC. In 1972 he told an IUE district women's conference that courts were beginning to investigate whether employers had to offer equal pay when jobs were different but entailed essentially the same skill, effort, and responsibility. At a conference on women and work at Wellesley College in 1975, Newman preached legal activism. After listening to one scholar after another call for more research on occupational segregation and sex discrimination, he insisted that "the best and quickest way to get meaningful change is to enforce existing laws and compel compliance[,] . . . to enforce the law by filing charges and lawsuits." In 1978, as general counsel for both the IUE and the Coalition of Labor Union Women, Newman criticized the EEOC for failing to file pay equity suits and urged the House Subcommittee on Employment Opportunities to prod the EEOC and the Department of Labor to make the issue "a priority item." After Newman left the IUE in 1980, he carried on the pay equity struggle, directing litigation strategy for the American Federation of State, County, and Municipal Employees.[44]

Merging Gender and Class Interests

Although the IUE leadership never did away with indifference or opposition to the antidiscrimination program among its membership, it was able to deflect open rebellion through a number of strategies. Overall, the national leadership and especially the Legal Department took care to cast the issue in terms that folded gender interests into class interests, stressing antidiscrimination efforts as part of the union's historical struggle against management's exploitation of workers, and emphasizing the benefits antidiscrimination policies could bring to men as well as women. In a five-page spread featuring International Women's Year (1975), the *IUE News* included a section entitled "When Women Win, Men Advance, Too." The article condemned employers' use of women "as a cheap labor pool who could be substituted for men" and gave specific examples of how men gained from gender equity, both as workers and as husbands of employed women. The article even challenged the gendered division of responsibilities in the family, concluding, "though union-backed goals like day care centers . . . commonly are treated as 'women's issues,' they aren't, really. Those are men's kids, too."[45]

The IUE foregrounded class interests when it acted in the relatively few situations where men suffered from disparate treatment, and leaders went out of their way to broadcast those actions to the rank and file. Women, union spokespersons pointed out, were not the only workers with something to gain from gender equity. When the IUE defeated General Electric's attempt to lower men's wage rates as a means of compliance with court rulings on equal pay, the *IUE News* featured that victory with the headline, "Equal Pay Case Pays Off Equally." The IUE also litigated against pension programs that allowed women to retire earlier with more generous pensions than men, filing a national EEOC charge against G.E. in 1973. Another suit, against Sperry Rand Corporation, put more than $2.5 million into the pockets of men whose early retirement benefits had been less than those of women with comparable employment histories. When the union issued a press release covering a favorable district court ruling on pregnancy discrimination, it made sure to point out its other antidiscrimination efforts, including those that benefited men. Even when publicizing its successful suit against G.E. on behalf of six women who were refused jobs at its Tyler, Texas, plant because they couldn't meet the 5′7″ height requirement, the IUE noted that some men, too, fell short of the minimum.[46]

Along with challenging practices that disadvantaged men, the IUE also defended its white male workers against the imposition of what was termed "fictional" or "prehire" seniority. In order to protect women and minority men, who because of past discrimination had only recently won jobs, from being the first workers laid off in times of retrenchment, some courts had begun to mandate prehire seniority. Nonetheless, in line with labor's longstanding adherence to the inviolability of seniority, the IUE opposed any layoff plans that did not operate strictly by date of hire. In the settlement of lawsuits, at the bargaining table, and in discussions with the EEOC, the union worked to establish the broadest possible seniority units for promotion and layoff purposes, but it clung to strict seniority even when this risked perpetuating racial and sex discrimination. Although union leaders and members articulated the union position on seniority as a class issue, it clearly served the interests of longtime white male employees and revealed the limits of labor union feminism.[47]

Gender interests proved more compatible with class interests in Newman's efforts to encourage leadership enthusiasm for the antidiscrimination program. He frequently presented the IUE's work for gender equity as an organizing device, and wherever possible he included women in unorganized plants in national EEOC charges and company-wide suits. Although the leadership never adopted Newman's strategy as fully as he wished, the IUE occasionally referred to its antidiscrimination program in recruitment campaigns. In an attempt to organize General Electric's Appliance Park—East factory in Maryland, for example, the IUE brochure featured its challenge to the G.E. height requirement. And it took care to note that the union was also representing men who were unable to meet the requirement.[48]

When powerful IUE executive board members complained about the amount of time and money spent on equity issues, Newman used his most powerful argument: the potential legal liability if the union did not act aggressively against discrimination. Newman appealed to the IUE's historical commitment to equal treatment and its moral responsibility to represent all workers, and occasionally he pointed out that equal pay also protected men's jobs. But he most consistently focused on protecting the union from liability, warning that "if we fail to take more forceful action . . . our present course could result in the financial ruin of the Union." Even though the IUE did not create the sex-segregated workplace, Newman argued, it could be held liable along with employers for discriminatory wage rates and job-assignment systems. "Our compliance program should be recognized as a defensive program," he insisted, "in addition to the gains it promotes for our members."[49]

Although in retrospect, Newman discounted the threat of substantial union liability, some women's obvious willingness to sue their union as well as their employer did put the IUE in a defensive position and spurred its antidiscrimination efforts. Women in Local 630 at the Bacharach Instrument Company in Pittsburgh rebelled when their leaders submitted a contract that did not address the issues of upgrading "female" jobs and eliminating pregnancy discrimination. After losing their fight to defeat the contract, the women's threats to take the union to court pushed the Legal Department to file Equal Pay and Title VII charges on their behalf.[50]

Even when women did not name the IUE as a defendant, management (especially at General Electric) routinely tried to shift liability to the union. In addition, the Legal Department also faced pressures from the EEOC, whose investigators sometimes found unions liable on the ground that they had approved discriminatory contracts. In fact, the EEOC's national discrimination charge against G.E. initially named the IUE along with the company as defendant. In such cases, the union's strategy was to try to realign the union as a plaintiff whenever possible; to provide EEOC investigators and the courts with evidence of its efforts to eliminate discriminatory contract provisions; and to use its antidiscrimination program as evidence of good faith. It was generally successful in its first tactic; the IUE did persuade the EEOC to drop the union as a defendant in its omnibus charge against G.E.[51]

Ultimately, the IUE helped persuade the EEOC to recognize the union's activities against discrimination and not find liability in cases where the union demonstrated "good faith" efforts. In adopting this position in 1980, the EEOC pointed to the IUE's compliance program as an example of such a voluntary effort.[52]

Although the antidiscrimination efforts of Newman, Weyand, and a part of the IUE leadership grew out of a pro-active commitment to equality that went beyond simple acquiescence in the law, legal imperatives clearly propelled their efforts and gave them a commanding argument to use on stubborn unionists. Newman repeatedly exaggerated the threat of union liability and portrayed antidiscrimination as a "defensive strategy," urging the leadership to make sure that it was "not simply regarded as a 'do-good' thing" by local unions and rank-and-file members. Reporting resistance from some locals on the grounds that "the membership won't stand for it, will strike, disaffiliate, revolt, etc.," Newman noted that disgruntled local leaders became amazingly "pliant . . . after they are sued and are really made to understand that the International policy is in their best interests." One way or another, union members were made to see that their class interests and the welfare of the union that upheld them depended on securing the women's gender-based interests.[53]

The Campaign to End Pregnancy Discrimination

If the Equal Pay Act and Title VII were the most powerful elements furthering the IUE's embrace of feminist goals, they were part of a larger, multifaceted, and interacting set of forces that distinguished this union as an ally of the women's movement. These complex forces can best be seen at work in the IUE's battle against pregnancy discrimination, the cause for which the union was most widely known.

The historical context for the pregnancy discrimination challenge began in the 1950s, when the IUE stated its position through convention resolutions and took the issue to the bargaining table. Once Title VII was passed, dozens of IUE women began to file grievances and charges, complaining that employers had forced them to take pregnancy leaves and then denied them seniority and pension service credits. Others charged that their employers refused to pay sickness and accident benefits for childbirth or pregnancy-related disabilities, even when those employers covered most other medical conditions. In fact, women's eagerness to charge pregnancy discrimination greatly surpassed their willingness to challenge the gender-segregated factory structure. If some women tended to think that men had a "right" to higher wages, they felt a strong sense of injustice when management forced pregnant women to quit, took away their seniority, or refused them sickness and accident benefits. Asserting their right to fair treatment as pregnant workers did not necessitate a challenge to male privilege; women made these claims as mothers, a role compatible with their own sense of femininity and with society's view of women's appropriate functions.[54]

The IUE Legal Department did its part to support these women by providing rank-and-file members with information about sex discrimination and encouraging them to file charges. At a district women's conference in 1971, for example, Weyand urged delegates to persuade victims of pregnancy discrimination to complain to the EEOC and promised that if the EEOC did not help them, the Legal Department would. *Keeping up with the Law* regularly reported on the status of pregnancy discrimination challenges, gave instructions on how to change contract language, and provided sample wording for EEOC charges. The Legal Department's influence at the grassroots level was apparent in Local 161, which represented G.E. workers in Salem, Virginia. Chief Steward Robert Gordon Delano became aware of the issue when other stewards informed him that the company was turning down claims for medical expenses related to pregnancy. He used *Keeping up with the Law* to educate himself about the status of pregnancy issues and forwarded sample language for grievance claims to the stewards who reported to him. Grievances originating in his local eventually became the basis of the IUE's pathbreaking pregnancy suit, *Gilbert v. General Electric.*[55]

In *Gilbert,* both the federal district and circuit courts ruled that differential treatment of pregnant workers constituted sex discrimination under Title VII. When the Supreme Court overturned that judgment, the IUE moved quickly for legislative relief. A number of feminist groups had supported the IUE in *Gilbert,* and they along with the union put together a coalition of more than three hundred organizations, including church and civil rights groups like the National Association for the Advancement of Colored People, other labor unions, NOW, the Women's Equity Action League, the National Women's Political Caucus, and other feminist organizations. Weyand co-chaired the coalition, called the Campaign to End Discrimination Against Pregnant Workers, along with Susan Deller Ross, representing the Women's Rights Project of the American Civil Liberties Union. The IUE president, David Fitzmaurice, and other union members testified before Congress, and Fitzmaurice wrote to all the locals urging them to put pressure on their representatives.[56]

So strong was the IUE's commitment to the pregnancy discrimination bill that it even entered the abortion fray over the issue. The union took no official position on abortion rights, but when the "pro-life" movement tried to attach anti-abortion amendments to the bill, Fitzmaurice urged members of the House Committee on Education and Labor to reject them. "It is inappropriate if not destructive to the general welfare of female workers," he insisted, "to indefinitely delay passage of this bill by saddling it with such amendments." Although Fitzmaurice based his plea on the desire for timely passage of the bill rather than on women's right to abortion, the union leadership clearly indicated that it would not sacrifice equity for women in order to avoid controversy on the abortion issue.[57]

The IUE's battle against pregnancy discrimination succeeded in part because conflicts between gender and class interests were minimal. Elimination of pregnancy discrimination did not threaten male privilege, and the gains won by women were compatible with popular perceptions of their appropriate roles. The Legal Department had little difficulty in committing rank-and-file members and the male leadership to a struggle based on motherhood, and this orientation also ensured its success in the larger political arena.

The pregnancy issue also revealed the profound entrenchment

of gender bias even within progressive unions. Two decades after the IUE formally committed itself to eliminate pregnancy discrimination, seven years after the union began to process its members' grievances, and just as it took the issue into the federal courts in 1972, Weyand examined the insurance plan for the union's own employees at international headquarters. And there she found some of the very provisions that formed the IUE's charge of sex discrimination against General Electric.[58]

The existence of the union's own discriminatory practices at the time it was challenging pregnancy discrimination by its members' employers indicates the gap between the union's avowed principles and meaningful action and structural change. That the union moved as far as it did to close the gap was due only in part to new laws and the revival of organized feminism. As we have seen, rank-and-file women in the IUE pressed their grievances independent of the largely middle-class women's movement and sometimes in advance of it. The union's comprehensive attack on sex discrimination is inconceivable without such activism on the part of women themselves.

Class Interests and the Feminism of Union Women

Eventually, IUE members and the union itself formed new relationships with such explicitly feminist organizations as ERA ratification coalitions, the Campaign to End Discrimination Against Pregnant Workers, and the National Committee on Pay Equity. Weyand took the lead in connecting the IUE to feminist groups involved in litigation. In 1973, for example, she conferred with thirty lawyers involved in gender equity issues at a meeting convened by the Ford Foundation. In 1974 she asked the NOW Legal Defense and Education Fund to file an amicus curiae brief on behalf of the IUE in a pension discrimination case. In turn, Weyand prepared amicus briefs for the Women's Law Fund in a pregnancy discrimination case involving public school teachers (*Cleveland v. LaFleur*) and for the suit by Equal Rights Advocates that challenged California's denial of pregnancy benefits to women (*Geduldig v. Aiello*).[59]

The union also developed links with the women's movement by inviting prominent activists, including Eleanor Smeal, president of NOW, and Joyce Miller, president of CLUW, to speak on women's concerns at national conventions. The most important new alliance was that between the IUE and CLUW, the Coalition of Labor Union Women, formed in 1974 to organize women workers, combat sex discrimination in the workplace, and increase women's involvement in political action and union leadership. Gloria Johnson and Mary Callahan were among the forty founders of CLUW. Johnson became its treasurer and Winn Newman its general counsel. In CLUW and other coalitions, the IUE contributed resources and publicity to women's causes, while its members gained knowledge, encouragement, and support.[60]

A common class position gave a similar cast to the feminism expressed in CLUW and the IUE, a feminism that differed in several ways from that of the largely white middle-class movement organizations. While the IUE focused on employment-related discrimination, middle-class feminists, who enjoyed the luxury of a more single-minded focus on gender, pursued broader agendas. The union supported day-care programs and began to address the issues of sexual harassment and domestic violence at the end of the 1970s, but that was about as far as it went in confronting needs that arose from women's private relationships with men. Nancy Gabin's description of the concerns of feminists in the United Auto Workers stands equally well for those of IUE women: "The elimination of gender inequality in the home, in marriage, or in the social arena outside the plants was not an explicit part of that agenda."[61]

Even when IUE women and feminist organizations both addressed employment issues, union women noticed a difference. Callahan, for example, called middle-class feminists "snobs. . . . Some of them are looking at, 'How can I become the manager.'

Not, 'How can we get along and improve our lot in life [but] How do I get up there.'" Mae Massie Eberhardt affirmed the class—and racial—lines separating the autonomous women's movement from its labor allies: "There are very few of us that . . . are in any position to be . . . executives. . . . The women's movement really got started within the middle-class white woman's back yard, and not the black woman's back yard."[62]

In fact, recognition that upward mobility lay beyond the reach of most working-class women undergirded the IUE legal strategy that focused on equal pay for work of comparable worth. In appealing to the EEOC to pursue a pay equity strategy, Newman argued that concentrating on opening up promotion opportunities for women would be of limited use in an industry that was losing jobs through globalization and technological change. Nor would a focus on access to different jobs help raise women's incomes much in factories where large numbers of women were employed. "Rather, women have a right to be paid fairly," he said, urging the commission to attack the systematic undervaluation and under-payment of traditionally female jobs. Eberhardt objected to the idea that women had to dig ditches, lay pipes, or climb telephone poles to make decent incomes. "Women's pay needs to be raised, not jobs changed," she insisted.[63]

Organized labor's emphasis on pay equity, pioneered in the IUE and uniquely suited to the needs of women who would remain in the working class, generally in pink-collar jobs, eventually reached the autonomous women's movement. As organized feminists faced accusations of class and racial bias, and the movement's momentum slowed, feminist groups responded with efforts to become more inclusive. The National Organization for Women's official endorsement of pay equity in 1978 demonstrated that the process of feminist change was not a one-way street. Although union attention to such issues as sexual harassment and domestic violence owed much to the women's movement, pay equity originated in the male-dominated labor movement, illustrating the capacity of mixed-sex liberal organizations to shape the agenda of the women's movement.

While working- and middle-class feminists could agree on pay equity, however, most union women chose solidarity with their male associates over support for organized feminism on the issue of seniority. In times of layoffs, middle-class feminists tended to favor saving the jobs of recently hired women or minority men over those of white men with greater seniority because previous discrimination had denied women and minority men the seniority that would have kept them their jobs. Many union women, on the other hand, stood by the timeworn labor tenet; as Callahan contended, any system that violated strict seniority "is just causing hatred among people. I mean, you have black versus white, male versus female." For her, the principle of labor unity took precedence over making up for past discrimination. Some union women remembered, too, that women workers had suffered when employers disregarded seniority in giving men jobs after World War II.[64]

Working-class feminists sometimes differed from the mainstream movement even when the two sought a common goal. The IUE, for example, put its own gloss on arguments favoring the ERA. In a full-page article appearing in the *IUE News* at the height of the ERA campaign, the writer insisted that the ERA was "not the same as women's liberation." The proposed amendment would not legalize homosexuality, affect abortion laws, or "undermine the family, the home, or any woman's femininity." Framing the issue in terms of class solidarity, the article presented the ERA as a matter of "simple justice," provided examples of how the amendment would help men, and pointed out that its opponents were the same groups that opposed labor.[65]

In the case of the IUE, the positive response of the male-dominated union to grievances raised by rank-and-file women depended on a number of factors, including its relatively large female membership and its historical commitment to equality. Key individuals who constituted women's strongest advocates had often had previous commitments to and experiences in the civil rights struggle. This was true for African Americans like Doris Austin, Mae Massie Eberhardt, Gloria Johnson, and William Gary. And it was true for Winn Newman and Ruth Weyand, whose political commitments and professional ambitions merged to fuel the Legal Department's drive for gender equity in the IUE.

Until 1972, however, the IUE lacked something that played a critical role in bringing the United Auto Workers to the forefront of the feminist struggle within organized labor. At the UAW's national headquarters there was a Women's Department, dating back to the 1940s, that made women's concerns more visible, facilitated communication among female members, and pressured the male leadership. Although Gloria Johnson undertook similar activities through her work first in the Research Department and then in the Social Action Department of the IUE, that union had no formal and visible structure and no specific women's organization, which in the UAW deployed greater resources and enjoyed the prestige and authority of an established entity.[66]

The IUE's Legal Department stepped into this institutional void, making shrewd use of the Equal Pay Act and Title VII. It informed members of their rights under the legislation and encouraged them to take advantage of it. The new policy and the IUE's efforts to educate its members gave new hope to women like Mary Klaric and Opal Greenfield, who had expressed gender-based grievances in the 1950s. Moreover, the IUE's attention to antidiscrimination policy increased awareness of the issue among women members who did not initially identify themselves as victims of sex discrimination. Winn Newman astutely used the threat of legal liability to convert national and local leadership to feminist goals, and he devised strategies that linked gender equity to the members' class interests and the good of the union as a whole. All unions confronted the demands of federal legislation and most faced pressures from women leaders and rank and file. The IUE inherited a progressive tradition on gender equity from the U.E., and its need to compete with its rival in an industry employing substantial numbers of women intensified that commitment in the 1950s, most visible in its pressure for national equal pay legislation. To an unusual degree, the role of key individuals in the IUE—men as well as women—distinguished its contribution to the gender-based struggle of the late twentieth century. And the union's leadership, particularly its professional staff, played a critical role.[67]

To be sure, the IUE was an imperfect vehicle of widespread feminist change. Focusing on the workplace, it addressed but a portion of the systematic gender inequity that existed throughout society. Moreover, labor union feminism flourished just before organized labor entered into a dramatic decline, measured by its members' decreasing percentage of the workforce, its lessened clout in the political arena, and its vulnerability to a hostile federal government and growing managerial power. Corporate restructuring and the decline in basic manufacturing exacerbated resistance to women's advances, especially in locals where women were greatly outnumbered. In Local 201, which represented workers in a large General Electric complex north of Boston, women constituted fewer than 20 percent of a ten thousand–person workforce that management cut in half during the 1980s. Activists had to overcome local leadership opposition to establish a Women's Committee there in 1978 and often experienced frustration in efforts to direct union attention to issues of child care, pregnancy discrimination, and sexual harassment.[68]

More remarkable than the IUE's limitations, nonetheless, were its actions on behalf of gender equity. Especially in the early years of the resurgent women's movement, the attention paid by male-dominated organizations to feminist concerns enhanced their visibility and legitimacy and provided resources necessary to fight sex discrimination. In this regard, the IUE made critical contributions. Union members and working-class people in general were much more likely to hear about and respond positively to union-generated ideas than they were to those promulgated by middle-class white women. Thus, the IUE increased awareness among people outside the reach of organized feminism. And the union's establishment in the workplace and policy arena enabled it to promote the implementation of antidiscrimination policy, an enterprise that lay beyond the capacity of the women's movement.

CHAPTER THREE

Litigating Feminist Principles
The American Civil Liberties Union

> I know that yours is almost always the lone feminist voice on the
> National Board, and I know that you take some abuse because of
> it. Perhaps we could drum up some support for a sister on the
> limb, and let these guys know that you have troops in the field to
> back you up. —Suzanne Post to Pauli Murray

Suzanne Post, chair of the Kentucky Civil Liberties
Union, wrote to fellow ACLU executive board member
Pauli Murray in October 1970, a watershed moment in
that organization's developing relationship with feminism. True, in singling out Murray as a "lone feminist," Post
neglected the critical efforts of Murray's fellow board members Dorothy Kenyon and Harriet Pilpel in mobilizing ACLU
support for women's rights. Yet she correctly recognized how
much the feminist positions taken by the organization up to
1970 depended upon the efforts of a few individuals. Thereafter, in part because of Post's own efforts, "troops in the field"
arose to push the national leadership toward a comprehensive
feminist agenda.

As was true for the IUE, the fundamental purpose and principles of the American Civil Liberties Union predisposed the
organization to campaign for women's rights. Founded during
World War I to protect freedom of speech, over the decades

the ACLU had moved from defending First Amendment guarantees to championing the entire Bill of Rights.

Like the IUE, the ACLU developed a strong commitment to racial justice that eventually created a favorable climate for feminist claims. In 1945 the organization identified eight "immediate tasks," five of which concerned racial discrimination; by 1950, its attorneys were urging the Supreme Court to reverse the "separate but equal" doctrine. And in 1964 the ACLU put sizable resources behind civil rights when it increased its budget by nearly one-third to create a Southern Regional Office in Atlanta.[1]

As an African American woman, Pauli Murray helped to stretch the ACLU's advocacy for civil rights into an equally zealous commitment to women's rights. In the words of civil rights lawyer Eleanor Holmes Norton, Murray was "a feminist when feminists could not be found." Dorothy Kenyon, whose feminism harked back to an even earlier time, and who struggled virtually alone on the ACLU board until Murray's arrival in 1965, recognized the younger woman's particular role when in 1970 she described the two of them as: "Pauli and I, she out in front with her double discriminations, I at the rear with my years of experience behind me and the prayer that the young ones may start out differently from us." [2] Kenyon understood the particular perspective and authority that Murray as a black woman brought to feminist issues; and she delighted in having an ally on the board.

Participation in the President's Commission on the Status of Women stirred feminist energies in the ACLU just as it had done in the IUE. Both Pilpel and Murray served on the commission's Committee on Civil and Political Rights, an experience of particular importance for Murray. Through the PCSW, Murray developed strong friendships with a number of feminists—including Marguerite Rawalt and Mary Eastwood—and helped create the network that eventually founded the National Organization for Women in 1966.[3]

To a much greater extent than was the case for the IUE, ACLU

Dorothy Kenyon at the biennial conference of the American Civil Liberties
Union, 1964 (Courtesy of Harvey Mudd Library, Princeton University).

advocates for women had ties to the mainstream women's movement, connections that ran in both directions. Kenyon linked up
with NOW and other new feminist groups, and women from
those organizations became active in the ACLU in the late 1960s
and early 1970s. Faith Seidenberg, a NOW leader, served on the
national ACLU board, and Wilma Scott Heide, chair of the NOW
board of directors, served on the ACLU's Equality Committee.
Another ACLU board member, Margie Pitts Hames, who argued
Doe v. Bolton (the companion abortion case to *Roe v. Wade*), was
also vice president of the Georgia Women's Political Caucus; and
ACLU board member Post helped found the Kentucky Women's
Political Caucus.

These women cast shrewd eyes on the resources that the ACLU
could bring to the feminist movement. In the 1960s and early
1970s, Post faced male resistance and indifference in both the
local and national ACLU. Working within women's organizations
was much more congenial; but she realized that no women's orga-

nization could command the dollars, reputation, and influence of the ACLU. In contrast to the other organizations studied here, the ACLU adopted a feminist agenda because of the deliberate efforts of card-carrying feminists to infiltrate and capture it.[4]

Like the IUE, the ACLU anticipated issues that became central to the resurgent women's movement. It preceded NOW in opposing employment discrimination, in advocating access to birth control and abortion, and in filing suits against sex discrimination. Board and committee meetings of the ACLU, as well as its biennial conference, provided arenas for feminists to gather information, develop arguments, and educate members. For example, Harriet Pilpel first introduced the issues of abortion and homosexual rights at the 1964 biennial conference.

The organization furnished expertise in lobbying as well as litigation as it pursued an expansive agenda that ranged from challenging Little League baseball's exclusion of girls to protecting poor women from compulsory sterilization to combating sex discrimination in prisons and in the military. By the mid-1970s, the ACLU stood as the premier litigator for women's rights and defender of reproductive freedom. Its women's rights project, in the view of sociologist Jo Freeman, provided "most of the legal planning and talent for the women's movement that the NAACP Inc. Fund provided for the black movement."[5]

The Pre-1960s Women's Rights Agenda

Feminists were never strangers to the ACLU. Lillian D. Wald, Jane Addams, Crystal Eastman, Elizabeth Gurley Flynn, Sophonisba Breckenridge, and other activist women numbered among the founders of its parent body, the American Union Against Militarism. Flynn served on the ACLU's executive board until 1940, when she was expelled for being a communist. Dorothy Kenyon joined the board in 1930 and remained on it for forty years. Nonetheless, white male New Yorkers controlled the executive board and committees, and they paid scant attention to women's issues.

Furthermore, the ACLU's early reticence on women's rights derived from its initial focus on the First Amendment rights to
freedom of speech and assembly. Only when issues concerning
women fit under that rubric did the ACLU act on their behalf.[6]

Thus, in the 1920s the organization supported Margaret Sanger's fight against Mayor James Curley for the right to speak about
birth control in a public hall in Boston; and it defended birth control advocate Mary Ware Dennett against prosecution for mailing
out her pamphlet, "The Sex Side of Life." In 1933 it deemed a
conference called by the National Committee on Federal Legislation for Birth Control as "covering matters outside our field,"
but in 1936, ACLU board member Morris Ernst argued a landmark birth control case. In *U.S. v. One Package,* Ernst defended
Dr. Hannah Stone, charged with importing contraceptives from
Japan, and won a federal appeals court ruling that in effect established physicians' right to dispense contraceptives.[7]

The ACLU moved more haltingly when it came to discrimination against women per se. In 1934 it charged the National
Recovery Administration with racial discrimination for sanction-
ing wage differentials in the South but remained indifferent to
the NRA's wage differentials for women. In 1939, however, the
organization offered its services to a group of teachers who were
refused reinstatement to their jobs after they had taken maternity
leaves. The women won their case, but they declined the aid of
the ACLU when their husbands marked it as a communist-front
organization.[8]

As was true for the United Electrical Workers, the ACLU's first
sustained attention to women's rights began during World War II.
Both organizations responded to the need for women's wartime
contributions, their rapidly expanding presence in the labor force,
and the wartime rhetoric stressing democracy and rights. In contrast to the U.E., however, which was spurred to action by its large
female membership, the ACLU began its support for women's
rights primarily because of the passion and labor of one woman.

At the center of ACLU action against sex discrimination in the 1940s and 1950s stood Dorothy Kenyon, who later described herself as "a Cassandra crying out in the A.C.L.U. wilderness against the crime of our abortion laws and man's inhumanity to women." Kenyon functioned as resident expert on women's rights until Harriet Pilpel and Pauli Murray joined the board and took up the struggle in the 1960s.[9]

Born into a wealthy family, Dorothy Kenyon graduated from Smith College in 1908. A foot soldier in the final stages of the suffrage movement, she remained a feminist until her death in 1972. At the beginning of her career, Kenyon experienced the discrimination regularly visited on women in a male-dominated profession. Barred by her sex from following her brothers to law school at Columbia and Harvard, Kenyon earned her law degree at New York University in 1917. It took twenty years more for her to fight her way into the New York City Bar Association; her prolonged battle against its exclusion of women included much ado about the availability of restrooms.[10]

The spirited, sharp-witted Kenyon combined practicing law with activism in a number of radical and reform movements and in the left wing of the Democratic Party. She held offices in such women's organizations as the League of Women Voters and the American Association of University Women, served on a League of Nations committee studying the condition of women in the 1930s, and represented the United States on the U.N. Commission on the Status of Women from 1947 to 1950. In the last years of her life, Kenyon joined NOW, addressed feminist rallies, marched down New York's Fifth Avenue with Betty Friedan and other activists during the National Women's Strike in 1970, and delighted in demonstrations by radical feminists. She described a women's liberation group's action at the Statue of Liberty as "a delicious little bit of midsummer nonsense, like tickling an old man's nose with a feather."[11] But her most significant work for women's rights occurred within the ACLU, where she connected the old feminism with the new and prodded that organization to act on women's behalf.

When World War II — and Dorothy Kenyon — compelled ACLU to pay attention to women's rights, the executive board created a Committee on Discrimination Against Women in Employment, with Kenyon as chair. In 1945 the ACLU adopted its first comprehensive statement on women's rights, recognizing that "the right to work is rapidly becoming for most women as important an economic right as it has always been for men." Emphasizing the right to work and equal pay, the ACLU adopted a legislative agenda that also included measures dealing with equality in jury service, guardianship of children, and control of property. Although it did not play as central a role as the IUE, the ACLU participated in the equal pay coalition, lobbied and testified at congressional hearings, and issued a press release when the Equal Pay Act passed in 1963.[12]

Like the IUE, other liberal organizations, and most women's organizations, the ACLU actively opposed an equal rights amendment — on the usual grounds that such a measure would eliminate labor laws protecting women. Kenyon herself deferred to the opinion of leading women trade unionists, "who are in a position to know what the overwhelming majority of industrial women want," and she frequently reminded women in the professions of their obligation to those in lower economic sectors. Conceding that the implication that women needed protection insulted professional women, she insisted that if they were truly concerned about the "economic exploitation to which the great masses of industrial women . . . are subjected," then to object to "a little matter of personal humiliation to those of us who are not so exploited seems to me both selfish and inhumane."[13]

Kenyon orchestrated the ACLU's stand on the ERA and represented the organization on various coalitions that opposed the amendment. Beginning in the 1940s these coalitions lobbied for a federal commission to investigate the status of women and to identify specific areas of discrimination that could be remedied with precise laws rather than by a blanket amendment. Jury service was one of these areas: in some states women were excluded from juries, while in others women had to volunteer to serve or could claim exemptions not available to men. In addition to supporting specific laws against sex discrimination, such as the Equal Pay Act, the ACLU also considered litigation. Its staff routinely sought Kenyon's comment on cases coming into the office that dealt with women, as she searched for a case that could establish the principle that sex discrimination violated the Fourteenth Amendment's equal protection clause.[14]

During the 1950s and early 1960s Kenyon considered a number of possible cases. She rejected an opportunity to challenge a municipal ban on female bartenders; although the ban clearly violated the equal protection clause, as an advocate for women's causes in an unfeminist era, Kenyon had endured her share of ridicule, and she wanted to find a case that was not susceptible to "leers and snickers." When two women challenged Texas A & M University in 1958 for its exclusion of women, she hoped for a ruling that the Fourteenth Amendment protected equal access to public education for women, but the Supreme Court refused to hear the case. Next, Kenyon seized on a criminal case, filing an amicus curiae brief on behalf of a woman convicted of second-degree murder by an all-male jury.[15]

The convicted woman, Gwendolyn Hoyt, had been tried in Florida, which like many states treated women differently in the juror-selection process. Women could be called for jury duty only if they took the initiative and filled out forms indicating their desire to serve. Thus the court drew the all-male jury that convicted Hoyt from a list of several thousand men and ten women. Kenyon and Phyllis Shampanier of the Florida Civil Liberties Union argued in the ACLU brief that such a selection process deprived Hoyt of a jury of her peers and consequently of equal protection under the Fourteenth Amendment. The Supreme Court didn't see it that way. The justices found Florida's system of jury selection "reasonable" because "woman is still regarded as the center of home and family life." More than a decade passed before ACLU lawyers were able to convince a federal court to dismiss *Hoyt* as "sterile precedent" and "outgrown dogma."[16]

In spite of the decision, Kenyon remained committed to the goal of persuading the Court to apply the Fourteenth Amendment to sex discrimination. Although she had to wait until 1970 and the *Reed v. Reed* decision, in the 1960s Congress and the federal courts did begin to write equal treatment of women into the law. The 1960s marked a turning point for the ACLU as well. In the 1940s and 1950s it had made a place for women's rights on its agenda but only at the margins. In fact, a pamphlet published in 1960 setting ACLU goals for the upcoming decade carried no mention of women or sex discrimination. Yet by 1971 the organization had positioned itself behind nearly all the goals of the resurgent liberal feminist movement.[17]

The Campaign for "Equal Protection"

As was true for other groups, external events shaped the ACLU's accelerating interest in women's issues in the 1960s. The President's Commission on the Status of Women not only touched ACLU individuals directly but also raised general awareness and set off a chain of events that led to the founding of new feminist organizations. Even more than was true for the IUE, the ACLU's involvement in civil rights activism laid a foundation for feminism and established precedents to which women's rights could be attached. Moreover, in the early 1960s there was growing national interest in government support of birth control and increased attention to the issue of abortion.

Kenyon's longstanding advocacy for these issues gained new life when Harriet Pilpel joined the ACLU executive board in 1962 and Pauli Murray followed at the end of 1965. Pilpel took the lead in shaping ACLU policies and litigation concerned with reproductive and sexual freedom, while Murray and Kenyon concentrated on establishing women's right to equal treatment under the law. By the time of Kenyon's death in 1972, several strong feminists had joined the executive board, and shortly thereafter the ACLU institutionalized its feminist commitment by establishing its Women's Rights Project.

Until 1970 Murray served as the key link between the ACLU and the independent feminist movement. Born in 1910, Murray lost her parents at an early age and was raised by relatives. She spent most of her youth in North Carolina, until her determination to attend an integrated school carried her to New York to Hunter College. While earning her law degree from Howard University in 1944, she led student sit-ins at segregated restaurants. Simultaneously, she developed her first awareness of sexism and expressed the desire to kill what she called "Jane Crow" as well as Jim Crow. As she later explained, at Howard "the racial factor was removed and the factor of gender was fully exposed." When she subsequently applied for graduate work in law at Harvard University, she found, as Kenyon had thirty years earlier, that the door was closed to women. After completing a master's degree at the University of California's Boalt Hall of Law, Murray moved to New York City, where she met Kenyon during her search for a job. Kenyon confirmed the younger woman's experience that law was "a long, hard battle for women," but urged her to "stick it out."[18]

Fifteen years later the two women formed a women's rights partnership after Murray agreed to serve on a subcommittee of the President's Commission on the Status of Women in 1962. Tackling the most difficult issue for the commission, Murray helped bridge the decades-long impasse between the advocates of an equal rights amendment and those like Kenyon who opposed it because it would threaten state laws protecting women workers. Murray prepared a long memorandum for the commission reviewing judicial interpretation of the Fourteenth Amendment and arguing that the Supreme Court could be persuaded to apply the equal protection clause to women. Providing a way to advance women's rights without a constitutional amendment, Murray's argument vindicated the approach that Kenyon had orchestrated for the ACLU. Kenyon summarized the memo for the ACLU executive board and won its "enthusiastic" endorsement. And when the commission issued its report, Kenyon engineered an approving statement from the ACLU offering its cooperation in actions against sex discrimination.[19]

Murray stayed in touch with PCSW women, particularly a handful of lawyers employed by the federal government. When Congress deliberated on whether to add a ban on sex discrimination to Title VII of the Civil Rights Act of 1964, Murray prepared a memorandum supporting the amendment, and her Washington friends circulated it to administration officials and senators. The ACLU as an organization also supported the act but not the amendment; in fact, during the deliberations, some board members urged the ACLU to oppose it openly. Like most liberals, they argued that it would be hard enough to pass the bill without the complication of gender equality; furthermore, if the measure succeeded, it would jeopardize protective legislation. But Kenyon asked the board to take no overt position on the amendment, and the board abided by her wishes.[20]

Once the bill passed, Murray continued to work with her network of Washington women to pressure the Equal Employment Opportunity Commission to enforce the sex-discrimination ban. She was one of those feminists whose frustrations with the EEOC's foot dragging eventually led them to found NOW. But by that time she had already begun to effect feminist change in the ACLU, having been elected to its national board in late 1965 under the sponsorship of Kenyon and civil rights leader James Farmer.[21]

Meanwhile, Kenyon and Murray continued their quest for a case to take to the Supreme Court that would extend the equal protection clause of the Fourteenth Amendment to women. They thought they had found one in 1965, when ACLU lawyers in a project entitled Operation Southern Justice filed *White v. Crook* on behalf of Gardinia White and other black residents of Lowndes county, Alabama, who were systematically excluded from serving on juries. Amending the suit to incorporate sex discrimination not only advanced Kenyon's strategy, it also served the purposes of lead attorney Charles Morgan, Jr., who wanted to get a case dealing with all-white juries to the Supreme Court as quickly as possible. Because the exclusion of women was based on state law (whereas the exclusion of African Americans was simply a matter of practice), the case could go directly to a three-judge federal court and from there to the Supreme Court. Thus, in *White v. Crook* the interests of white women, black women, and black men merged and reinforced one another. Although the ACLU leadership considered the addition of sex discrimination "a side interest" of the case, Kenyon and Murray produced a brief arguing that exclusion of women from juries violated women's rights under the Fourteenth Amendment.[22]

In addition to working with Kenyon on the ACLU brief, Murray and her colleagues in the federal government also maneuvered behind the scenes to persuade the Justice Department to include the sex-discrimination issue in its own brief. Their work paid off. Ruling on a much more blatant form of sex discrimination than obtained in the *Hoyt* case, the lower court agreed that jury service was "one of the basic rights and obligations of citizenship" to which women were entitled under the Fourteenth Amendment. Unfortunately for the plaintiffs, the state's attorney decided not to appeal, a move that deprived them of a Supreme Court affirmation.[23]

Nonetheless, if most men in the ACLU celebrated the victory over racial discrimination and saw the ruling on sex discrimination as "a secondary aspect of the case," feminists were elated. Marguerite Rawalt, longtime advocate of an equal rights amendment and one of the most ardent Washington feminists, cheered, "Sound the tocsin! a Federal Court has ruled that women are within the equal protection clause of the 14th amendment." Heaping praise on Kenyon and Murray, she regretted that her own organizations, the National Association of Women Lawyers and the National Federation of Business and Professional Women, could take no credit for the victory. The work of Kenyon and Murray in *White* clearly established the ACLU's leadership in the area of sex discrimination and the law.[24]

Even before the district court ruled in *White v. Crook,* Kenyon and Murray found themselves once more making the argument that efforts to guarantee equal access for African Americans should also stress equal treatment of women. At issue was a proposed civil rights bill that included jury selection provisions. Kenyon and Murray insisted that the bill should cover sex discrimination as thoroughly as it did racial discrimination. But their ACLU colleagues expressed reluctance to challenge the Leadership Conference on Civil Rights, where the bill was drafted; these men worried that adding sex provisions could threaten northern support for the bill by "burdening an already heavily loaded bill." Kenyon scorned the "old argument not to muddy the waters by including women," but Murray clinched the debate by stressing the interrelationship of women's and black rights. Without a ban on sex discrimination, she insisted, black *women* would continue to be disadvantaged. In addition to accepting the Kenyon-Murray position on that bill, the ACLU issued a more general statement, calling for an "affirmative policy that the equal rights of women are an integral part of the whole movement to protect the civil rights and civil liberties of all individuals in the United States."[25]

After persuading the ACLU board, Kenyon and Murray prepared a sixty-page memo in support of gender equity in jury service. Murray contacted feminists she knew from the PCSW, African American women leaders, women's organizations, and congresswomen in a broad effort to convert the Leadership Conference on Civil Rights, Congress, and the administration to their position. Despite their success with the administration, Congress remained unconvinced; the bill did not ban gender distinctions in state juror selection. Moreover, Alabama's decision not to appeal the *White v. Crook* ruling thwarted Kenyon and Murray's expectation that the Supreme Court would rule for gender equity under the Fourteenth Amendment. Not until the 1970s, when Supreme Court decisions in ACLU-argued cases finally supported their claim, did women achieve complete equity in the juror selection process. Yet Murray and Kenyon went far in tying the cause of women's rights to their organization's longstanding advocacy of civil rights.[26]

The Right to Reproductive Freedom

Just as the ACLU challenged sex discrimination in jury service before the rise of feminist organizations, so it anticipated and subsequently advanced feminist activism for reproductive freedom. As we have seen, the ACLU involved itself early on in issues of birth control and sexuality when First Amendment rights were at stake. In these cases, organization lawyers stressed freedom of speech and assembly rather than women's autonomy and focused on the right to disseminate contraceptive *information*. A critical change came in the 1960s, when the ACLU developed arguments based on the right to privacy, expanded its position to include the right to abortion, and framed its stance on reproductive freedom in terms of women's rights.[27]

As usual, Dorothy Kenyon marched in front of the ACLU. An advocate for the birth control movement back in the 1920s, by the 1950s she was urging her ACLU colleagues to support liberalization of abortion laws. She failed to win a single ally. Instead, the ACLU board kept its distance, leaving the issue of abortion law reform to be dealt with "by social agencies in the field." In 1959, in a speech to the Albert Einstein College of Medicine, Kenyon took her case outside the ACLU.[28]

Kenyon's interest in abortion in the late 1950s paralleled movement in the legal and medical professions, whose arguments clearly influenced her thinking. But she was one of the first to make abortion a feminist issue. In her 1959 speech she complained that birth control had advanced "as a health measure, never in terms of personal choice. . . . No account is taken of the woman's individual wishes." Referring to laws banning abortion, Kenyon asked, "What are women? Simply breeders? Why not permit them a choice?" Anticipating the demands of young woman of the next decade, she insisted, "Women have a right to choose what shall happen to their bodies."[29]

As doctors and lawyers—mainly men—joined the movement for abortion law reform, Kenyon grew impatient with the failure of women to take the lead in fighting restrictions. "Where are all the women in this great fight we are waging against our cruel and unconstitutional Abortion Laws?" she demanded in 1967. "The spokesmen for the change are men and what they suggest is good but woefully inadequate." By the time women began to assume leadership of the freedom of choice movement, Kenyon had helped prepare the way for them with her uncompromising feminist position on abortion.[30]

While Kenyon went after reproductive freedom with an absolutist approach, Harriet Pilpel shaped a position on abortion that could win consensus from the ACLU board. Coming along twenty years after Kenyon, Pilpel was able to attend one of the law schools that had been closed to her colleague. In 1936, along with a dozen women, she earned her law degree from Columbia University, ranking second in a class of 259 students. Hired by the firm of Greenbaum, Wolff, and Ernst, Pilpel served her apprenticeship under Morris Ernst, principal lawyer to Margaret Sanger and the Planned Parenthood Federation of America and longtime member of the ACLU executive board.[31]

Within a multifaceted practice that included copyright, literary and entertainment, and matrimonial law, Pilpel labored to expand civil liberties in the areas of obscenity, defamation, and privacy. Fresh out of law school, she assisted Ernst on the *One Package* (contraceptives) case. Eventually taking her mentor's place as counsel to Planned Parenthood, Pilpel participated in every significant birth control case up through *Griswold v. Connecticut*, which established a right to privacy by striking down restrictions on the use of contraceptives. Pilpel traced her commitment to reproductive rights back to her family circumstances. Her maternal grandfather had fathered sixteen children by two wives, and she grew up hearing "my mother and all her sisters lamenting the fact that women can't have lives of their own because they're prey to every biological event." She contributed her legal talents to the movement for reproductive rights in both Planned Parenthood and the ACLU and shaped the evolution of abortion policy within the latter. Like Murray, Pilpel found inspiration in Kenyon, who "was a beacon light for all of us . . . and epitomized so many of my goals and ideals." [32]

Two events in the early 1960s broadened the discussion about abortion law reform that lawyers and doctors had quietly begun in the 1950s. In 1962 national publicity spotlighted the case of Sherri Finkbine, who tried to get an abortion at an Arizona hospital after she learned that a drug she had taken, thalidomide, caused deformities in fetuses, and was denied. Around the same time, the United States experienced an epidemic of German measles, a disease that caused fetal defects. It was in this context of heightened attention to the abortion issue that Pilpel, who had joined the ACLU board in 1962, reintroduced the issue that Kenyon had advocated unsuccessfully several years earlier.

At a workshop entitled "Civil Liberties and the War on Crime" during the ACLU's biennial conference of 1964, Pilpel criticized laws on birth control, compulsory sterilization, prostitution, miscegenation, homosexuality, and other forms of private behavior between consenting adults. Laws restricting abortions, she said, "raise fundamental civil liberties questions particularly for two groups in our population—the women and the doctors." Without mentioning Kenyon's name, she noted that a board member had raised "the question of the right of a woman to control what happens to her own body" in 1956. Urging the ACLU to support at least a mild reform proposed by the American Law Institute, "although it doesn't go nearly far enough," she won a resolution instructing the board to study the constitutionality of abortion laws.[33]

While the ACLU leadership examined the issue, affiliate groups moved ahead of the national body. The New York Civil Liberties Union advocated women's right to abortion in 1965 and helped establish a movement for a national abortion referral service by providing legal advice to the founders of the Clergy Consultation Service. In 1966, the NYCLU began a campaign for the first abortion reform bill in New York, sending Pilpel to testify at legislative hearings in 1967. Although Pilpel presented various pragmatic and constitutional arguments, she also insisted that New York's restrictions on abortions deprived "women of the liberty to plan their families" and that "a therapeutic abortion should be performed whenever the woman and her doctor agree."[34]

Taking a similarly strong stand, in 1966 the ACLU of Southern California affirmed "the individual's fundamental personal right to determine when and whether to produce offspring without interference by the state." In 1967 the Miami chapter followed suit; and the Colorado affiliate's campaign for liberalization won modest reforms that produced the most liberal abortion law at that time.[35]

In February 1967, the ACLU board began a year-long struggle over a national policy on abortion. Dorothy Kenyon, with only a few allies, took an absolutist position, insisting on a woman's unfettered right to an abortion. The state, she argued, had no legitimate interest in the fate of a fetus at any time in a pregnancy that superseded the woman's interest in her own life and health. Pilpel took a more moderate stance. She fought down a proposal requiring a husband's consent to abortion but went along with a mandate that abortions be performed only by licensed physicians and agreed to restrictions on abortions after the twentieth week of pregnancy. In February 1967 the board endorsed the right to abortion during the first three months of pregnancy but reached an impasse over what stand to take on abortions after the first trimester.[36]

Subsequently, the ACLU leadership wrangled for several months over the question of a woman's rights versus those of her fetus. It rejected a proposal from Kenyon, Pilpel, and others that simply asserted a woman's right to have an abortion and a doctor's right to perform one, without specifying any time limit. (Pilpel, having succeeded in her first aim, now broadened her scope.) Instead, in January 1968 it adopted its final position, which affirmed abortion rights to women and physicians before the viability of the fetus (defined in a footnote as sometime after the twentieth week of pregnancy) and called for repeal of all criminal penalties for abortions.[37]

One of the earliest organizations to call for abortion law repeal, the ACLU followed NOW by just two months. The ACLU position was all the more important because, as Susan Staggenborg has shown, NOW's activities concerning abortion were limited during the early years. Moreover, while independent feminists could generate grassroots activism and publicity, a tactic at which radical feminists proved particularly effective beginning in 1969, they lacked the treasuries and other kinds of resources that the ACLU could devote to abortion rights. Its affiliate structure positioned legal talent and lobbying capacity at the state level, the point at which litigation or legislative reform had to begin. Keeping affiliates informed about abortion, the national office strongly encouraged them to "take all possible steps to bring about repeal or substantial liberalization of the laws." By the beginning of 1969, at least ten affiliates had joined the national campaign.[38]

In 1969, ACLU representatives helped found the National Association for Repeal of Abortion Laws (NARAL, later renamed the National Abortion Rights Action League), the first national organization that focused solely on abortion rights. But the ACLU's major aid to the movement was its addition of abortion to its litigation docket. Before January 1973, when the Supreme Court issued its decision in *Roe v. Wade,* the ACLU and its affiliates had filed more than thirty lawsuits and amici curiae briefs challenging abortion restrictions, helping not only to change laws in seventeen states but also to alter public attitudes about abortion. The New York, Connecticut, and New Jersey affiliates generated the most activity, but ACLU chapters in more than a dozen states and the District of Columbia also took abortion laws to the courts, including the Georgia affiliate, whose counsel Margie Pitts Hames argued *Doe v. Bolton,* the companion case to *Roe.*[39] Once the *Roe* decision established women's right to abortion, the ACLU took on an even more central role as a defender of that right.

Grassroots ACLU Women Mobilize for Feminist Change

While Pilpel was fighting the issue of reproductive freedom, Pauli Murray and Dorothy Kenyon were contending with the ACLU leadership over policy regarding sex-based classifications in the law. Not only did they have to persuade board members of the gravity of sex discrimination, but they had to deal with the organization's historic support of protective legislation. As was true of the IUE, before the ACLU could advocate legal gender equality, it had to do an about-face on a position it had held for decades and one that Kenyon herself had supported. After Murray gently worked to change Kenyon's mind, she and Kenyon tried to persuade fellow board members. Although various outside events added punch to their arguments, it ultimately took the mobilization of women delegates at the ACLU biennial conference of 1970 to align the organization with one of the two key goals of liberal feminism.

Unlike Kenyon and other ACLU board members, Murray did not have a longstanding investment in opposition to an equal rights amendment. On the one hand, she supported basic labor standards for all workers and expressed the hope that certain protections against exploitative conditions afforded women could also be applied to men. But she also saw how protective laws restricted women, and as an African American woman she realized that these laws had "very little meaning for a large sector of the Negro, female working population," the vast majority of whom worked in occupations untouched by protective laws. Gradually, she converted Kenyon to the position that any distinctions based solely on sex were "inherently discriminatory and unreasonable." Murray proposed instead a "functional approach" that would apply only to those women for whom laws were relevant; for example, laws designed to protect mothers would apply only to pregnant women or mothers, not to all women.[40]

Such a position was compatible with Title VII of the Civil Rights Act of 1964, the law for which Murray had lobbied and which she worked to persuade the EEOC to enforce. To that end, she worked both with her network of women in Washington and within the ACLU national board. Part of those efforts involved persuading the EEOC that laws ostensibly protecting women workers actually discriminated against them—as some union women recognized—by keeping them out of higher paying jobs. In 1966 Murray began a campaign, which Kenyon soon joined, to win the ACLU board to a new policy that (1) supported the inclusion of sex in all civil rights legislation and regulations; and (2) committed the ACLU to challenging any legislation that classified individuals by sex as "inherently discriminatory and unconstitutional."[41]

One obstacle confronting the two women came from men —white and black—who dismissed sex discrimination as "relatively unimportant" when compared to race discrimination. Floyd McKissick, director of the Congress on Racial Equality (CORE) and a member of the ACLU Equality Committee in the late 1960s, reported that CORE had decided to emphasize "black male power"; "tomorrow [it will] concentrate on the equality of women." McKissick's position was echoed three years later by another committee member, who queried whether removing "restrictions upon women [would] be a blow to the precarious position of the black man" and insisted that priority must be given to "the liberation of the black male."[42]

The second and more difficult objection to overcome was the ACLU's historic support for protective legislation. Like the IUE, the ACLU struggled for years over this key policy reversal. In fact, representatives of organized labor at both the affiliate and national levels of the ACLU fought to preserve the traditional position. The Michigan chapter, for example, affirmed the stand of its member Myra K. Wolfgang, vice president of the Hotel and Restaurant Employees and Bartenders International union. She disputed the assertion that special laws for women were no longer necessary and urged the national board to maintain its support for current protective legislation until sex-neutral laws covered men and women alike. One of the national board members, Howard D. Samuel, also held the post of vice president of the Amalgamated Clothing Workers of America, and he too advocated continued support for protective laws for women.[43]

Although Murray and Kenyon failed to win a majority of board members to their side, they did begin to attract allies. The ACLU's general counsel, Norman Dorsen, asked one of his New York University law students to prepare a strong memorandum in favor of the proposal. Louise Noun, who represented the Iowa affiliate on the national board, became more active on women's issues after she wrote a book about Iowa suffragists. She asked Murray to bring her up to speed "on the current status of women's rights," and made a special effort to attend an Equality Committee meeting, where she argued on behalf of the Murray-Kenyon proposal. Murray also kept the entire board abreast of the status of sex-discrimination cases, and she reported on developments in the emerging women's movement. In addition, she used her authority as a black woman to urge the organization to "recognize that classification by race and sex are equally immoral." Kenyon reminded her fellow board members of her history "as a long time supporter of and battler for" special laws for women and documented her own conversion to gender neutrality in the law.[44]

In 1968, at the age of eighty, Kenyon found her patience running out. After a heated board meeting she felt compelled to apologize to fellow members "for my temper tantrum," the result of being "outraged at being classified as something less than a 'person.'" Her words revealed the cost of struggling nearly single-handedly to advance feminist convictions in a male-dominated organization. One of those costs was the need to resort to tactics that devalued women and feminist aims; Kenyon concluded her apology: "I am far from being a feminist and am not greatly interested in women, certainly not nearly as much as I am in men."[45]

Even these wiles proved fruitless. The ACLU board clung to differential treatment until 1970, when it was swept away by outside events and the actions of its own membership. As Kenyon had argued, "the long anticipated head-on collision of the greatly respected but now partially obsolete laws limiting the working hours of women with the facts and laws of modern life" had arrived. First came the EEOC shift of position in 1969. The commission issued a guideline stating that Title VII superseded protective legislation. This policy, moreover, coincided with a clear trend set by federal courts in striking down protective laws as violations of Title VII. In addition, at least one ACLU affiliate went on record against special treatment of women under the law. And some of the ACLU leadership began to express concern about the consequences of "supporting laws which every major women's rights organization finds discriminatory."[46]

An organization whose leaders liked to view it as a vanguard in the fight for citizens' rights could not long resist the growing women's movement, particularly when its own members were involved. An ACLU member from Pennsylvania, Nancy Van

Vuuren, expressed the grassroots exasperation with the leadership when she wrote to Murray, "Women in Pittsburgh are about to completely bypass the ACLU." In contrast to women in the IUE, many ACLU members had strong ties to feminist organizations; some, like Karen DeCrow, president of the central New York NOW chapter, wrote to the ACLU as early as 1968 urging that it take a strong position on women's rights, including support for the ERA. Alan Reitman, ACLU associate director, took such letters seriously and expressed concern about "the flabby policy position" of the ACLU on women's rights. At the same time, Murray made sure that Reitman and others knew about the "mood of organized women today," as more and more women's groups shifted to support the Equal Rights Amendment.[47]

In the end it took pressure from below to break the leadership's attachment to protective legislation and align it behind the ERA. The relentless efforts of Kenyon, Murray, and Pilpel over the years did heighten their colleagues' understanding of women's grievances. But not until women from the affiliates mobilized at the organization's national conference did the ACLU embrace the feminist commitments that thrust it into the vanguard of women's rights litigation.

The mobilization of women at the grass roots coincided with the advent of a new climate at ACLU headquarters, as Aryeh Neier stepped into the position of executive director in 1970. Neier had held the same position in the New York City affiliate, which had an unusually strong record in promoting the rights of previously unchampioned groups. Energetic and impatient, Neier helped push the ACLU to spearhead a "rights revolution." He obtained foundation money for special projects dealing with such groups as voters, prisoners, students, and the mentally ill; and he initiated a series of publications informing specific groups about their rights. While critics charged that the ACLU was being "politicized" and straying from its original purpose with its support for "excessive individualism," membership soared to a record high of 275,000 in

1974. As women developed their own power within the organization by mobilizing as a group, they also benefited from the vision and energy Neier brought to the executive director's position.[48]

Feminist demands on the ACLU executive board came along with efforts to increase the presence of women in leadership positions within the organization. In 1969, Murray wrote Norman Dorsen, chair of the national nominating committee, about the dearth of women proposed for top positions and urged him to add more women to the slate. Two months later, Suzanne Post, chair of the Kentucky Civil Liberties Union, called for more leadership positions for women in the ACLU as a means to attract women to the organization and keep them there. She criticized the paucity of women on affiliate boards and suggested that affiliates create women's rights committees. Post described the plans of her own chapter for a program on abortion and other civil liberties that were of particular importance to women as an example of ways to attract women to the organization.[49]

The 1970 biennial conference was a stark reminder of women's limited presence in the national organization. Twenty women comprised just 15 percent of the delegates, and another twenty-two alternates represented 29 percent of that category, making women's attendance roughly the same as it had been in 1968. Although women's rights were not among the four major topics of the conference, the program did include a lawyers' workshop on "Legal Rights of Women." Chaired by Kenyon, the workshop served as a catalyst for the women delegates. Post, a mother of five who had defeated the old guard in her state affiliate, was ready to take on the national leadership. So was Faith Seidenberg, a civil rights lawyer who had worked with the movement in Mississippi and Louisiana. A national officer in NOW, Seidenberg had a year earlier hauled McSorleys' Old Ale House into court to challenge its 115-year-old tradition of refusing to serve women.[50]

With the help of Kenyon and Murray, these and other women formed an ad hoc committee on women's rights and drew up a resolution insisting that the ACLU "respond with greater speed and intensity in this growing crisis." Their resolution began by documenting women's virtual exclusion from policymaking areas of the ACLU—the national board, affiliate boards, committees, national staff—and demanding that the ACLU "take affirmative and vigorous action" to increase women's representation "significantly. . . . Token representation will no longer be acceptable." [51]

In addition to condemning internal sex discrimination, the resolution demanded action on a broad range of women's rights issues, several of which Murray and Kenyon had been fruitlessly pursuing on the board. The document called for ACLU opposition to all laws that classified individuals by sex, to discrimination in education, and to discrimination based on pregnancy or motherhood. It urged the organization to advocate support for a woman's control over her own body, including the right to abortion and sterilization as well as protection from involuntary sterilization. [52]

Resolution proponents contended with the ACLU leadership for a place on the agenda. Relegated to a time slot at the end of an evening session, the resolution failed for lack of a quorum. At the next session, the delegates adopted it, 116–0 and 8 abstentions, with the understanding that the convention was voting on the general substance of the resolution rather than its exact language. Seidenberg attributed the lack of negative votes and sparse discussion to the resolution's appearance at the end of the convention and to the failure of many delegates to take it seriously. Regardless of the reasons for its overwhelming adoption, the resolution proved a victory for the women of the ACLU because it *required* action by the executive board and thus provided women board members and their allies with sorely needed leverage. [53]

The resolution immediately galvanized the ACLU staff. In July 1970 the outgoing executive director, Jack Pemberton, sent a strongly worded memo to ACLU staff and affiliate leaders throughout the country. Pointing to the organization's efforts against outside sex discrimination, he confessed, "It is embarrassing, therefore, to be caught engaging in employment discrimination against women ourselves." The handful of high-level women on the staff and in a few affiliates could be considered tokens. "While we are going about the country as busy-bodies attacking other peoples [sic] faults," he chided, "we might as well look to the consistency of our own practices."[54]

"Bravo!" responded Pauli Murray, requesting twenty-five copies of Pemberton's memo. The directive supported Murray, who had been campaigning behind the scenes for the nomination of women to policymaking positions in the ACLU. Murray wanted not just women but women who would promote feminist goals, as was clear from the individuals she nominated: they included Aileen Hernandez and Wilma Scott Heide, both national NOW leaders, and Eleanor Holmes Norton, who had recently pursued a sex-discrimination case against *Newsweek* for the NYCLU.[55]

Although women did not gain a sizable presence on the executive board until 1974, Suzanne Post was elected in 1970. She was eager to light fires under the white male lawyers who in her view had "been exposed to so little they are frozen in time and space." The way to do it, she believed, was to get more women involved informally and formally. She contacted Murray about reactivating and expanding the women's caucus that had engineered the resolutions at the June conference "in order to agitate all across the board (or Boards) for equal opportunity." Under Post's nurturance, the caucus thrived and enabled board members to strategize on feminist issues. Eventually, a few men began attending, and the caucus expanded to include racial issues.[56]

The national board formally endorsed the first part of the 1970 resolution on women at its December meeting. In a new policy statement, it committed the ACLU to "affirmative and vigorous action" to increase "significantly the representation of women on all policy-making bodies and committees." Mindful as well of the organization's paid staff positions, it called for parallel efforts to open up high-level staff positions to women and to provide equal pay for equal work. Like Pemberton, the board agreed with the resolution writers that "token representation" was "no longer acceptable."[57]

But the organization did not move fast enough for ACLU feminists. At the 1972 biennial convention, Post presented statistics on women's presence on the national and affiliate boards showing that the new policy "had not been implemented." A resolution requiring the addition of women board members narrowly failed, but delegates did approve the creation of a national Status of Women Committee to address the issue. Feminists took the close vote to mean that "radical change can occur in the organization this year" and organized behind a proposal that "frankly set quotas" for a limited period of time.[58]

The proposal drew fire not only from individuals opposed to quotas but also from those determined to defend affiliates' autonomy against national directives. As the board struggled with the issue, its feminist members did not present a united front. Assuming a moderate stance that considered quotas "radical surgery," Murray adopted Kenyon's style, using "creative feminism on our male-dominated ACLU, by disarming them and then 'leading them.'" Representing a younger generation, Post preferred to confront men directly and expressed impatience with an organization that was "overweighted with isolated lawyers who do not know the daily horrors . . . all too real to many of our people." Post assured Murray that she respected her centrist position. "In this struggle," she wrote Murray, "we need women with footholds everywhere," and the two worked together with a caucus of women board members to determine strategy for the meeting that would decide the issue. Although the board rejected quotas, it ultimately adopted a policy that mandated steps that stopped just short of quotas to increase women's representation; and these measures, combined with the awareness kindled by feminists' demands, resulted in substantial progress. In 1974, for example, women claimed 30 percent of the national board seats (up from 9 percent in 1968 and 1972) and constituted 40 percent of the delegates (up from 25 percent in 1972). Although men continued to hold the top leadership positions, women also began to move into the higher-level and higher-salary positions at national headquarters.[59]

The 1970 resolution also forced the ACLU to move on outside issues, thus helping to break down the executive board's resistance to Murray and Kenyon's campaign for a policy statement challenging all sex-based legal classifications. Events outside the ACLU accelerated the pressure on board members, including Murray and Kenyon, to endorse the Equal Rights Amendment. Murray's close ties to outside feminists alerted her to a groundswell of pro-ERA sentiment in women's organizations, sentiment that moved the House of Representatives to approve the amendment in August 1970. In addition, President Richard M. Nixon appointed justices to the Supreme Court who seemed unlikely to rule in favor of adding sex-based legal classifications to the understanding of the Fourteenth Amendment. "We better have the Equal Rights Amendment in a hurry," Kenyon told a reporter, "because I'm afraid the Supreme Court is going in a backward wave for the next 20 years."[60]

Although both Dorsen and Murray testified for the amendment at Senate hearings in September 1970, they could not claim to represent the ACLU. With the Senate poised to debate the ERA, Kenyon and Murray beseeched the ACLU board to emulate their conversion to the ERA. "How long must women wait?" they asked. Pointing out that "in spite of heroic efforts on the part of women as well as of A.C.L.U.," the Supreme Court had not given them the Fourteenth Amendment ruling they had so long sought, they insisted: "There comes a time when you cannot wait any longer, when you must find new tools for the tools that have failed you."[61]

Given its decades of resistance to the principle of gender-neutral law, the ACLU board moved relatively quickly to support the ERA. With only the briefest debate and just one question about unisex bathrooms, it resolved to support the amendment by a vote of 52–1, with one abstention.[62] Kenyon and Murray had planted the seeds for this reversal and had nourished them with dogged persistence. But it took more than the struggles of two women and a handful of allies on the board. External events provided a powerful push: federal court and EEOC rulings that protective legislation violated Title VII, the growing support of traditional women's groups for the amendment, and the prospect of more conservative justices occasioned by Nixon's presidency. Above all, the mobilization of women from ACLU affiliates that produced the resolution at the 1970 biennial convention provided the muscle to align the still heavily male-dominated ACLU with the goals of mainstream feminism.

The ACLU Women's Rights Project

Endorsement of the ERA was just the beginning. The most important outcome of the women's organizing in 1970 was the creation of the Women's Rights Project (WRP), a unit within the ACLU national office devoted solely to the fight against sex discrimination. Through the WRP, the ACLU furnished substantial amounts of money and personnel to ERA ratification efforts. Furthermore, the WRP monitored and planned strategy for increasing women's voices throughout the ACLU and its affiliates. But its greatest impact lay in the area of feminist litigation. The WRP ultimately achieved the struggle for equal protection that Dorothy Kenyon and Pauli Murray had begun in the early 1960s.

With an ailing Kenyon unable to attend board meetings by the end of 1971, Suzanne Post stepped into the void. At the October board meeting she implored her colleagues to move more quickly on gender equity within and outside the organization. Her earlier argument that ACLU support for women's rights would increase female membership had already impressed the national office. In 1971 the ACLU issued a pamphlet entitled "Sexual Equality: This Is the Law," which discussed women's rights in jury service and voting, employment, education, and reproductive rights, pointed to ACLU activities in these areas, and urged readers to join the organization. In October 1971 the board designated women's rights as an issue of great urgency. It asked all affiliates to give it "a high priority in funding and litigative activity" and instructed the Equality Committee to prepare a plan of action for the national office.[63]

Thanks to Murray's efforts, strong feminists and NOW members Wilma Scott Heide and Faith Seidenberg now sat on the Equality Committee. The committee moved rapidly to comply with the board's directive, and at the board's December meeting Seidenberg, Heide, Post, and Ruth Bader Ginsburg (the future Supreme Court Justice) presented an argument and a plan for the Women's Rights Project. They won board approval and an initial budget of $30,000—not a small amount given that the organization had cut $200,000 from its budget in 1971. Just four months later, in March 1972, the WRP was formed, with Ginsburg and Brenda Feigen Fasteau at the helm. Feigen Fasteau had earned a law degree in 1969 from Harvard, "an infuriating experience throughout which I was treated as an unwelcome phenomenon." She channeled her anger into work for NOW, the New York Women's Political Caucus, and the Women's Action Alliance, which she co-founded with her friend Gloria Steinem. Nominally, Feigen Fasteau and Ginsburg co-directed the WRP, but it was Ginsburg who orchestrated its strategy.[64]

Born in 1933, Ginsburg represented a generation of women lawyers quite distinct from both Kenyon and Murray, for she found her way through doors that had been firmly shut to the older women. One of nine women who entered Harvard Law School in 1956, she transferred to Columbia Law School when her husband's work took them to New York. She was elected to both law reviews. Unlike Kenyon and Murray, she was married; she reared a preschool-age daughter while still a law student and bore her second child while teaching law. After receiving her law degree at the top of her class at Columbia in 1959, Ginsburg served a federal district clerkship and then conducted a legal research project in Sweden. With her service on committees of the American Bar Association and the Association of American Law Schools and on the editorial board of the *ABA Journal,* she established a name in the legal profession.[65]

Ginsburg's feminism developed through her teaching at Rutgers University and her work with the New Jersey affiliate of the ACLU. At Rutgers, where she became the second woman to join the law faculty, her students pushed for a Law Day program on sex discrimination and caused her to think about women's rights issues. At the same time, in the late 1960s, the New Jersey ACLU began to receive complaints of sex discrimination, which found their way to Ginsburg because, as she recalled, "sex discrimination was regarded as a woman's job." [66]

Ginsburg's first national case for the ACLU marked a feminist changing of the guard in the ACLU and a watershed in women's legal status. Implementing the strategy pushed by Kenyon and Murray, legal director Melvin L. Wulf in 1970 inserted the ACLU into *Reed v. Reed,* a case in which the Idaho Supreme Court upheld a state law giving preference to men as executors of estates. When Ginsburg became aware that the U.S. Supreme Court would hear an appeal, she contacted Wulf and soon joined the case. Although the ACLU named Kenyon and Murray along with Wulf and Ginsburg as lawyers on the case, the listing of the two feminist pioneers was clearly a courtesy. Ginsburg and other young feminist lawyers were stepping into the shoes of Dorothy Kenyon, who died in 1972, and Pauli Murray, who left the ACLU in 1974 to study for the Episcopal priesthood. As one of her last activities in the organization and symbolizing the transition, Murray wrote the essay that accompanied Ginsburg's nomination to the national board.

Happily, both pioneers were around to celebrate the *Reed* decision, the first time the Supreme Court struck down a law on the grounds of sex discrimination.[67]

As Ginsburg assumed leadership of the WRP, she also became the first woman to join the tenured faculty at Columbia University Law School. Obtaining partial leave from her Columbia position, Ginsburg shaped the WRP's legal strategy first as director and then as general counsel until President Jimmy Carter appointed her to the federal bench in 1979. Ginsburg's primary interest and the focus of WRP efforts was litigation, but the WRP also monitored and promoted women's rights legislation and applied substantial energy to ERA ratification efforts across the nation.

Within a year after Congress passed the ERA, ACLU representatives could be found in ten states testifying before state legislatures and organizing ratification efforts. For most of 1973, the WRP assigned a full-time staff member to help affiliates in the seventeen unratified states mobilize ERA coalitions and lobby. The ACLU executive board appropriated extra funds for ratification, supporting, among others, field organizers in Indiana, Nevada, and Oklahoma in 1976. Like the IUE, it also played a key role in ERAmerica.[68]

The ultimate defeat of the ERA made the ACLU's litigation achievements all the more critical. When the WRP began, ACLU affiliates had already filed a number of suits relating to sex discrimination. What Ginsburg brought to the WRP—along with her inestimable legal talents—was insistence on the need for strategy. Her goal was Kenyon's old dream: to move the Supreme Court from *Hoyt,* the jury decision that had so bitterly disappointed Kenyon, to a ruling that the Fourteenth Amendment required equal treatment of women under the law. This meant improved communication among groups and individuals who were initiating sex-discrimination suits as well as shrewd choices about what cases to pursue. Ginsburg wanted to prevent the Supreme

Court from hearing a case that could result in a decision establishing "bad" precedent and a setback to the goal of equal treatment.[69]

To this end the WRP made itself a monitoring and information center for feminist litigation. It published a monthly newsletter and a quarterly docket of sex-discrimination cases pending throughout the nation. Ginsburg and Sylvia Roberts, president of NOW's Legal Defense and Education Fund, obtained money and sponsorship from the Ford Foundation for a conference on feminist litigation in April 1973. Pauli Murray participated, along with representatives from feminist groups, lawyers from other organizations (including Ruth Weyand from the IUE), and government officials involved in antidiscrimination policy. Although one case that made a particularly bad fit with Ginsburg's strategy did go to the Supreme Court (which upheld Florida's tax law that gave an exemption for widows but not for widowers), the WRP brought considerable order and focus to feminist litigation.[70]

In fact, the Women's Rights Project was by far the most active litigator for gender equity before the Supreme Court. Even though mainstream feminist organizations like the National Organization for Women and the Women's Equity Action League had legal defense arms, the feminist groups did not command the resources of the WRP, which employed four full-time attorneys by the late 1970s. The ACLU not only got the WRP started by providing its initial support, but the prestige and track record of the fifty-year-old organization also helped the project obtain foundation support, including a $1 million grant from the Ford Foundation in the 1970s. While all feminist groups filed amicus curiae briefs in various sex-discrimination cases, the WRP actually sponsored the vast majority of suits that transformed women's legal status in the 1970s.[71]

Ginsburg had set her sights high, aiming for a Supreme Court decision that would interpret the equal protection clause to require the same strict judicial scrutiny for gender classifications as it did for race. In 1973, in *Frontiero v. Richardson,* she carried four justices over to her position, yet the Court never equated sex with race. The WRP nevertheless whittled away at gender distinctions affecting women in the military, in employment and social security benefits, and in jury service. Although she did not persuade the Court that sex-based distinctions required "strict scrutiny," Ginsburg did convince a majority of justices to establish a "heightened level of scrutiny" for laws that treated men and women differently.[72]

The ACLU's litigation efforts ranged broadly and embraced issues that were critical to women but that mainstream feminists often overlooked. Before the WRP came into existence, the ACLU participated in two important cases affecting poor women that were filed by poverty activists. *King v. Smith* (1968) overturned a welfare policy that denied benefits to children in homes where there was a "man in the house," while *Goldberg v. Kelly* (1970) guaranteed welfare recipients notice and a hearing before benefits could be terminated. Various ACLU affiliates also challenged federal guidelines discriminating against poor women in job training programs, and in 1979 the WRP won a Supreme Court decision that extended welfare benefits to children of unemployed mothers as well as fathers. In addition, ACLU litigation opened police and blue-collar jobs to women, protected women from strip searches, and secured equal treatment for women and men in prison. And its expansive approach to reproductive rights likewise placed it out in front of feminist organizations in addressing the needs and interests of poor and minority women.[73]

A Feminist Agenda for Diverse Groups of Women

Harriet Pilpel's concern for the protection of sexual privacy helped determine ACLU policy on both reproductive rights and gay rights. At the ACLU biennial conference in 1964 she took a position in the vanguard of most civil libertarians in calling the criminalization of abortion and homosexuality "a dagger aimed at the heart of some of our most fundamental freedoms." In 1966 the national board modified ACLU policy, and in 1973 it established the Sexual Privacy Project, which included among its purposes protecting the rights of homosexuals. Women especially benefited from the ACLU's litigation on behalf of lesbian mothers for custody of their children.[74]

Playing a key role in the development of ACLU policy on reproductive freedom, Pilpel directed particular attention to the differential impact of restrictive policies on birth control: women with money could circumvent the restrictions, while the poor could not. Thus, her leadership on reproductive issues as well as the ACLU's growing attention to the poor and racial minorities in the 1960s meant that the organization early and consistently attended to the interests of poor women and women of color.

From the start, Pilpel argued for both aspects of reproductive freedom — the right to limit childbearing, which included access to contraception, abortion, and sterilization; and the right to bear children, which meant freedom from coerced sterilization. Seeking to make contraception available to all women, in 1965 she charged that "birth control legislation and policy is often class legislation." The government must "democratize birth control," Pilpel maintained, by incorporating contraceptive services into public health and welfare budgets. When the Johnson administration provided family planning funds in its War on Poverty, she and Kenyon persuaded the ACLU executive board to challenge Office of Economic Opportunity restrictions that, for example, banned the use of federal funds for services to single women.[75]

It was Pilpel's profound commitment to individual liberty in sexual matters, not population control motives, that drove her concern for reproductive freedom for poor women. Her call to "democratize birth control" was in fact one voiced by the Urban League in the early 1960s. Moreover, her emphasis on privacy as a civil liberty extended beyond reproductive freedom to protect homosexuals from government surveillance, for example, and to eliminate "midnight raids" on welfare recipients to see if there was a man in the house. She denounced compulsory sterilization in the same breath that she called on government to provide birth control services for the poor. Testifying for abortion law reform on behalf of the NYCLU before a state legislative committee in 1967, she grounded her argument on women's "liberty to plan their families," but she emphasized that the burden of unwanted children "falls most heavily on the poor," who also "suffer most severely" from illegal abortions.[76]

The policy and actions of the ACLU on sterilization reflected Pilpel's inclusive position. Up until *Roe v. Wade* in 1973, it filed a number of suits against hospitals that refused to sterilize women who requested it; often these were materially secure married women who had already borne several children. On the other hand, in 1969 the board of directors adopted a policy opposing "all compulsory sterilization," and in 1973 the organization began to put its muscle behind the policy. The ACLU filed a class-action suit against the state of North Carolina, where pregnant teenagers, thinking that the procedure was temporary, had been sterilized under the threat that their families would lose welfare benefits. In South Carolina the ACLU went to court on behalf of women welfare recipients who had been intimidated by loss of assistance if they did not agree to sterilization. A third case that year pitted the Northern California Civil Liberties Union against the state to stop a father from having his thirty-two-year-old daughter, who was mildly retarded, sterilized.[77]

The publicity brought by the ACLU and National Welfare Rights Organization suits pushed the Department of Health, Education, and Welfare to develop regulations in 1973 for sterilization under its auspices. Here too the ACLU fought for poor and minority women. Endeavoring to stiffen protections for potential victims of coercion, the WRP submitted a twenty-three-page critique of the proposed guidelines and threatened "to go to court to try to protect the rights we have advocated here." Moreover,

ACLU representatives pushed for stricter guidelines than even NOW, NARAL, and Planned Parenthood wanted. These organizations expressed more concern with guaranteeing women's *access* to sterilization, while the ACLU assumed the perspective of poor and minority women *victimized* by coerced sterilization.[78]

Initially, the WRP handled reproductive freedom issues, but as the litigation docket grew, executive director Aryeh Neier's fundraising prowess enabled the organization to spin off a Reproductive Freedom Project (RFP). In March 1974, the project was organized with two goals: enforcing compliance with the Supreme Court's ruling on abortion and ensuring that abortions and voluntary sterilizations were available to all who wanted them but protecting women from coerced sterilization.[79]

Increasingly in the post-*Roe* years, the ACLU strove to defend the right to abortion. It sent out model complaints for affiliates to use against public hospitals that refused to perform abortions or against state or county policies that restricted Medicaid reimbursement for abortions. And the national office summoned affiliates to lobby against state bills restricting abortion and to challenge restrictions that had already been enacted. In 1977, after the Supreme Court upheld the right of states to deny Medicaid reimbursement for abortions, the ACLU made reproductive freedom its top priority and involved itself in every important case on the issue at the federal and state levels. Although the RFP failed to prevent all restrictions on women's access to abortion, its legal talents and financial assets filled a gap in the resources available to the women's movement and helped keep the basic right established in *Roe* intact.[80]

At Dorothy Kenyon's memorial service, Pauli Murray applauded her "unflagging efforts to make the issue of women's rights an integral part of the work" of the ACLU, noting that "she had often been a lone voice among her male colleagues for whom this issue had low priority if, indeed, they were concerned at all." Kenyon's labors in the 1940s and 1950s, joined by those of Pilpel and Murray in the 1960s, helped prepare their colleagues and society in general for demands that would subsequently issue from the independent feminist movement. These efforts enabled the ACLU to play a substantial role in the reproductive rights movement and to become the preeminent litigator on behalf of gender equity in the law. Its work was critical to the legal change that transformed women from dependents into autonomous individuals entitled to equal treatment.

To a much greater extent than in the IUE, whose male legal counsel was a driving force, women in the ACLU repositioned the organization behind feminist demands. Beginning at the biennial conference of 1970, their collective force broke the national board's resistance to policies that Kenyon, Murray, and Pilpel had been pushing unsuccessfully for years. Moreover, although the feminist inclinations of these pioneers antedated their associations with NOW and other groups, many activists in the ACLU also belonged to the new feminist groups that sprang up in the late 1960s and early 1970s. More than in the other organizations under study, feminists active in the autonomous women's movement, in Jo Freeman's words, "coopted the resources of the ACLU to its ends." [81]

Yet the ACLU's feminist commitments proved broader and more inclusive than those of most independent women's organizations. The ACLU's commitment to sexual privacy rights included advocacy on behalf of lesbian rights, an issue the NOW leadership resisted until 1972. Moreover, years before mainstream feminism took up the challenge from women of color to broaden abortion rights into a multiracial, multi-issue movement, the ACLU promoted disadvantaged women's access to contraception, advocated on behalf of welfare recipients, and litigated against sterilization abuse suffered by poor and minority women. As was true for independent feminist organizations, privileged white individuals controlled ACLU policy. But the organization's fundamental purpose and its preexisting commitment to minorities and the poor enabled women like Pauli Murray and Harriet Pilpel to form its advocacy for women in ways that substantially expanded the scope of feminism in the 1970s.

CHAPTER FOUR

Establishing Feminism's Moral Authority
The National Council of Churches

Out of long commitment to women [we] understood at once
what the secular feminists were struggling with and in revolt
against. These intelligent, angry younger women articulated our
frustrations also. Their analyses deepened our understanding of
the systemic oppression of women. Their determination to revise
patriarchal culture and politics energized us. —Theressa Hoover

heressa Hoover's 1983 description of the relationship
between secular and religious feminists referred specifically to the Women's Division of the United Methodist Church, which she directed from 1968 to 1990.
Yet her words applied as well to women in such religious institutions as Church Women United (CWU), an organization
of denominational women's groups and individuals, and the
National Council of Churches of Christ in the U.S.A. (NCC),
a federation of Protestant churches and ecumenical organizations. Hoover's strong ecumenical interests and those of the
United Methodist Church propelled her into feminist projects
in these two organizations as well as in her own church.[1]

Before an independent feminist movement arose, as
Hoover suggested, women in religious organizations were already experiencing—and expressing—"frustrations" related to
"women's oppression." If feminist stirrings in the secular world

"energized" religious women, those women had already given voice to some of the issues that would engage the new movement, just as women of the International Union of Electrical Workers and the American Civil Liberties Union had done. Unlike these two groups, however, the NCC was tied to a robust and vibrant women's organization, Church Women United, that helped spur women's activism. In 1965, a year before the founding of NOW, CWU sponsored a Committee on the Changing Role of Women, which insisted on the need to make "a radical challenge to the Church . . . and raise the question of why the Church is not practicing what it preaches."[2]

The feminist convictions of religious women grew in part from their historical experience in the churches. On the one hand, women exercised leadership in their own groups, where they raised and disbursed large sums of money on projects that stretched across the world. But the authorities in their male-dominated denominations expected women to serve rather than lead, to contribute rather than to decide important questions. One CWU leader, Claire Randall, maintained in 1970, "Men in the church have no idea of how long and how much women within the church have talked among themselves with deep concern and frustration about their inability to have a real part in shaping the church." The conflict between women's actual abilities and contributions and the roles to which churchmen relegated churchwomen generated a rise in feminist consciousness within organized religion.[3]

The churches' engagement with the claims of the civil rights movement in the 1960s also spurred the development of feminism among church women, just as it did in the secular realm. In responding to demands for racial and economic justice, the large white liberal denominations and the NCC realigned their agendas to address the needs of oppressed groups and emphasized concepts of liberation, of inclusiveness, and of the oneness of all

Claire Randall, general secretary of the National Council of Churches, at the 1983 press conference announcing publication of *The Inclusive Language Lectionary* (Courtesy of the NCC).

humans in Christ. These developments then created an agenda and rhetoric that feminists could expand to include women. In fact, the theological bases for their assertion of women's equality gave religious feminists a special confidence and commitment to their cause. To them, sexism was a sin, and feminism became a part of spreading Christ's gospel in the world.

The liberal orientation of the National Council of Churches, which regarded social reform as being as central to Christianity as personal salvation, provided a relatively open climate for feminism. Founded in 1908 by the social gospel arm of the Progressive movement, and enlarged and renamed in 1950, the NCC in the 1960s was the largest ecumenical organization in the United States. Thirty-three Orthodox and Protestant denominations (about one-half of all Protestants), representing more than 30 million Christians, comprised the council. African Americans made up one-fourth of the NCC membership, although the largest denominations—United Methodist, Presbyterian, Episcopal, and United Church of Christ—were predominantly white.

The NCC's historic commitment to reform intensified dramatically in 1963, when the council aligned itself with the civil rights movement. Led by high-ranking staff members at national headquarters in New York City, the council took an increasingly activist stance, supporting a variety of black leaders and organizations, lobbying for federal antidiscrimination and antipoverty legislation, and organizing a community development project in the Mississippi Delta. The NCC opposed the Vietnam War, and it manifested the influence of liberation theology growing out of Latin American Catholicism in aligning itself with dispossessed peoples around the globe.[4]

As an African American woman, Theressa Hoover lent particular authority to the task of incorporating women into a civil rights and social justice agenda, just as Pauli Murray had done in the ACLU. Nor was Hoover alone. Black women provided inspiration and leadership to the feminist cause within the National Council of Churches at a greater level than in any of the other organizations considered here. African American women's considerable presence and leadership among NCC activists ensured that inclusivity and antiracism formed an integral core of the feminism they constructed.

If the NCC's commitment to social justice predisposed the council to care about women's concerns, feminists at first faced barriers within the organization. Both the council professional staff and its governing bodies were dominated by churchmen whose previous experience had given them little exposure to women leaders. Among high-ranking staff, the majority had attended exclusively male seminaries and had little parish experience that might have accustomed them to working with women. Moreover, like many organizations in the 1970s, the NCC struggled with shrinking budgets and staff retrenchments. New activities would have to compete for scarce resources. Finally, adoption of feminist causes could threaten the council's ecumenism by alienating the more conservative Orthodox Catholic churches that were already members and by impairing its active pursuit of Roman Catholic membership in the late 1960s.[5]

The four-page spread on women and the church in the council's periodical *Tempo* in 1969 marked an exception to the virtual absence of women's issues in NCC activities and deliberations up to that time.[6] That year, however, everything changed: a women's caucus was formed and a woman was elected president of the NCC. By the mid-1970s a white feminist held the highest professional position at NCC headquarters, and a black feminist served as associate director of the council and head of one of its three divisions. Actions taken by the NCC or by one of its subunits reflected the feminist leadership and the collective efforts of women on spiritual as well as secular issues. These actions encompassed support for women—including women of color and lesbians—as ministers and church professionals; promotion of nonsexist language in religious practice and Scripture; advocacy for the Equal Rights Amendment and abortion rights, particularly access to abortion for poor women; and defense of lesbians and radical feminists against official harassment.

Church Women United and the Seeds of Feminism

Feminist pressures on the NCC arose first in Church Women United. Founded as the United Council of Church Women in 1941 by a group of denominational women's organizations, CWU became a general department in the National Council of Churches in 1950. There it operated, in the words of a historian of the NCC, as "a bit of a burr under the saddle to the overwhelmingly male leadership" of the organization.[7]

Spiritual and social missionary work claimed most of CWU's attention, and it took an early and consistent stance against racial discrimination. In 1945 national board members stayed in private homes rather than patronize District of Columbia hotels that refused to serve African Americans. In 1948 the organization issued a strong statement against school segregation as "contrary to our Christian principles and inimical to the democratic pattern." African American women held important paid and volunteer positions in CWU, and in 1971 the organization chose Clare Collins Harvey, the granddaughter of a slave, as its president.[8]

From its inception, CWU leaders chafed at the disparity between women's vast contributions to church work and their near absence in decision making. During the 1950s and 1960s, CWU held conferences with women of various denominations and persuaded the council to sponsor committees and surveys investigating denominational policies and practices regarding the ordination of women and their participation in policymaking. Long before the resurgence of feminism in secular life, the CWU expressed dissatisfaction at the exclusion of women from church administration and decision making. In 1954, for example, it drew up guidelines for local and state chapters to use when considering membership in councils of churches; listed among the criteria was that such affiliation "provide for a more adequate participation of the Council of Church Women in policy building."[9]

To a lesser extent, CWU acted on issues concerning women in the secular world. In 1959 it took steps to facilitate women's employment outside the home by issuing a study and discussion guide on the issue for church groups. Although the organization had supported the principle of equal pay for women since 1950, its members could not testify before Congress on behalf of federal legislation until CWU's parent body, the NCC, approved. Not until the eleventh hour did CWU obtain that approval, when the general board of the council adopted a resolution in support of equal pay legislation in February 1963. Subsequently, the NCC sent a representative to express its support at congressional hearings, and CWU submitted a written statement.[10]

Church Women United also had close ties with another organization of the early 1960s that helped raise consciousness and spark the feminist resurgence. As was true for the IUE and the ACLU, key CWU individuals served on the President's Commission on the Status of Women: Cynthia Wedel, a past president of CWU and a member of the executive staff of the NCC, and Dorothy Height, president of the National Council of Negro Women, who would subsequently join the NCC governing board. Undoubtedly influenced by the work of the PCSW, CWU heightened its attention to feminist issues.

In 1965, CWU created a Committee on the Changing Role of Women charged with studying, in cooperation with appropriate NCC bodies, the role of women in the United States. The committee went about its work boldly. It assumed the authority to study theology and the interpretation of Scripture and to evaluate the churches' teachings about women. Moreover, the committee invited a small group of consultants to discuss the relation between the church and contemporary women. The consultants, in turn, issued a forceful statement calling for "a radical challenge to the Church" and rebuking it and its male leaders for interpreting Scripture "in such a way as to minimize the personhood of women." Several years before "consciousness-raising" swept through the secular women's movement, the report articulated the need to "help women to validate their interior feelings" and gain confidence in themselves. It anticipated that "forces of both men and women will rise against us if we really move" but argued that women's roles were already changing and the churches had to respond. The report's ideas and rhetoric borrowed much from the civil rights movement and at the same time demonstrated the feminist stirrings present within organized religion before the secular movement took shape.[11]

When the NCC reorganized in 1966, CWU lost its status as a general department and moved with other interdenominational bodies into the new Division of Christian Unity, headed by Cynthia Wedel. Although CWU enjoyed the staunch support of

Wedel, its former president, organization leaders chafed under the authority of the council. According to Margaret Shannon, executive director of CWU, they felt "hamstrung by a group of uniform regulations to which every department must conform." In 1969, Wedel pointed to "some very bad tensions" resulting from the ability of women "to go out and take a much more far out stand, and perhaps, some of us say, a far more Christian stand on certain things than the structures of the churches could do."[12]

Church women resented the gap between the CWU's substantial financial contributions to the council and women's actual influence and presence in the larger organization. In 1968 Shannon complained to R. H. Edwin Espy, general secretary and highest executive officer of the NCC, that CWU was being asked to contribute to such priority budgets as the peace fund, but the council refused to include a woman in pacifist delegations to Vietnam unless CWU also picked up the tab for her expenses. Claire Randall, associate executive director of CWU, put it even more bluntly: "This has been the role of women in the church—to be used. We are used to dispense the ideas men have decided upon, to feed the money to support the projects that men have decided on and are running."[13]

Further troubling the relationship between the NCC and the CWU was the NCC's sluggish response to CWU's interest in getting women into executive positions on the council. In 1969, CWU sponsored a Consultation on Recruiting, Training, and Employing Women Professional Church Workers and called on the NCC to make special efforts in this area. Speaking for the NCC leadership, Espy promised to take the recommendations seriously but cautioned women about obstacles to employing more women in high-level posts: budget cuts and the consequent reduction of personnel; the council's commitment to increase black representation in executive posts; and the scarcity of experienced women. The NCC leadership adopted specific targets for the employment of minority individuals in executive positions; with regard to women it simply affirmed that the minority goals "must be seen in relationship also to the need to include more women."[14]

The NCC leadership's implicit equation of black with male, evident in the factors that Espy indicated would inhibit the hiring of women, prompted another CWU challenge. In the summer of 1969, black activists led by James Forman occupied NCC headquarters and those of several denominations and issued a Black Manifesto, calling on the churches to marshal their treasuries and other resources behind economic development projects that would alleviate black poverty. Leaders in the CWU expressed dismay at the "missing dimensions" of the NCC and churches' responses to the manifesto. The organizations, claimed CWU, evinced a "lack of concern for women disadvantaged by poverty," and there were too few women in "the decision-making bodies to which the church is promising large funds." In September 1969, CWU called together black women leaders and representatives of national women's organizations from the denominations to discuss economic justice for women. Their resulting statement demanded that religious bodies and the organizations they funded "include women in significant numbers from varied segments of our society in the decision-making processes," and that "major funds be secured for innovative projects which encourage the economic development of women." In addition, CWU created its own Commission on Economic Justice for Women, chaired by Coretta Scott King; but it did not let the NCC off the hook. Shannon communicated the CWU's displeasure to the council, telling its leaders that women "will be expecting some radical adjustments in the national programs and funds that will include their goals."[15]

Over the next decade the NCC did adopt many CWU goals but only after the women's organization had decided to declare their independence of the council. In addition to feeling "somewhat paralyzed" by the NCC—their contributions unappreciated, their presence unwanted for important occasions and decisions—CWU leaders recognized other difficulties. Both organizations represented many denominations, but the CWU also enrolled individual women from all Christian churches, including the Roman Catholic Church and other communions that did not belong to the NCC. Although council leaders urged CWU to delay separation and attempt yet another redefinition of their relationship, in March 1970, CWU decided to go its own way. It became a "related movement [to the NCC] not subject to the benefits and obligations of administrative relationships," but it kept its offices in the Interfaith Center that housed the council and several denominations. Further, CWU retained its ability to participate in program boards of the council.[16]

As it split from the NCC, CWU intensified its feminist efforts, identifying as two of its three emphases for 1970 economic justice for women, especially those living in poverty, and the "whole participation for woman as a person in church and society." Likewise, in March 1970, CWU's board of managers took positions supporting both the Equal Rights Amendment and a woman's right to terminate an unwanted pregnancy.[17]

Even as these efforts intensified, however, CWU's board of managers gave notice that "Church Women United must not be the substitute for the fuller participation of women as individuals and church representatives in the NCCC." Integration of women into the NCC, insisted CWU's president, Dorothy M. Dolbey, "must increasingly be fulfilled by the women who are members of the General Board and Program Boards as representatives of their denominations." In fact, the organization's withdrawal from the NCC made it more likely that feminist issues would gain consideration throughout various divisions of the council, for now it no longer held a unit exclusively focused on women. Moreover, a new body of women, most of whom had ties to CWU as well, arose within the NCC to take up CWU's old role but with greater determination and on behalf of a much broader agenda than had attended CWU's efforts in the 1960s.[18]

Feminist Networks in the NCC

In December 1969, three months before CWU declared its independence, it gave birth to a women's caucus at the NCC's triennial general assembly meeting in Detroit. As CWU leaders searched for a way to "place the question of women's liberation in the main stream of the church's concern," they looked to the NCC meeting as a "launching base" for their struggle and invited all the women attending the assembly to a briefing. That briefing turned into a full-fledged caucus, as individuals worked through the night to draw up a statement. The next morning, the group gathered again. It was time to "alert the churches that the era of tokenism was over."[19]

In the midst of a tumultuous meeting, during which African American and American Indian delegates issued demands and antiwar protesters poured red paint over the papers of NCC leaders, Peggy Billings, an executive in the United Methodist Church, read the women's statement. As she did so, every one of the more than one hundred women delegates and observers stood up to demonstrate that Billings spoke for all of them. The women's statement affirmed support "for the movement to liberate women in the United States," but it focused on "women's liberation in the life of the Church." Mirroring the first women's caucus in the ACLU, it highlighted the scarcity of women delegates, citing statistics showing that women comprised just 12 percent of the assembly and held only 6 percent of the seats on the general board responsible for conducting council business between the triennial assemblies. "Women are rising," Billings read, "black and white, red and brown, to demand change" in an institution dominated by "white-skinned male clergy over 40." Acknowledging that the caucus had just begun to find its voice, she asserted that it was here to stay: "You will be sick of this theme, but we will not stop raising it." Afterward, two of the caucus leaders rejoiced, "For the first time in history men made no effort to laugh us off and made no funny remarks all week."[20]

The women's caucus raised the feminist theme throughout the 1970s and beyond. Women confronted the next general assembly in 1972 with the issues of female representation and sexist language. By 1974 the caucus had achieved a greater degree of organization, with three meetings scheduled around NCC sessions and attended by three-fourths of the women delegates, including significant representation of black women. Women's ability to wield influence strengthened with the reorganization of the NCC in 1972, which replaced the general assembly and the general board with a single governing board. As a result of the restructuring, a smaller number but a larger percentage of women attended (the new governing board was about one-third the size of the general assembly), and the frequency of board meetings (twice a year compared to the triennial meetings of the assembly) enabled women to achieve greater cohesion. African American women continued to be highly visible in the caucus. Beginning in 1977, the Reverend Joan M. Martin, a black woman on the NCC professional staff, served as its convener.[21]

The caucus functioned in a number of ways that enabled feminists to influence the NCC. It not only brought women delegates together, it also increased contact between delegates and women on the staff who implemented NCC programs. The caucus persistently raised the issue that had provided the immediate spark for its birth—representation of women in policymaking positions. It helped push bylaw changes that required minimal percentages of women delegates for the governing board. It monitored nominations to committees, exerting quiet pressure on the denominations and NCC staff members not only to increase the numbers of women but to appoint specific women experienced in council affairs. Similarly, the caucus pushed for more women on the professional staff at NCC headquarters. By 1979 it could report that women's share of seats on the governing board had increased from 6 to 24 percent, while the proportion of women on the NCC professional staff had grown from 10 to 35 percent. Moreover, the caucus claimed an important victory in the selection of former CWU administrator Claire Randall as executive secretary, the highest position in the NCC and a post that Randall held from 1974 to 1984.[22]

In addition to creating a community of women that enabled them to draw "upon our strength and support for mutual empowerment," the caucus taught women how to participate effectively in board meetings. Caucus members explained the importance of sitting close to a microphone, arranged beforehand which women were to speak on specific points, and strategized at caucus meetings on ways to attract attention to their concerns. Because resolutions were frequently read and approved with little or no discussion, the caucus devised ways to expand the amount of time and attention spent on feminist agenda issues. When a resolution supporting the creation of a memorial to black leader Mary McLeod Bethune was introduced, for example, all of the women present stood up at the same time to second the motion, and then several spoke about her life. These actions demonstrate not just the caucus's attention to strategy and tactics but the cooperation between black and white women that characterized much of its activity.[23]

Finally, the caucus worked on women delegates. Caucus leaders sought to attract women who did not identify themselves as feminists by devoting a portion of the meetings to general issues. But they also arranged discussions of topics that initially disquieted nonfeminists. When feminists expressed concern about male-oriented language in the governing board worship in May 1977, they found that some caucus members did not consider the matter important. Consequently, the next caucus meeting included a discussion and workshop on sexist language led by two women theologians who were involved in efforts to make the language of Scripture and liturgy express the value of women as effectively as it did that of men.[24]

Feminist activism in the NCC paralleled developments in the denominations. Separate women's groups had existed in most churches since the nineteenth century, and women frequently belonged to those organizations as well as to Church Women United. In the 1960s many of these denominational groups began to raise feminist issues. In some cases, feminist consciousness increased when churches absorbed their women's organizations into the church as a whole in the 1960s. Betty Johns, a CWU staff member and a member of the United Church of Christ, regretted the reorganization of her church that resulted in the merger of the women's organization: "You see, there is no base of power at all for women if you don't have a national women's group." And women in churches where women continued to maintain an autonomous organization recognized their strength. "Our funds are own. This gives us the power," asserted Carol Wilhelm, a staff member from the women's division of the United Methodist Church. Assessing what happened when women lost their separate organizations, Cynthia Wedel concluded in 1969, "Women aren't really integrated and they've lost the power they had." [25]

Regardless of whether women had autonomous organizations in their denominations, they supported projects to heighten awareness of women's issues and improve women's position both within the church and outside, and they pressured their churches' governing bodies to take up the issue of sex discrimination. In the early 1970s several denominations, including the United Methodist Church, the United Church of Christ, the (northern) United Presbyterian Church, and the (southern) Presbyterian Church in the United States established task forces on women.[26]

Frequently, feminist networks overlapped, affecting the denominational governing body, the denominational women's organization, CWU, and the NCC. Wedel, for example, served as president of CWU and on the national board of Episcopal Church Women and held a staff position at the NCC. The Reverend Davida F. Crabtree and Valerie E. Russell were on the United Church of Christ's task force on women and active in the NCC women's caucus. Both Peggy Billings, who had read the caucus' declaration at the 1969 NCC assembly, and caucus member Theressa Hoover held executive positions in the Women's Division of the United Methodist Church. Thelma Stevens promoted feminist goals through the women's caucus, CWU's Commission on Women in Today's World, and the Women's Division of the United Methodist Church. The sense of community and feminist reinforcement women received in multiple arenas balanced the difficulties of sustaining active and meaningful membership in several bodies.

The birth of the women's caucus coincided with the election of the first woman president of the National Council of Churches. The wife of an Episcopal clergyman and holder of a Ph.D. in psychology, Cynthia Wedel had presided over CWU in the 1950s before joining the NCC as a division head in the 1960s. Her nomination predated the caucus and probably only marginally reflected the influence of women's rising complaints about their exclusion from decision-making positions. In fact, the council experienced much greater pressure to elect its first black president. The black caucus had nominated its own (male) candidate and solicited support from the women's caucus. But Wedel refused to withdraw, and the caucus women stood behind her.[27] Although we do not know how black women as a group responded to this choice between a white woman and black man, they continued to join with white women in a commitment to interracial work.

An important symbolic achievement, Wedel's election gave a tremendous lift to feminists, even though they realized that "Mrs. Wedel is not unconditionally ours, either." She publicly characterized herself as not especially militant about feminist issues, "because I was always one of the few lucky women who happened to be in positions of some power." Nonetheless, she had accumulated considerable feminist experience through her work in CWU, on the President's Commission on the Status of Women, and with its successor, the Citizens' Advisory Council on the Status of Women. Wedel professed to understand the frustrations of other women and affirmed that "when this frustration comes to the surface in action, it's all to the good." Clearly influenced by the "young and sometimes rather militant women . . . pressing for opportunities" and finding opposition "in the church more than any place else," Wedel recognized in 1969 that organized religion needed to respond to these secular feminists. Shortly after her election, Wedel placed equal opportunity for women and new structures in which "we would no longer be relegated to the 'women's work' " on the NCC's "agenda for the future." [28]

Even more beneficial to church feminists was the election of Claire Randall as general secretary of the NCC in October 1974, an event the *New York Times* characterized as "a break with 2,000 years of tradition." Although the council president changed every three years, the general secretary served five-year terms; in addition, Randall was reelected in 1979. Moreover, the general secretary, not the president, was in charge of running the organization on a day-to-day basis. Henry Pratt has demonstrated the considerable power exercised by NCC staff executives in moving the organization to the left in the 1960s. They attended governing board meetings, where they affected decisions made by delegates with formal voting power. Moreover, staff executives wielded significant influence as they carried out their responsibility of implementing policies, especially because most policy statements were broad enough to allow for a vast range of actions. Randall's election as the highest staff executive was thus much more than symbolic for NCC feminism.[29]

Randall came to her office from Church Women United, where she had worked since 1962, rising to the position of associate executive director. Especially in her last few years at CWU, much of her work had revolved around feminist issues, and she was a central figure in the group that initiated the NCC's women's caucus. At the NCC general board meeting in 1971, she reported on the status of women in the churches, asserting that CWU had moved beyond concern with "status and rights" to "liberation, which is more fundamental." In 1972, Randall organized a conference at which women from across the country spent several days in a retreat. Their discussions paralleled in form the consciousness-raising and nonhierarchical processes that marked the radical branch of secular feminism. Along with theological concerns, the women talked about specific strategies to bring their demands to the churches. But Randall's activities extended to secular feminist issues. She chaired the NCC's task force on abortion in 1972 and 1973, and she publicly approved the Supreme Court decision in *Roe v. Wade*, even though the council itself could muster consensus only to distribute a study paper on the issue.[30]

There were limitations to what Randall could do on behalf of women. And secular activists pressuring the federal government on behalf of feminist policy found that having a highly placed ally was not an unmitigated blessing. As Irene Tinker has shown for secular feminism, women who wished to retain power in their organizations had to make compromises, and they could not always produce what the activists wanted.[31] On the other hand, feminists on the outside found it difficult or unwise to criticize their insider allies. The obligations of her position constrained Randall's ability to muster unequivocal support on women's issues, as did the council's structure, which located considerable power in the governing board and in the various divisions of the national organization. Yet these limitations were offset by the boost Randall was able to give to a number of feminist projects.

As general secretary, Randall continued her support of the women's caucus, which she frequently invited to her suite at governing board meetings. She also championed resistance to the use of masculine language and imagery. When such usage crept into board meetings, she refused to let it pass, calling for stronger efforts to guard against it. She acted on feminist proposals from staff women when such actions did not require governing board approval. And she imparted added force to feminist resolutions approved by the board by implementing them in the strongest fashion possible. When she was invited to participate in secular feminist activities, she responded enthusiastically, speaking, for example, at ERA ratification rallies and serving on the National Commission on the Observance of International Women's Year and on the President's Advisory Committee for Women.[32]

Feminists Exploit a Decentralized Structure

Throughout the 1970s, the women's caucus made itself felt at the semiannual meetings of the NCC governing board. In 1975 and again in 1979, caucus representatives gave lengthy reports on NCC activities concerning women. At several meetings, caucus members rose to protest the use of male-specific pronouns in NCC documents, in statements of board members, and in the worship services that accompanied each meeting. On other occasions they obtained amendments to resolutions specifying that women be represented in bodies convened to implement those resolutions.[33]

Feminists also persuaded the board to take positions supporting various projects of the secular women's movement. The NCC board approved the observance of International Women's Year and the National Women's Conference held in Houston in 1977, and it urged member communions to encourage participation and discussion of women's issues. In 1977 the board called upon the federal government to fund safe and wholesome day-care facilities for children of working parents. The next year the NCC leapt to the aid of the federal government's increasingly beleaguered affirmative action policy; it urged churches to reaffirm their support for the policy by pursuing educational efforts and legal strategies, including the filing of amicus curiae briefs. And in 1980 the board prodded the government to ratify the U.N. Convention on the Elimination of All Forms of Discrimination Against Women.[34]

The NCC governing board also passed three resolutions backing ratification of the Equal Rights Amendment. Following its endorsement of the amendment in 1975, the board in 1977 committed the NCC to support the NOW-led boycott of unratified states and commended member denominations that had already done so. In 1980, as the national ratification campaign concentrated on Illinois, the board passed another resolution, aimed at the state legislature. Under Randall's direction, the NCC staff placed special emphasis on implementing that resolution. The NCC sent mailgrams to key legislators and to Governor Tommy Thompson; staff member Joan Martin represented the NCC in a prayer vigil and ERA march in Chicago; Randall called Thompson to urge his active support; and she joined with other leaders of church organizations to lobby Thompson and Illinois legislators directly.[35]

The decentralized structure of the NCC enabled specific divisions of the council to go further in support for the ERA without having to obtain governing board approval. In 1976, largely upon the initiative of CWU, more than twenty representatives of Catholic, Jewish, and Protestant organizations formed the Religious Committee for the ERA (RCERA) to demonstrate widespread religious support for the amendment. Claire Randall and William P. Thompson, president of the NCC, became individual sponsors of the committee, and Randall was one of five speakers at the press conference announcing its founding. The council as a whole did not join the coalition, but its Division of Church and Society did so and played a critical role in coalition work. The RCERA's national office was housed by the Division of Church and Society; in addition, the division donated funds and part of the time of staff member Joan Martin. Martin's office developed resource materials, helped train church activists, and produced handbooks for organizers as well as a brochure explaining religious groups' support for the amendment. Although its advocacy for the ERA ultimately proved futile, the NCC efforts were nonetheless significant in publicly aligning the moral authority of organized religion with feminist aspirations.[36]

Although feminists were able to obtain NCC support for the ERA without apparent controversy among member denominations, they could not obtain equal unanimity on the issue of abortion rights. By 1970 a number of NCC member denominations, as well as Church Women United and state councils of churches in New York and Washington, had called for liberalizing or repealing laws restricting abortion. The NCC general board discussed the issue in 1970 and authorized a special committee to study it. Unable to reach consensus, the Committee on Responsible Family Planning and Abortion simply presented a number of working papers to the board. The board then voted to establish a Task Force on Abortion and charged it with preparing a policy statement.[37]

The outcome on abortion revealed the limits of what feminists could accomplish within the NCC even when they held commanding positions. President Cynthia Wedel appointed Claire Randall—at that time still with Church Women United—to chair the task force, which included a majority of women as well as representatives from the Roman Catholic and Orthodox churches. Placing women's needs at the center of the discussion, the task force drafted a statement emphasizing the fact that poor and minority women suffered the most from restrictive abortion laws. It insisted that "a woman's conscience must be given priority in the decision-making" about abortion, and it called for the removal of abortion from the legal arena. But three task force members, including a Roman Catholic and a Greek Orthodox representative, dissented from the statement. And their disagreement foreshadowed its fate before the governing board.[38]

At its second reading before the board in March 1973—after

the Supreme Court had established the right to abortion—the statement occasioned two hours of discussion, with a final vote that it be presented to member churches as a document for study and consideration rather than a policy statement. The failure of the board to adopt a policy statement on abortion derived, above all, from concern about the ecumenical repercussions of such a course. For the past few years, the council had been seriously exploring the possibility of Roman Catholic membership; indeed, that ranked second in its list of priorities in 1971. Moreover, the eight Orthodox churches, already NCC members, had become increasingly disenchanted with the liberal direction taken by the council, and a pro-abortion statement would intensify that problem. During the board discussion, the Reverend Robert G. Stephenopoulos, who had served on the task force, warned that "a policy statement of this sort . . . would seriously jeopardize our continued relationship with the NCCC." [39]

Themselves deeply committed to ecumenism, women board members accepted the need to accommodate different theological perspectives on abortion. Nevertheless, they pointed out the anomaly of predominantly male bodies making decisions on issues affecting women. And they did not allow the board to forget their concern. At a 1976 board meeting, Lacy Camp spoke for members of the women's caucus: "To have the major voice of Protestantism silenced by lack of policy . . . hurts me at a very deep level, and I have heard that pain echoed by my sisters as the women's group met last night." Camp did not call for action, intending instead to hammer the board with the "pain and frustration we feel because the Council is silent." [40]

In 1977, after Congress began to restrict federal funding for abortions, two caucus members found a way to end the council's silence on the issue. Peggy Billings suggested an NCC resolution opposing the denial of federal Medicaid funds for abortion, and Chris Cowap, staff member in the Division of Education and Ministry, found a previous policy statement on which to base such a stand. In 1963, the council had adopted a policy asserting the rights of all individuals to receive government benefits or services without discrimination. On this foundation, caucus members persuaded the governing board to adopt a resolution in 1977 disclaiming any policy on the merits of abortion but supporting the principle that a right guaranteed to all must not be denied to some because of economic status. Moreover, the resolution urged governments to guarantee equal access to legal abortions by ensuring adequate funding. Using that resolution as a basis, in 1980 the Division of Church and Society recommended that the NCC file an amicus curiae brief with the Supreme Court in cases challenging the denial of Medicaid reimbursements for abortions. As general secretary, Randall acted on the recommendation, which did not require governing board approval, and the NCC joined with a number of churches in efforts to protect poor women's access to abortions. As was true in the ACLU, the NCC feminists adopted an expansive definition of reproductive freedom that addressed the specific needs of poor and minority women and targeted sterilization abuse.[41]

The degree of autonomy possessed by NCC divisions that had allowed them to actively support the ERA and poor women's access to abortion facilitated a number of other NCC initiatives on behalf of women. Each NCC division had a unit committee composed of representatives from the denominations that approved specific projects. Instead of going to the governing board for permission to act, divisions could secure the consent of their unit committees and obtain funding from denominations.[42] Thus, the Division of Church and Society established a Justice for Women program, and the Division of Education and Ministry created a Commission on Women in Ministry as well as a Task Force on Sexism in the Bible. African American women headed two of these bodies, which undertook a vast range of projects that gave priority to the needs of disadvantaged women.

Because it focused on secular issues, the Division of Church and Society (DCS) provided an obvious vehicle for NCC feminism. Moreover, by 1974 two feminists active in the women's caucus held positions in the division that allowed them to draw attention to women's concerns. Chris Cowap, an Episcopalian and former staff employee of CWU, was Staff Associate for Economic Justice, and Peggy Billings represented the United Methodist Church on the division's unit committee, the body that approved the division's programs and activities. In 1975, Billings and Cowap brought up concerns about harassment of the women's movement by the Federal Bureau of Investigation and other law-enforcement agencies. As part of a nationwide search for radical fugitives, including Katharine Ann Power and Susan Saxe, FBI agents interrogated members of radical feminist and lesbian communities and employed a variety of threats to pry information from feminists about their associates. Several women went to jail for refusing to answer FBI or grand jury questions. Billings and Cowap believed that these officials' actions made a mockery of civil liberties and amounted to intimidation of the women's movement. Concerned also about the spread of harassment of women's centers supported by religious bodies, they formed a Committee of Concern along with women representing CWU and denominational organizations.[43]

Billings reported the situation to the DCS unit committee and asked the division to endorse the Committee of Concern and shelter it under the division's aegis. As a staff member, Cowap also spoke for the motion, and the unit committee agreed. Subsequently, the Committee of Concern persuaded the NCC to file an amicus curiae brief on behalf of two women who were imprisoned for refusing to testify before a New Haven grand jury. Although the judge refused the plea and sentenced the women to eighteen months in jail, NCC intervention signaled religious support for the women's movement, attracted publicity to the case, and warned the government that FBI and grand jury actions would receive close scrutiny. The Committee of Concern also sponsored public briefings on the issue, contacted legislators, and wrote to seven hundred women's organizations asking them to report instances of harassment and offering information and support. These NCC actions resulted specifically from initiatives taken by Billings, Cowap, and other women linked to the council through their denominations or as staff members. Their efforts enabled women from various denominations to join forces and linked the country's largest ecumenical organization with the radical branch of secular feminism.[44]

In 1975 the DCS also began planning for a formal mechanism to deal with women's concerns. It named justice for women among its top four priorities and authorized a staff position for coordinating such a program. As was true for many NCC programs, the new project depended upon member organizations providing financial support for that specific purpose. By 1977 the division had gathered funds for at least a year, and the Justice for Women (JFW) program began with the Rev. Joan M. Martin as its staff associate.[45]

In addition to her work on the NCC's professional staff, Martin was active in the council's Commission on Women in Ministry and convener of its Ethnic Women in Ministry Task Force. In her training at Princeton Theological Seminary she had experienced "otherness" both as a black and as a woman, and like Pauli Murray she had decided that for women of color, "the luxurious choice of which oppression to fight is not an option." Dedicating her work to "doing what I dare call Black feminist theology," Martin sought racial diversity among the representatives to the Justice for Women program, which operated in the "collective feminist style" that characterized most other women's groups within the council.[46]

Martin quickly assumed responsibility for coordinating activities of the NCC's women's caucus and for overseeing the council's contributions to the Religious Committee for the Equal Rights Amendment. She grounded her new project in a Justice for Women Working Group, whose members came from denominations, ecumenical organizations, and secular women's groups. The working group furnished opportunities for ecumenical action on secular issues of concern to women while it helped to sustain JFW by raising funds and pressuring the DCS's unit committee to establish it as a core program with full-time staffing. By 1979 the unit committee had approved the first but not the second objective.[47]

Justice for Women and its working group involved themselves in a broad assortment of issues, including domestic violence, sterilization abuse, affirmative action, connections between sexism and racism, prison conditions for incarcerated women, and relations between churches and right-wing politicians. At congressional hearings, a JFW representative communicated NCC support for a federal program against domestic violence. Martin and members of the working group acted behind the scenes to encourage NCC's amicus curiae brief supporting Medicaid funding for abortions. In addition, JFW promoted links between the NCC and secular organizations through its representation on the National Affirmative Action Task Force, for example, and at the first National Hispanic Women's conference. It furnished materials and services for women's groups and for denominations like the Church of the Brethren, whose conference on feminism and faith was designed and facilitated by JFW staff. Martin's office cooperated with such other NCC women's groups as the Commission on Women in Ministry, and it combated the ghettoization of women's issues by bringing them to the attention of other units in the division.[48]

Justice for Women thus served feminist needs in a variety of ways. It provided both an arena for women to find others with mutual concerns. Support from other women and the possibility of joint action was especially important to those who felt isolated in their denominations. Although the NCC provided minimal financial support for the group, and JFW had to obtain its own funding, NCC sponsorship lent credibility and strength to program activities. Correspondence went out on stationery that named the Division of Church and Society, but the top line in even larger letters bore the imprint "National Council of Churches of Christ in the U.S.A." In reporting activities of divisions within the NCC, the press frequently attributed the actions to the council rather than to the particular agency. When the Committee of Concern protested grand jury abuse and FBI harassment of radical feminists and lesbians, the *Boston Globe* identified Chris Cowap as spokesperson for the National Council of Churches and reported that the NCC had sent letters to women's organizations, when the actions had in fact been the work of the Committee of Concern.[49] Acting under the council's imprimatur gave women's groups within the organization the appearance of greater support than they probably could have gotten from the governing board.

Justice for Women was not the only feminist subunit in the NCC. While JFW focused on women's issues in the secular world, the Commission on Women in Ministry (COWIM) attacked sex discrimination in the churches and worked to advance women's opportunities as ministers, professionals, and support staff in the denominations. With more than a hundred members, it flourished in the Division of Education and Ministry (DEM), headed by Emily V. Gibbes. The first African American woman named associate general secretary of the NCC, Gibbes had served as executive secretary for United Presbyterian Women and as president of CWU in Pennsylvania.[50]

Gibbes had been head of the DEM for less than a year when Linda Brebner from the United Presbyterian Church proposed creating a center to encourage the employment of women in the churches. Gibbes responded enthusiastically. She assembled an advisory committee to consider the proposal, and on Claire Randall's suggestion sponsored a consultation on women in ministry held in December 1973 and chaired by Randall. After two days of discussion the thirty-four women and men from several denominations recommended that a commission be created. Further planning, in which Randall continued her involvement, resulted, in September 1974, in the first gathering of COWIM, a subunit of Professional Church Leadership, a program unit in DEM. Like the Justice for Women program, COWIM had to find its own financial support.[51]

Women appointed by their denominations or by ecumenical organizations comprised most of the COWIM membership, but Roman Catholics and women from other churches not affiliated with the NCC also participated, as did a few men. Usually attracting about fifty people, the commission's semiannual meetings incorporated consciousness-raising sessions and structures that encouraged everyone to participate. Funds contributed by a dozen denominations enabled COWIM to hire a part-time consultant; the commission also relied on staff assistance from Burnice Fjellman, who headed DEM's Professional Church Leadership program and had helped found COWIM.[52]

The paucity of ordained women and the difficulties women experienced as ministers claimed a large part of COWIM's attention. The commission's very first activity announced its militant intentions. At Riverside Church in New York City, COWIM sponsored a "Service in Celebration of Women in Ministry," where three women who had recently been ordained in violation of their Episcopal Church's hierarchy celebrated the Eucharist. Although the service did not have or need the sanction of the NCC as a whole, the proceeding appeared to suggest council support of the female priests, and some Episcopal bishops expressed displeasure at NCC "involvement" in what they considered the internal affairs of their church.[53]

In a less subversive effort to "lift up the ministry of women in the churches" and increase its visibility, COWIM asked Randall to give the group responsibility for the worship services at the NCC board meeting in March 1975. Its request granted, COWIM chose a text from Proverbs that personified wisdom as a female. The meditation, given by Ella P. Mitchell, a black minister, presented a model of womanhood that included "sagacity, wisdom, and intellectual power" combined with passion derived from close contact with human realities and concerns. Of this ideal woman, Mitchell said, "Her *feelings* are deeply involved in the use of her wisdom." Thus, the meditation reflected COWIM's purpose not only to advance the right and necessity of women's ministry but also to create a new concept of ministry that drew on strengths and characteristics traditionally associated with women.[54]

It was not coincidental that an African American woman led the governing board worship service planned by COWIM, for the concerns of minority women claimed high priority for the commission from its inception. At its first meeting COWIM addressed the issue of how few minority women were in attendance and made plans to remedy that underrepresentation. With a goal of 50 percent ethnic representation, the commission pressed denominations to appoint women of color and sought out minority women to join as individuals. Every meeting occasioned discussion on strategies for recruiting minority women, and although the commission fell short of its goal, nonwhites usually comprised about 30 percent of attendance at meetings. The commission ensured minority participation in leadership by expanding its steering committee to include three women who were appointed by its Task Force on Ethnic Women in Ministry.[55]

More broadly, COWIM organized a conference of minority women in ministry, the first of its kind. Some two hundred women — African American, Latina, Asian American, and Native American — gathered in Washington, D.C., in 1978 to explore the particular concerns of minority women serving as ministers and church employees. They agreed on more than twenty resolutions, including demands for greater attention to women ministers in storefront and independent churches; religious support for Native American treaty rights; and ratification of the Equal Rights Amendment. Pauli Murray, who had become the first black

Participants in the Minority Women in Ministry conference in Washington, D.C., sponsored by the National Council of Churches, 1978 (Courtesy of the NCC).

woman Episcopal priest after more than a decade of feminist activism in NOW and the ACLU, led a Sunday worship service at the conference.[56]

White feminists in COWIM tackled racial oppression with greater intensity and commitment than did most of their secular sisters. In part, this reflected the leadership of Emily Gibbes and the persistence of Joan Martin and other women of color on the commission. White women proved responsive to the claims of these women and willing to combat their own racism by engaging in the consciousness-raising sessions that became a regular part of COWIM meetings. These women, like men, had been sensitized to racial issues through their participation in denominational and ecumenical affairs in the 1960s and early 1970s when liberal churches allied themselves with the civil rights movement. But these white women also saw their part in the struggle against racism as inseparable from their feminism. Susan Savell, a consultant to COWIM, characterized its confrontation with racial oppression as a "chaotic and creative process of giving birth to a feminist model of ministry in our midst," one that grew out of an examination of "the relationship between *all* forms and experiences of oppression." [57]

The commission also fought discrimination against homosexuals. At its second meeting, COWIM created a Task Force on Gay Women in Ministry to inform the commission about issues facing lesbians in the church and society. As they had with racism, COWIM members confronted their own attitudes and emotions about sexuality through consciousness-raising and role-playing sessions at commission meetings. The commission also sought to educate church members throughout the country by publishing and distributing to member denominations a resource packet on gay issues and ministry. And it helped establish a support network for lesbians by co-sponsoring a conference called "Journey to Freedom, Lesbian-Feminist-Christian," in March 1979. [58]

In addition to a general policy of support, COWIM protested specific instances of discrimination against homosexuals by churches and public agencies. After the United Methodist Church decided against using its resources to support homosexuals, COWIM wrote to several Methodist seminaries that expelled or refused to admit gay students. When the UMC fired a female staff member who declared her homosexuality, the commission sent a letter of protest and urged members to do the same. It also passed a resolution against the proposed Briggs referendum, a California proposition designed to restrict the rights of homosexuals as well as of those who advocated homosexual rights. The commission's failure to obtain a similar resolution from the NCC governing board demonstrated once again the importance of the council's decentralized structure in facilitating feminism within its walls. [59]

While the intensity of its commitment to fight discrimination against racial and ethnic minorities and against lesbians and gay men formed COWIM's most distinguishing feature, the commission worked in multifarious ways to support and empower all women in the ministry. It published a resource guide for women in seminaries and co-sponsored an annual national conference for female seminarians. For already ordained women, it held Women in Ministry weeks, gathering together women from across the country and from diverse denominations and ministerial responsibilities. The commission assisted women in the Division of Education and Ministry in the struggle against sexist language by convening a forum on sexism in the Bible in 1977. And it reached out beyond the NCC's constituency, writing a letter in support of Sister Teresa Kane, who confronted Pope John Paul II on the issue of women's ordination during his visit to Washington, D.C., in 1979.[60]

Although the existence of COWIM risked pushing women's concerns to the margins of the NCC, that seemed more desirable to its members than any available alternative. Commission members responded positively when COWIM's parent body, Professional Church Leadership (PCL), requested a closer relationship; but they also revealed deep pessimism about the prospects for integrating feminist issues into PCL. At a meeting of the two bodies' steering committees, COWIM members pointed out that only two PCL members had bothered to show up and that only 10 percent of PCL members were women. Women also noted that PCL had evinced no interest in such key concerns of COWIM as lesbian and minority issues. In fact, COWIM saw itself as unique among ecumenical groups in commitment to "the tough issues relating to sexism, racism, heterosexism, and classism and their interrelationships." [61] For feminists isolated in their denominations, COWIM provided affirmation and a lever to apply pressure to the denominations. Although the commission had limited impact on the men who ruled the churches and seminaries, COWIM's presence made it impossible for them to ignore

women's concerns, and it provided invaluable support and leadership training for the women it served.

The Challenge to Gendered Language

More visible and even more controversial than COWIM was a
second feminist enterprise undertaken by Gibbes' Division of
Education and Ministry, the elimination of sexism from religious
language. As we have seen, the use of male-gendered language in
worship and discussion at governing board meetings constituted
an early grievance of the NCC's women's caucus. Feminists in
member denominations, too, voiced their discomfort with sexist
language. By 1974 several churches, including the United Church
of Christ, the United Presbyterian Church, and the Lutheran
Church of America, had established committees to examine language in religious materials and had published guides to more
inclusive speech.[62]

Soon attention turned to the NCC and its Division of Education and Ministry, which held copyright to the Revised Standard
Version of the Bible (RSV Bible), and under whose charge a body
of distinguished scholars, the RSV Bible Committee (RSVBC),
periodically updated and issued new editions of the Scripture.
The first proposal dealing with sexist language came from Edward
Powers, whose own denomination, the United Church of Christ,
had already begun to address the issue. On his suggestion, in May
1974 the executive committee of DEM recommended creation of
a task force to study sexist language in the RSV Bible and inclusion of women in the all-male RSVBC. The division's governing
body, the Unit Committee, hinted at the contention that would
surround the subject for the next decade when it approved the
recommendations only after discussing them in "great detail" and
limiting their scope.[63]

Professional, practical, and spiritual considerations posed
mighty obstacles to the feminist project of eliminating male lan-

guage from the Bible. As scholars, members of the RSVBC possessed a vested interest in the Scripture as they and men like
them had translated it. Feminist claims against this "ownership"
challenged both their ingrained professional standards and their
masculine authority. Bruce M. Metzger, professor of theology at
Princeton Theological Seminary and chair of the RSVBC, declared that he was "unwilling to monkey around with God language." Furthermore, biblical revision bore implications for the
division's million-dollar budget, which depended in part on roy-
alties from the RSV Bible. Finally, the male theologians worried
about the effects of transforming biblical language on the many
Christians—men and women—who actually did encounter God
as a "he" and held sacred the Scripture that they had learned and
made part of their lives. As much as the RSVBC respected "those
offended by male God language," they were concerned for "those
distressed by the efforts to alter that language." [64]

Feminists set to work on dealing with sexism in the Bible in an-
ticipation of the strife that lay ahead. In gathering members of the
Task Force on Sexism in the Bible, Emily Gibbes sought women
with solid credentials as biblical scholars. Phyllis Trible special-
ized in the Old Testament as an associate professor at Andover
Newton Theological Seminary. A prolific writer, Elisabeth Schüss-
ler Fiorenza was associate professor of theology at the University of
Notre Dame and a member of task forces for the National Council of Catholic Bishops and the Catholic Theological Society.
Letty M. Russell had served as pastor of a Presbyterian Church
in East Harlem and taught theology at the Yale Divinity School.
Two other members of the task force were completing doctoral
degrees in theology, and Valerie Russell, the chair, was assistant
to the president of the United Church of Christ. Gibbes herself,
along with Burnice Fjellman, represented the NCC staff on the
task force. The task force spoke for women striving to reconcile
their Christianity with their feminist aspiration to be fully equal

under God. Describing herself as "a feminist who loves the Bible," Phyllis Trible later portrayed their task as that of "redeem[ing] the past (an ancient document) and the present (its continuing use) from the confines of patriarchy." [65]

No doubt aware that it fished in troubled waters, the Task Force on Sexism in the Bible cast its net beyond the RSVBC. It provided the committee with the names of women competent to work with the male theologians, although when four vacancies occurred in the thirty-five-member body, the committee added only two women along with two men. Members of the task force expressed their interest in working with the RSVBC "in any areas related to our concerns for the inclusion of women's perspectives." But they looked as well to cooperation with other groups interested in inclusive language, such as the World Council of Churches and ecumenical women's organizations, and to sponsoring workshops at divinity schools. Most important, the task force began preparation of a study guide on nonsexist interpretation of the Bible.[66]

Published in 1976, *The Liberating Word: A Guide to Nonsexist Interpretation of the Bible* contained chapters written by four task force members, all professors of theology. The authors explained the power of language and the necessity "to liberate the interpretation of God's Word from male bias." They demonstrated how biblical texts reflected the patriarchal environment of their construction and provided examples of feminist readings of particular narratives. Acknowledging that altering language used to describe God was both "difficult and dangerous," they suggested such changes as avoiding the use of patriarchal terms like Master and Father to refer to God and speaking of Jesus as male only when referring to his earthly life as a man. Designed for religious leaders and seminarians as well as for lay study groups, the 120-page paperback attracted attention in major media, including *Time* and the *Washington Post,* as well as in church magazines.[67]

The task force made little headway with the RSVBC. After lengthy discussion in June 1976, the committee agreed to eliminate male expressions that did not appear in the original Greek or Hebrew, but it refused to consider changing language that identified God as male. Metzger refused "to cut myself off from the combined Judeo-Christian tradition and cease calling God Father." According to the male theologians, changing passages that "reflect the historical situation of ancient patriarchal and masculine-oriented society" would result in "betrayal of what translation is supposed to be." These men devoted primary allegiance to the context out of which Scripture arose, while feminists placed more importance on the community into which it was conveyed. Although the men in charge of the RSV Bible had considerable independence, Gibbes and the Unit Committee were able to insist that they engage in further discussion with the task force and others concerned about sexism in the Bible.[68]

Consequently, in June 1977 the chair and vice-chair of the RSVBC and two members from the Task Force on Sexism and the Bible met with the Unit Committee. An "intense" discussion failed to move the RSVBC representatives, who dug in their heels especially hard on the issue of language referring to God, and the meeting came to an inconclusive end. On the one hand, the Unit Committee voted to send a copy of *The Liberating Word* to each RSVBC member; but at the same time it expressed its "deep gratitude" to the committee, implicitly acknowledging that it could not or would not tell the male theologians what to do.[69]

The outcome disheartened feminists, who regretted that only the RSVBC had the opportunity to present a statement and who believed that committee members "were not hearing the questions or issues being raised." In response, the Commission on Women in Ministry decided to sponsor a public forum where both feminists and traditionalists could be heard. Convened at NCC headquarters in December 1977, the forum attracted some hundred participants and was covered by the *New York Times* and the *Christian Science Monitor.* Moreover, in 1978, the Unit Committee mandated further dialogue between feminists and the RSVBC by authorizing yet another body, a Task Force on Issues of Biblical Translation, with representation from both the RSVBC and the Task Force on Sexism in the Bible.[70]

The final recommendations of the Task Force on Issues of Biblical Translation revealed both the influence of feminists in the NCC and the confines of their power. The report, representing the views of five women and eight men, defined a fundamental dilemma: the RSV Bible "must not lend aid and comfort to sexist attitudes and interpretations," but it must also provide readers with "access to the language and conceptuality of the ages in which the biblical texts took shape." Resolution of the quandary essentially acknowledged the RSVBC's independence and its hold on tradition. The report did praise the committee's "good beginning" in avoiding sexist translations and encouraged "more substantial revisions in the interest of . . . fully inclusive language," providing a series of recommendations that resembled those in *The Liberating Word.* It also recommended appointment of scholars "with feminist perspectives" as regular members of the RSVBC. But the task force's most important recommendation indicated that feminist concerns would have to be met outside the RSV Bible.[71]

The task force proposed to meet the demand for nonsexist Scripture through the development of a new lectionary, a series of primary Bible passages that are read aloud at services throughout the church year. Such a project could provide the opportunity to try out new language and give people a chance to get used to it. Most important, it was appropriate to focus on the worship service, ensuring "that the connotation of the words used will not impede the thrust of God's liberating truth." The proposal clearly represented a momentous step for DEM. Its Unit Committee spent an entire day hearing and discussing the report and delayed action for five months while members examined the lectionary proposal with their denominations. After spending the better part of a day in November discussing, amending, and voting on the report, the Unit Committee authorized the lectionary project.[72]

Even before the Unit Committee took final action, thousands of letters poured into the NCC denouncing the lectionary project as an effort to "de-sex" the Bible. "You sound and act like Communists," blasted one, while a disgusted women asserted that "people in this country . . . have gone crazy over this women's liberation idea." Some of the letters resulted from a direct mail campaign conducted by groups of the religious right, including the Religious Roundtable, which castigated "Bible butchers" for "tampering with the word of God." Even the more temperate correspondents displayed misconceptions, assuming, for example, that the project dealt with the RSV Bible itself. Careful to explain what the project was intended to do and why, the DEM, backed by the NCC leadership, carried it through. The division appointed a Lectionary Committee of six women and five men, all but one of whom were scholars at theological seminaries or universities, and the committee published the first volume of the *Inclusive Language Lectionary* in 1983.[73]

Reference to God as "Father and Mother," substitution of "the Human One" for "the Son of Man," bracketed additions of the names of patriarchs' wives when Abraham, Isaac, and Jacob were mentioned, and a host of other changes proved too much for representatives of some NCC denominations. The nine Eastern Orthodox churches urged the NCC governing board to dissociate itself from the lectionary. Advising his parishes not to use it, the president of the Lutheran Church in America (the denomination of Victor Gold, the chair of the lectionary committee) claimed that the lectionary was "often inaccurate and sometimes written in a poor and inadequate linguistic style." Bruce Metzger deemed "altogether unacceptable" the new language referring to the Deity.[74]

The NCC stuck with the lectionary, reminding critics that it was "experimental and voluntary" and not meant to replace the Bible. It completed the project with new volumes in 1984 and 1985. Although most ministers refused to use the lectionary, worshipers in a sizable minority of churches became accustomed to hearing the Scripture in woman-affirming language. The Presbyterian Church U.S.A., born when the northern and southern Presbyterian denominations merged in 1983, took no official position on the lectionary. But it began immediately to educate its 3.2 million members about the lectionary, and its spokesman called the book a step toward "breaking down some of the walls of separation felt by women and others who feel excluded by male language and imagery."[75]

Moreover, NCC sponsorship of projects related to inclusive language, beginning with the Task Force on Sexism in the Bible in 1975, had an impact ranging beyond the lectionary. The Lutheran Church in America, after advising its ministers not to use the NCC lectionary, published its own in 1987. Advertised as more conservative than the NCC's lectionary, the Lutheran version nonetheless excised masculine pronouns for God and eliminated many of the male references to Jesus. And NCC feminists did influence the RSVBC, still overwhelmingly male in the 1980s. In the new edition of the RSV Bible, which made its appearance in 1989, the editors held steadfast to the masculine references to God, but they eliminated many of the masculine pronouns referring to humans.[76]

Although feminist influence on the language of religious practice had limits, in the words of one of the lectionary authors, it was "immensely important to me because as an evangelical woman, I know first-hand the oppression of women who are linguistically and structurally excluded." Virginia Mollenkott spoke for many devout Christian women alienated by the traditional language of worship. "If God is always manlike, and never womanlike," she protested, "then men are Godlike and women are not." Stemming from a different source than that of secular feminists, religious women's distress with sexist language reached a different audience, broadening public consciousness about the power of words.[77]

Since the early decades of the nineteenth century, religion had inspired women's challenges to the status quo. The first American-born woman to claim a right to speak in public, African American Maria Stewart, based her claim on Scripture. "What if I am a woman?" she argued in 1833. "Did [God] not raise up Deborah to be a mother, and a judge in Israel: Did not queen Esther save the lives of the Jews?" Abolitionist and feminist Sarah Grimké insisted in 1837 that "no where does God say that he made any distinction between [men and women] as moral and intelligent beings." On the contrary, in the Sermon on the Mount, "I find the Lord Jesus . . . giving the same directions to women as to men, never even referring to the distinction now so strenuously insisted upon between masculine and feminine virtues."[78]

The scriptural justification and inspiration that women found through the ages for their challenges to patriarchy rested uneasily within a thoroughly patriarchal institution. Some feminists, like Elizabeth Cady Stanton, simply withdrew from traditional religion, which she identified as "the chief obstacle in the way of women's elevation." In her presidential address to the Woman's Christian Temperance Union in 1888, Frances Willard acknowledged an impulse to separate from a church that denied "women's equality within the house of God." She, however, would remain, because "I love my mother-church so well and recognize so thoroughly that the base and body of the great pyramid she forms is broader than its apex, that I would fain give her a little time in which to deal justly by the great household of her loving, loyal and devoted daughters."[79] As was true for Willard, strong and often lifelong bonds tied NCC feminists to their traditional religious institutions. They saw the church as their church, too, based on women's strong presence and myriad contributions; and they were determined to make liberal Protestantism embrace their feminist claims.

The ecumenical purpose and attendant concern for inclusiveness of the National Council of Churches, along with its previous commitment to the black freedom struggle, enabled these claims to be heard. When that same ecumenical priority foreclosed a feminist objective, as was the case with reproductive freedom, feminists exploited the council's decentralized structure to realize at least partially their goals. In addition, the presence of feminists in leadership positions helped position the NCC as an ally of secular feminism. That some of these leaders were African Americans meant that the feminism practiced by the NCC and the goals it rallied behind incorporated the particular concerns of women of color.

The actions of the NCC encouraged feminist demands for leadership positions in the church and a wording of Scripture that included and valued women. The council lent moral authority to such secular feminist demands as the ERA, reproductive freedom, and nonsexist language. And especially in its subunits where women wielded particular leverage, the NCC attacked the compound forms of oppression experienced by poor women, lesbians, and women of color. Through all of these actions, the council served as a counterweight to the religious arguments marshaled by antifeminists, and it prevented the religious right from monopolizing the church's voice on feminist issues.

CHAPTER FIVE

Financing Feminism

The Ford Foundation

> What they've been doing is applying pressures rather judiciously,
> never to the point where the male leadership feels so threatened
> that he reacts negatively. . . . The screw is tightened each day
> very carefully. — Mitchell Sviridoff

In November 1972, during a Ford Foundation discussion of women's roles across cultures, Vice President Mitchell Sviridoff offered his impressions of feminist strategy at the foundation. Noting that efforts at other institutions had been "counterproductive," he pointed out that when the women "are judicious, they get a response." Nonetheless, he encouraged feminists "to keep the pressure on all the time" at Ford and anticipated that women would achieve a "position of empowerment" there.

One of those women was twenty-nine-year-old Susan Berresford, who, upon taking a job at the foundation in 1970, fared better than many college-educated women of her generation. A 1965 Radcliffe graduate, Berresford first worked in two of New York City's antipoverty agencies that focused on job training and employment. She joined the Ford Foundation as a researcher, while other women with college degrees who worked there held lower positions. More than 25 percent of women holding support-staff positions at Ford had bachelor's degrees; one in every five women in the secretary–staff assistant category had graduated from college.[1]

Berresford did share one dilemma with other employed women —how to combine a career with motherhood. Raising a small child while working full time primed Berresford to respond positively to the resurgence of feminism in the 1960s. She took a keen interest in day care and asked to research that issue as part of her assignment at Ford. Moreover, she had grown up expecting to have a career, and at Vassar, where she had spent her first two college years, her professors had introduced her to the ideas of Simone de Beauvoir and other feminists. Fortunate to work in an environment that was hospitable to new ideas, Berresford concentrated her feminist energies on work at the Ford Foundation rather than in the independent women's movement. Along with a group of like-minded coworkers, she pushed the foundation to actions that later caused NOW leader Mary Jean Tully to declare, "Among the giants, only the Ford Foundation has moved in all the appropriate ways to meet the needs of feminists."[2]

Like women at the ACLU and NCC, Berresford and her colleagues focused first on improving the position of women within the organization. Motivated in part by the disparity between their credentials and their jobs, women at Ford initially pressured the foundation to clean its own house by offering equal opportunities for staff women. But their feminist concerns expanded rapidly; soon they were pushing programs designed to redress the gender-based handicaps of women nation- and worldwide. Their efforts put Ford in the vanguard of philanthropies both in the money expended on feminist projects and in the variety of issues addressed. By 1980 the Ford Foundation had dispersed more than $30 million to combat sex discrimination and increase women's well-being and opportunities. Foundation funds assisted mainstream feminist organizations, including the National Organization for Women, the Women's Equity Action League (WEAL),

Left: Members of the Self-Employed Women's Association of Ahmedabad. *Below:* Participant in the Coal Employment Project. Both programs were designed to promote the economic security of women and supported by Ford Foundation grants (Copyright © Ford Foundation, 1982, 1984).

Ms. magazine, the Women's Action Alliance, and the Feminist Press. Ford supported projects on behalf of professional women, blue- and pink-collar workers, welfare mothers, students, African American and Native American women and Chicanas, and women throughout the world. And its programs touched various aspects of women's lives, including education and socialization, employment and economic status, legal rights, political participation, childrearing, pregnancy, and abortion. Ford's greatest contributions were focused in two areas: litigation on behalf of women's rights and the development of university-based women's studies.

The sheer size of the Ford Foundation made it an important ally to feminists. The largest foundation in the late twentieth century, Ford possessed assets of $3.8 billion and dispersed more than $200 million in 1968, dwarfing even its closest ranking peer, the Rockefeller Foundation, whose assets totaled $890 million. In some cases, Ford money alone enabled feminist projects to come into being or to survive, for example, the Women's Law Fund, which depended upon the foundation for 70 percent of its budget.[3] But the significance of the Ford Foundation to the feminist movement cannot be measured solely by the size of its expenditures. Even at peak support, the foundation allocated only about 10 percent of its annual budget to women's programs. But its size gave it considerable importance as a pacesetter in the philanthropic world as well as substantial influence with government and educational institutions. Ford threw its professional authority behind sex equity and furnished not just money but also visibility and legitimacy to feminist goals.

Challenging Institutional Discrimination

In contrast to the IUE, the ACLU, and the NCC, which began to tackle feminist demands between 1965 and 1969, feminist initiatives came relatively late to the Ford Foundation. In 1971 all thirteen of its senior officers were men, as was every member of the board of trustees.[4] Assistant general counsel Sheila McLean was the highest placed woman at the foundation, and only a handful of women served at the next level, as program officers. Some of these senior women—especially McLean, Siobhan Oppenheimer-Nicolau, a program officer in the National Affairs division, and Mariam Chamberlain, a program officer in the Education and Research division—supported feminist initiatives, but they did so in response to initiatives junior-level women had set in motion.

As was true in other liberal organizations, the general national climate as well as the particular environment of the Ford Foundation nourished feminist ambitions in the women who worked there. As part of a widespread trend among philanthropies in the late 1960s and early 1970s—which followed the groundswell of social activism—private foundations increased their grants to social-movement organizations more than fivefold (measured in constant dollars) between 1964 and 1980. Ford boosted its own support for social action and research from $7 million in 1960 (out of total outlay of $160 million) to $42 million in 1970, more than 20 percent of total spending. Even more dramatic, its investment in projects relating to minorities and civil rights shot up from 2.5 percent of total expenditures in 1960 to 40 percent in 1970.[5]

The strong support of civil rights objectives reflected the foundation's new activist approach, directed by McGeorge Bundy, who became its president in 1966. Bundy's brilliance and elite credentials had so impressed Harvard's governors in the 1950s that they awarded him tenure in the Department of Government even though he had never taken a course in the subject and then made him dean of Harvard College, although he had not earned a Ph.D. He then moved on to the White House, where he served as national security adviser from 1961 to 1966 and where his arrogance was legendary, but when he arrived at the Ford Foundation, staff members appreciated his quick mind, loose rein, and openness to their ideas. Although he presided over the foundation during a time of retrenchment, Bundy helped make Ford a part of the social and political change that characterized the era.[6]

In 1966 the board of trustees designated equal opportunity "the first concern of the foundation domestically." Like the other liberal organizations considered here, the foundation began with civil rights, and its work there provided the basis for subsequent feminist projects. For the first time, Ford began to support activist organizations, including the NAACP, CORE, and the Urban League, as well as more radical groups. The foundation edged closer to the political domain by subsidizing voter registration and community-action groups. It entered the litigation arena with grants to the NAACP Legal Defense and Educational Fund and to the Mexican-American Legal Defense and Educational Fund. And it allocated $7.2 million for the development of ethnic studies programs in colleges and universities. Funding in each of these areas—activist organizations, political participation, litigation, and nontraditional scholarship—established a framework in which the Ford Foundation would ultimately target women as well as minorities.[7]

Nonetheless, Ford virtually ignored women in its equal opportunity initiatives throughout the 1960s. As part of its antipoverty and minority-assistance drive, the foundation began to help minority and low-income groups attract federal funds for day-care centers in 1969; and it supported programs to improve conditions for domestic workers. Also during the 1960s, Ford sponsored programs to encourage women's careers in mathematics, science, and engineering, and it supported fellowships for independent study at the Radcliffe Institute, a research center that fostered women's scholarly and professional activities. Women benefited from general foundation activities in education, the arts, and national affairs, but as a 1974 foundation report conceded, women's representation had "been as proportionately low in these activities as in many other parts of American life." The foundation dispensed massive support for research, education, and policy development related to birth control, but the desire to limit population growth, not an effort to meet women's needs, drove those programs.[8]

The relatively late date at which feminism became a major concern of the Ford Foundation reflected the scarcity of women in positions of authority as well as the absence of older women with ties to traditional women's organizations or to public activities concerning women's status. No woman at Ford had Dorothy Kenyon's links to the suffrage movement or the experience that she and Claire Randall of the NCC had with organizations like the American Association of University Women or Church Women United. There were no women like Mary Callahan of the IUE, Pauli Murray of the ACLU, or Cynthia Wedel of the NCC who had been members of the President's Commission on the Status of Women and participated in the equal pay movement in the 1950s and early 1960s. Unlike the IUE, the ACLU, and the NCC, feminism had no history at the Ford Foundation.

The first feminist stirrings at Ford sprang from the rank and file and spotlighted the status of women within the organization itself. Although not actively engaged in feminist organizations, these junior-level staff members expressed a general interest in women's issues and kept abreast of the developing women's movement. Several found themselves in jobs that failed to match either their expectations or their educational attainment. This was especially true for minority women, only three of whom held positions among the professional staff of 55 women and 226 men. Women of color pressed for minority women to be an integral part of foundation projects, coordinating their activities both as individuals within largely white groups of women and in an independent group, Concerned Minority Women at Ford.[9]

The absence of women at the top, where policymaking occurred, attracted the first surge of feminist activity. In May 1970, Janet Koriath, a white staff assistant in the National Affairs division, submitted a memo to President Bundy. Signed by 150 employees, the memo pointed to the absence of women on the board of trustees and listed the names of twenty women qualified to serve as members. That same month, staff members brought up the status of women and minorities at Ford when the foundation held an all-day convocation in response to the invasion of Cambodia and the killing of students at Kent State and Jackson State universities.[10]

In June, another young white employee, who had never met Bundy and had not attended the May convocation, took it upon herself to push the issue with him. Gail Spangenberg had worked at the foundation since 1965; as staff assistant in the Education and Research division, she performed professional work without the commensurate status. She clipped articles on women's issues and attended a few NOW meetings, but her connection to the organized women's movement was as a dues payer not as an activist. Instead, as her feminist consciousness developed, she directed her considerable energies to her own workplace. In a long memo, Spangenberg urged Bundy to appoint women to the board of trustees, examine foundation practices affecting women, hold seminars on the women's movement, and set up a task force to implement these suggestions. Bundy responded by inviting Spangenberg to his office, where they talked for more than an hour. Shortly thereafter, he appointed a committee to examine the role of women at the Ford Foundation.[11]

Bundy gave clout to the committee by assigning Vice President for Administration Arthur D. Trottenberg as its chair. Given the opportunity to select half of its members, Spangenberg chose two high-ranking men, hoping that what they learned from their committee work would direct the attention of powerful officials to gender inequities. The committee also included two of the most senior women, Elinor Barber and Siobhan Oppenheimer-Nicolau, as well as Kathryn Mitchell and Carmen Turay, two women of color who made sure that the committee's recommendations did not focus exclusively on the interests of white women.[12]

In July 1971 the Trottenberg committee released its report, along with a series of wide-ranging recommendations, most of which the foundation implemented within the next three years.

In December 1971 the board of trustees elected its first women members: Dorothy Napper Marshall, provost at the University of Massachusetts, Boston, and Patricia Wald, a public-interest lawyer. A sign of Ford's commitment to alleviating sex discrimination, this move also provided staff members with influential allies. Wald, for example, established contacts with staff members working on women's programs. When she had served on the board for less than two years, Harold Howe II, head of the Education and Research division, wrote to her, "I am glad you are pushing on behalf of women's privileges [sic] in this shop."[13]

Staff women won direct benefits as the foundation set in motion other recommendations of the Trottenberg committee. Female professionals saw their paychecks increase as the foundation moved to eliminate a male-female salary gap. Prodded by Sheila McLean, the committee had investigated the foundation's maternity leave policy, and as a result, Ford changed its policy so that pregnancy was treated in the same way as other extended medical absences. In accordance with recommendations of a special committee on day care that was an offshoot of the Trottenberg committee, the foundation became one of the first employers to subsidize day care for its workers.[14]

Staff women also benefited from efforts to make Ford's professional corps more diverse. By 1974 women had achieved a net gain of twenty-five professional staff positions, upping their share of such posts from 20 to 25 percent. Starting from a base of three, the number of minority women in professional slots grew to eleven, or 13.5 percent of all women in such posts. These gains occurred as the foundation hired women to fill open positions and upgraded lower-level positions. Among those benefiting were several of the women who had agitated for equal opportunity. In the National Affairs division, Susan Berresford was promoted to program officer, and Janet Koriath and Kathryn Mitchell became assistant administrative officers; in Education and Research, Gail

Spangenberg moved up to assistant program officer and Terry N. Saario became program officer.[15]

The movement of women into program officer posts made a big difference to the women whose programs they funded. Ruth Mandel, head of the Center for the American Woman and Politics, which was established in 1971 as part of a larger Ford grant to the Eagleton Institute of Politics at Rutgers University, had found her initial program officer, a man, tough and condescending. When she proposed a program of grants to be named after Florence Eagleton, the center's benefactor, he had quipped in agreement that he would "buy a couple of Flo-ies." When Susan Berresford took over, Mandel found her much easier to work with: Berresford treated the relationship as a partnership, worked with Mandel on fund-raising strategies, and helped emphasize the importance of the center to top administrators at Rutgers.[16]

Although more than a dozen women managed to break into the ranks of program officer by the mid-1970s, they found it much harder to break out of the middle levels of the organization. Foundation officers acknowledged that women lagged woefully behind men in the three highest classifications. As late as 1978, McLean remained the only woman among twenty-seven senior staff. The foundation's overall attractiveness as a place of employment meant that it had a low rate of turnover, especially in higher-level positions. Moreover, Ford underwent a financial retrenchment that eliminated a hundred professional jobs between 1973 and 1977. Berresford eventually made the most spectacular break through the "glass ceiling," becoming a vice president in 1980 and president in 1996.[17]

Feminist Initiatives in Grant Making

Not content with gaining an affirmative action program inside the foundation, junior-level women also urged the Ford leadership to take steps to ensure that women and minorities enjoyed equal opportunity in Ford-supported projects. In October 1971, Berresford, McLean, Mitchell, Oppenheimer-Nicolau, Spangenberg, and five other women addressed the issue in their recommendations for women's programs in the National Affairs division. Surveying the division's 340 grants, the group found that women held high-level positions at only 6 percent of the grantee institutions; furthermore, these women earned lower salaries than did men in equivalent positions. The foundation, they insisted, should require grantees to practice affirmative action both for racial minorities and for women.[18]

When Bundy hesitated to implement such a policy in what he considered a "sensitive and complex" matter, 122 employees signed a petition supporting an external affirmative action program. Meeting with some of the petitioners in January 1972, Bundy explained that the foundation had equity issues of its own to address before it could make demands of its grantees. But he set staff members to work on the issue, and in 1974, Ford launched its external affirmative action program for grantee organizations. Policy guidelines offered a great deal of flexibility, avoiding "mandatory requirements or standards," taking into account the "often critical constraints that may operate on [grantees]," and assuming the grantees' "good faith." Nonetheless, the new Ford policy required grant applicants to submit a statement of their policies and practices relating to opportunities for women and minorities, and it clearly alerted grant seekers to the fact that their performance in this area would affect their chances of obtaining funding.[19]

Although feminist initiatives in the Ford Foundation usually built on those launched earlier on behalf of racial minorities, the external affirmative action policy was an exception. It did not represent a policy designed for minorities that was later applied to women. Rather, it grew out of women's efforts to expand opportunities for women *and* minorities. Black women played a central role in pushing Ford's executives, and their participation on this issue led to further activity. The women of color who attended the January 1972 meeting with Bundy created an independent group of minority women to work on other issues in the future.[20]

Even before inaugurating its external affirmative action program, the Ford Foundation had moved to support feminist goals in society at large. Beginning in 1970, Ford undertook an extensive and diverse range of grant-making activities that made the foundation the premier philanthropy dealing with feminist issues. As was the case with the Trottenberg committee and external affirmative action, junior-level women spearheaded the efforts, which centered in the Division of Education and Research (E&R) and the Division of National Affairs (N.A.). Staff women armed themselves with a handful of proposals for women's programs that came to the foundation in 1971, but they also took the initiative in suggesting funding possibilities. They quickly gained support from some key higher-ranking women, as well as the attention of a few powerful men. By November 1971, both E&R and N.A. had begun to educate staff members about women's issues and to seek the advice of outside experts. Within a year the foundation was well on its way to developing a comprehensive approach to funding feminist objectives.

Not content with her successes in helping women within the foundation, Gail Spangenberg also applied her energies to incorporating women's issues in grant making. An administrative assistant in the Division of Education and Research, Spangenberg remained part of the support staff until her promotion to assistant program officer in 1972, but her low status did not inhibit her efforts. In December 1970 she drew up a list of college and university funding possibilities that included fellowships for women, assistance to women's studies programs, and a survey of women in academics.[21]

Spangenberg cultivated higher-ranking women, particularly Mariam Chamberlain and Elinor Barber, program officers in the E&R and International divisions, respectively. In the early months of 1971, the three women met with a number of women leaders in the educational field. Shirley McCune, an official of the American Association of University Women who taught at George Washington University, discussed the status of women in higher education and the need for more adequate counseling of younger women. Patricia Albjerg Graham, a professor at Barnard College, and Cynthia Epstein, who had just published a book on women in the professions, talked about improving women's status in college-level teaching and administration. Sheila Tobias, associate provost at Wesleyan University, outlined the importance of women's studies programs. Most of these women did not come to the foundation out of simple altruism. They brought with them proposals for which they sought foundation support, and these, along with other proposals for projects concerning women in education being received by Ford, created outside pressures on the foundation to develop funding programs for women's programs.[22]

In mid-1971, leadership of the drive for women's programs in the Division of Education and Research passed from Spangenberg to Mariam Chamberlain. As a program officer, she surpassed Spangenberg in experience and influence, but initially she lacked the younger woman's feminist zeal. After earning a Ph.D. in economics from Harvard in 1950, Chamberlain had adapted her career moves to fit those of her husband, working at a succession of jobs that included college teaching, consulting for the Ford Foundation, and doing economic analyses for the Central Intelligence Agency. She joined Ford as a program officer in 1967. "Program officers have the responsibility to respond to needs when we see them" was her later assessment of her position. And Spangenberg and the feminists who visited the foundation in 1971, especially McCune and Tobias, made sure that Chamberlain saw the need for women's programs. In May 1971, Chamberlain identified a couple of projects "worthy of serious consideration[,] budgets permitting." And within months, she became the staff member most closely identified with funding for women's projects in E&R. Chamberlain joined NOW and later served on the national board of WEAL. But like most feminists at Ford as well as at the NCC and the IUE, her major efforts on behalf of women occurred in her workplace rather than in the national women's movement.[23]

The male leadership of E&R also soon adopted feminist goals. In September 1971 a discussion paper prepared for the board of trustees stressed the division's focus of many years—expanding educational opportunities for minorities. The document paid only modest attention to women, suggesting that "usually they are probably as well served as men, but when not, we should recognize and do something about it." Such activity would be "a checkpoint rather than . . . an area of special involvement." Just five months later, in February 1972, the division set women's concerns at the top of a list of new program options. That shift represented the culmination of activities begun by Spangenberg in 1970 and owed a great deal to a meeting held at the foundation in November 1971.[24]

Chamberlain had seized on Sheila Tobias' suggestion that E&R sponsor a discussion between academic feminists and foundation staff. Here was an opportunity to impress upon powerful men in the organization the importance of supporting educational equity for women. For this proposal, Chamberlain won the backing of Harold Howe II, vice president and head of the division. The former commissioner of education in the Johnson administration, Howe already knew and respected Tobias. Like Bundy, he was open to new ideas, and he had an unusual eagerness to hear about issues with which he was unfamiliar. Chamberlain scheduled the meeting in President Bundy's conference room, sent Bundy an invitation to drop in, and persuaded Howe to reinforce the invitation. "It would be good to have you tune in with these ladies at any point you would find possible," Howe wrote Bundy. The president did more. He attended the entire meeting, and his presence, along with that of Howe and Deputy Vice President Marshall A. Robinson, meant that the feminists' ideas reached an audience empowered to act on them.[25]

The thirteen women invited to the meeting represented various facets of feminist issues in higher education. Bernice Sandler, with assistance from WEAL, had filed the first sex-discrimination suit against universities under the executive order banning discrimination by federal contractors. Florence Howe of the State University of New York, Westbury, and Alice Rossi from Goucher College pioneered the field of women's studies. Ruth Mandel of the Center for the American Woman and Politics at Rutgers University was present. Tobias, Graham, Epstein, and McCune returned, and Chamberlain, Barber, and McLean were among the foundation women present.[26]

Although Ford routinely held meetings on various issues, this gathering became a catalyst in orienting the foundation toward goals of the women's movement. In a wide-ranging discussion, the academic feminists documented and deplored both the gender-stereotyped socialization and the outright discrimination that limited the presence of women in teaching and administrative positions. Chamberlain had arranged the meeting to give outsiders the force of numbers. The thirteen women did not always agree on specific points or remedies, but they generally reinforced one another. Because the women present greatly outnumbered the men — probably a first for the foundation — they spoke in an atmosphere of support. For the most part, the academic feminists obeyed Bundy's injunction at the outset of the meeting to refrain from proposing how the foundation should spend its money. But Mandel took the opportunity to suggest that the women's movement needed seed money. And Sandler averred that money for lawsuits might do more to help sex equity in higher education than funds for fellowships. Several of the women followed up the meeting with letters to Bundy and others outlining the needs of women and possibilities for Ford activities.[27]

At around the same time, feminist ideas were gaining currency in the National Affairs division, which Bundy had assigned to tackle "the larger dimensions of the role of women in our society" while the Trottenberg committee dealt with women inside the foundation. Throughout the 1960s, N.A. had concentrated on urban crises, funding projects to decrease poverty, unemployment, and crime and to improve housing and education for disadvantaged residents of the inner cities, especially African Americans. National Affairs became even more involved in social-action programs after Mitchell Sviridoff, a former labor leader and head of New York City's Human Resources Administration, became division director. Given these circumstances, it is not surprising that when N.A. began to consider the needs of women, it focused on those who were often slighted by the national feminist movement: poor and working-class women and women of color.[28]

Junior-level staff women laid the groundwork for the expansion of N.A.'s agenda in a forty-page paper, "Recommendations for Women's Programs," which they submitted to Sviridoff and Bundy in October 1971. Assistant counsel McLean and program officer Oppenheimer-Nicolau helped write the paper, but none of the other eight women in the group held professional staff positions. All worked in National Affairs, except for Gail Spangenberg, who managed to push a feminist agenda in that division as well as in her home base of E&R; and the group included only one woman of color, Kathryn Mitchell. It nonetheless produced a comprehensive analysis of existing programs, pointing out how they could be revised to serve women or how they offered models for new women's programs. The group's survey of fellowship, leadership, and job-training and education programs found women severely underrepresented both in general programs and in programs for minorities. The document boldly recommended a budget of $2 million for women's programs in five areas, including women's rights litigation, employment, and the women's movement.[29]

As was true in E&R, external pressures on N.A. helped fuel the push for women's programming. The division had already funded a proposal to establish the Center for the American Woman and Politics. (The women's report called this "a welcome precedent," but at $50,000 over a two-year period, "too small . . . to bear the burden of major expectations in programming for women.") Proposals to establish women's rights law firms modeled after those created by the civil rights movement had also arrived at the foundation. At about the same time that E&R held its meeting with academic feminists, in October and November 1971, National Affairs entertained a parade of experts on women.[30]

Leading off was Esther Peterson, a former trade unionist, prime mover in the President's Commission on the Status of Women, and assistant secretary of labor in the Kennedy and Johnson administrations. At Sviridoff's request, Peterson came with a forty-three-page paper exploring women's status and concerns and recommending potential program activities for foundations. In keeping with the recent focus of N.A. funding and of her own career, Peterson urged Ford to target "the average woman, the poor woman, and the minority woman." Although sex discrimination was universal, the "well-educated, well-heeled" woman had greater resources to improve her lot; "if the most disadvantaged group can be lifted, it lifts all." Peterson's recommendations paralleled those of the N.A. staff, some of whom had helped with the research. They touched nearly every feminist base and concluded with an appeal for Ford to transform itself into a model of equal opportunity. After Peterson came Aileen Hernandez, former president of NOW; Adele Simmons of Tufts University, who spoke about continuing education for inner-city women; Eleanor Holmes Norton, a lawyer and chair of New York City's Commission on Human Rights, who discussed litigation in the field of women's rights and minority women's perspectives on the women's movement; and Barbara Wertheimer and Alice Cook of the New York State School of Industrial Relations, who educated the Ford staff about women in the labor movement.[31]

Institutionalizing Feminist Funding

Formal and informal networks facilitated feminist efforts at Ford. In February 1972 thirty-seven minority women added their collective voice to calls for funding projects targeting disadvantaged women. Employed in support-staff positions throughout the foundation, Concerned Minority Women at Ford keyed in on N. A.'s antipoverty and community development programs. In all of the strategies aimed at the urban poor, they asserted, "one of the major and more constant victims of poverty has been almost completely overlooked—the minority women." Noting the high proportion of single mothers in the black population, they concluded that "minority women need jobs as much or more than men." They pressured the foundation to expand existing programs to provide more training for women, make day care a top priority, and tackle problems associated with teenage pregnancy. Concerned Minority Women at Ford urged the foundation to support training programs for women to help them move beyond clerical occupations. Dovetailing self-interest with community needs, they suggested a pilot program for minority women in the foundation.[32]

Another network grew up primarily around white women. By the end of 1971, Ford employees had begun to notice that a handful of women who were known to be interested in women's issues frequently sat together at lunch. Although the composition of the group varied, Berresford, Chamberlain, McLean, Spangenberg, and Terry Saario, who worked on elementary and secondary education, formed its core. Over lunch, these women discussed the proposals coming across their desks and considered possibilities for foundation initiatives. The women formed close friendships as well as an informal network for promoting a feminist agenda at Ford. In April 1972 the informal networks would take institutional shape with the creation of a Task Force on Women.[33]

Feminists at Ford also became involved in an outside network in 1972 when women from several philanthropies in New York City began to get together. Calling their group Women in Foundations, they exchanged information about women's issues and ideas for women's projects and strategized about making their foundations more receptive to feminist proposals. One of the members, Avery Russell from the Carnegie Corporation, published an article in the journal *Foundation News* announcing the group's creation and calling for more attention to women's issues from the foundation world. Susan Berresford co-chaired Women in Foundations; Miriam Chamberlain and other Ford colleagues were members.[34]

Berresford also had a hand in creating a national network concerned with women and philanthropy. At the 1975 annual conference of the Council on Foundations, women met separately to discuss women's issues. That meeting led to a new organization, Women and Foundations/Corporate Philanthropy, which was established in May 1977 to work for greater funding of programs for women and girls and to advance women in the profession of philanthropy. Women and Foundations grew to include more than a hundred supporting organizations and several hundred individual members. Berresford was a member of the planning committee and served on its board of directors, while the Ford Foundation provided modest grants in its first few years of operation.[35]

At Ford, the push for attention to women's issues got a boost from President Bundy's interest in more rational, systematic, and long-range planning on the part of the foundation. In January 1972 he announced a revision of planning and budgeting processes and asked all divisions to identify new fields for foundation activity. Harold Howe wanted to clarify foundation priorities with regard to women's programming. "Mariam Chamberlain is stirring up quite a lot of activity about women," he noted. "The way projects are coming in and with all the discussion that is going on, we can get nickeled and dimed to death . . . without having a really clear policy about it." [36]

In response to Bundy's request for potential new areas of funding, both National Affairs and Education and Research identified equal opportunity and equal treatment for women as important targets. Howe reported that as a result of the November meeting with the feminists in higher education, his division had under consideration a number of small grants as well as the establishment of a task force on women and education. Sviridoff forwarded the recommendations of N.A. staff women and of Concerned Minority Women at Ford, reported on recent grants for day care and litigation projects, and suggested focusing on the special problems of minority women. Both Howe and Sviridoff recognized that women's issues crossed divisional lines, and they supported the creation of a foundation-wide planning group as well as additional staff meetings with outside experts. [37]

Further advocacy for a foundation-wide approach to women's issues came from Oppenheimer-Nicolau, the sole female program officer in National Affairs. Reflecting on the precedents that civil rights activism had set for feminism in general, her paper recalled the foundation's response to the civil rights movement in the 1960s. Without diminishing its commitment to minorities, she argued, the foundation should move with equal determination to address issues raised by the women's movement. Just as Ford had begun its programming for minorities with a foundation-wide study committee, it should establish a similar body "to explore how Foundation research and action can help achieve a world free of sexism as well as racism." [38]

Bundy incorporated these suggestions into a paper presented to the trustees in March 1972. He acknowledged that the foundation "has been relatively insensitive to the special . . . problems and needs of women, and the unfair, often unreasonable obstacles and barriers" they faced. Promising vigorous internal affirmative action, Bundy identified equal opportunity and treatment of women as one of ten potential new fields for future funding emphasis. Viewing foundation activity as "complementary to the massive forces beyond our walls," he named education and employment, law and public policy, information and communication, and sex-role socialization in education as areas where Ford "should be able to foster change and social progress." With the informal consent of the trustees, Bundy created a Task Force on Women to explore potential areas for philanthropy.[39]

Bundy's selection of vice presidents Howe and Sviridoff to co-chair the task force signified the importance of male support for the new funding area. Although women initiated the focus on women and exercised day-to-day responsibility for applications and grants, without the help of the most powerful men at Ford, they could not move ahead. In accordance with Howe's recommendations, Bundy filled out the task force roster with nine women, most of whom were already involved in feminist activities. Six, including Chamberlain, McLean, and Oppenheimer-Nicolau, were among the highest-ranking women at the foundation. Two others, Berresford and Saario, moved up the professional ladder when they became program officers in 1972.

Even though National Affairs had targeted minority women as one of its primary interests, Bundy's appointees were all white. Women of color had to achieve representation through their own efforts, working through Concerned Minority Women at Ford. The group's chair, Beatrice Colebrooke, a staff assistant at N.A., wrote to Howe insisting that the lack of minority women at the professional level should not be an excuse to exclude minority representation on the task force. In response, Howe penciled a note on the bottom of her memo: "We don't want to leave anyone out." He invited her to "join our informal group at its next meeting." Despite Howe's laconic response, at least one woman of color served on the task force and its successors.[40]

With representatives from the four major divisions, the task force involved a broad range of programs, thereby providing widespread visibility for women's concerns. Its very creation, in addition to the selection of its co-chairs, further invested women's issues with importance and legitimacy and captured the attention of those empowered to make decisions. The task force could prod foundation officials who were not yet engaged in women's programming to consider possibilities in this area. And its meetings continued the consciousness-raising begun in 1971, providing a regular audience for new ideas and a systematic mechanism of support and reinforcement for the promotion of feminist goals.

The task force helped spur the International division to catch up to National Affairs and Education and Research in support for women's programs. David E. Bell, a vice president and head of International, noted that "cultural constraints" limited actions in many of the division's operations abroad. Even though the division gave high priority to birth control and family planning, experts on developing nations had not yet recognized women's critical role in food production or the connection between elevating women's status and lowering the birth rate. Thus, the International division had no focus on women as such. Its representative on the task force, Elinor Barber, had been involved in the early foundation activities concerning women, however, and she began discussions within the division about possibilities for targeting women. She distributed task force documents to staff in New York and abroad and asked overseas representatives to submit reports about women's needs and problems in their areas. As co-chair of the task force, Howe prodded Bell, commenting on activities already under way and reminding him that "action is likely to take place where it is strongly supported by Vice Presidents." Barber's efforts and Howe's urgings encouraged Bell to give serious attention to women's programs. In April 1974 he convened a general division meeting and established a Committee on Women in International Programs with Barber as chair. Bell's appointment

of Mariam Chamberlain from E&R to the new committee demonstrated the continuing cross-divisional influence in stimulating
international activities on women's behalf.[41]

The task force completed its most important duty, preparation
of a report and recommendations for the trustees, in March 1973.
Its twenty-five-page paper surveyed the women's movement, explained feminist issues, and reported on feminist initiatives the
foundation had already undertaken. It recommended four lines of
action: vigorous pursuit of internal affirmative action; attention
to every grant to ensure that women's concerns were addressed
wherever appropriate; foundation-wide grant making focused on
women's economic status but also including educational equity,
family issues, and changing attitudes toward women; and the creation of a standing committee to monitor progress and recommend strategy changes as new needs and issues arose. With trustee
approval, Bundy created a Coordinating Committee on Women
to carry on when the task force completed its work at the end
of 1973.[42]

Four members of the task force joined the coordinating
committee: Berresford, Barber, Howe, and Chamberlain, whom
Bundy appointed chair. Esther Schacter from National Affairs and
Adrienne Germain from the International division's Population
Office had had little previous involvement with feminist issues but
would contribute significantly to future activities. The remaining
five members came from other offices, representing all major program areas. In 1976, Schacter replaced Chamberlain as chair, and
several changes in membership occurred throughout the 1970s.
But leadership in women's programming remained stable, resid-
ing in a small group consisting of Berresford and Schacter in
National Affairs; Howe, Chamberlain, and Saario in Education;
and Barber and Germain in International.[43]

The coordinating committee institutionalized the long-term
commitment of the Ford Foundation to promote feminist objectives. Its composition meant that no foundation office could

ignore the concerns of women, and its responsibility to report directly to Bundy carried these concerns to the top of the institution. Much of the grant making for women developed within specific program areas in response to proposals from individuals and women's groups. Yet the coordinating committee also took the initiative in defining areas in which Ford should act and in recruiting proposals. As had been the case with the task force, the coordinating committee's monthly meetings and sessions with outside feminists provided a regular vehicle for exchanging information and raising awareness about problems women faced.

The coordinating committee also provided a structure for women to raise issues that involved the foundation itself. The committee monitored affirmative action for foundation staff, prodding the Internal Affirmative Action Committee to meet more regularly and inform staff about its activities. The coordinating committee took up the complaints of support-staff women that they were underutilized and capable of doing work that was being contracted to consultants; and it struggled to eliminate the sex discrimination in retirement benefits practiced by TIAA-CREF, the foundation's insurance company. By 1976 the committee was regularly making recommendations to the trustees' proxy committee on how foundation stock shares should be voted at shareholders' meetings when the issues involved corporation practices concerning women.[44]

Consciousness-Raising

Like feminists in the National Council of Churches, those at the Ford Foundation found certain structures and practices conducive to consciousness-raising about women's issues. Continuing the meetings with outside experts that National Affairs and Education and Research had begun in 1971, both the task force and the coordinating committee served to encourage discussion and increase awareness of women's issues among women and men alike. Task force discussions began in May 1972 with law professors

Ruth Bader Ginsburg and Jane Picker and concluded in January 1973 with Baltimore County councilwoman Barbara Mikulski, who spoke on white ethnic women. Foundation staff also heard from, among others, Inez Reid, head of the Black Women's Community Development Foundation; Elizabeth Koontz, director of the Women's Bureau of the Department of Labor; feminist lawyers Ann Freedman and Rhonda Schoenbrod; and sociologists Elise Boulding, Alva Myrdal, and Lee Rainwater. Even the foundation staff most savvy about feminist issues found these sessions exhilarating. "Fascinating," declared Oppenheimer-Nicolau at the end of a meeting. "These are things I just never get to hear." [45]

Vice President Sviridoff had a different response: "Why do these sessions always turn into sensitivity meetings?" he asked during one of the visits. Though exaggerating the amount of "sensitivity" talk, his question acknowledged how much the character of the sessions depended on who attended. Sviridoff, Howe, and Paul A. Strasburg, Bundy's assistant, were usually the only men present. Commanding a majority of the gathering and with support from outside experts, foundation women boldly expressed their own frustrations and in so doing further enlightened other staff members who attended the sessions. During the discussion on employed women, for example, Oppenheimer-Nicolau noted that "personally I have suffered very directly" from accusations of being an "irresponsible, selfish, rotten woman who is not paying proper attention to her children." Chamberlain aired her annoyance at charges that employed women were "taking somebody else's job who needs it more than you do." And Berresford expressed her exasperation with media stereotypes about childrearing: "You know, the ads for babies' things drive me crazy. I get so angry. . . . You never see an advertisement of a man feeding an infant." Women from the outside also disclosed frustrations. Elise Boulding, for example, described the stresses of working within male-dominated groups, noting, "I have to decide any time I go into a meeting whether I'm going to call any statements . . . that are essentially denigrating to women."[46]

In these settings, where they had the power of numbers, women occasionally challenged men. Staff women displayed mild impatience when sociologist Lee Rainwater talked about women only in terms of their relationship to the family. They sought to turn his attention to women as individuals and disputed his comments on the "possible destructive" effects of the women's movement. Occasionally, the outside experts directly confronted foundation leaders about gender equity, as when Boulding asked, "Can you see what I'm looking at?" To Sviridoff's response, "No, what is that?" she shot back, "I'm looking at the [overwhelmingly male] staff of the Ford Foundation." And when Sviridoff complained about feeling "slightly flagellated" at the end of another session, Elizabeth Koontz gently reprimanded him for taking the discussion personally.[47]

Sviridoff frequently interrupted the conversations with wisecracks. When sociologist Janet Giele suggested that married women would have a better chance of pursuing careers when "boys grow up not having been taken care of so much hand and foot," Sviridoff retorted, "There goes another great institution — the Jewish mother." And when Berresford mentioned a film that presented abortion in a positive light, he queried, "Like abortion can be fun?" While the vice president's efforts at humor may have reflected some discomfort in dealing directly with gender issues, he also made clear that the sessions were having a positive effect on him. As we have seen, he approved the "judicious" application of pressure by feminists while declaring more extreme actions "counterproductive." Although Sviridoff clearly hoped to contain feminist activism at Ford, he also revealed that the male leadership's receptivity to feminist claims resulted from both internal pressures and external events. "Nobody wants a *Newsweek* sit-in at the Ford Foundation!" he said.[48]

Professionally socialized to be accessible to new ideas and issues and determined to avoid headline-grabbing demonstrations, male leaders at the Ford Foundation responded positively to feminist visitors and the urgings of their female subordinates. Although Paul Strasburg downplayed the amount of expertise needed by the task force on women, it quickly became obvious that foundation staff had a lot to learn from the visiting experts. Sviridoff, for example, expressed surprise upon learning from Boulding that women's traditional roles in West Africa involved considerable political and economic power. And he noted near the close of the session with Koontz, "I really got the message as I've never gotten it before." [49]

As a result of these meetings and other activities involving programs for women, Ford staff members became experts themselves on women's issues and extended the foundation's influence beyond the projects it funded. Terry Saario, for example, was co-author of an article on sex-role stereotyping in the public schools for the *Harvard Educational Review;* and she delivered a lecture on how schools discriminated against women to the National School Board Association in 1973. When the Senate Subcommittee on Education held hearings on the Women's Educational Equity Act of 1973, Howe testified along with educators and representatives of feminist organizations. Citing his experience with the task force at the foundation as well as research done by Saario, Howe made a forceful case for the significance of the women's movement and the need for society to adopt sweeping changes in gender roles. He called for educational materials and programs to counter conventional sex-role socialization and stereotypes, support for research about women, and "a major Federal effort in the child care area." He did not see the proposed bill as a "categorical aid to education" but rather as "human rights legislation that affects one-half the population directly and the rest of it . . . importantly." When Title IX of the Higher Education Amendments Act (1972) mandated an end to sex discrimination in all aspects of education and university presidents fought to keep football expenditures out of the calculation of equitable spending, Howe chastised the leaders and spoke out on behalf of gender equity.[50]

Meetings with outside experts in various areas were not uncommon at Ford, but the sessions with the feminists stood out for their scope, frequency, and intensity. These conversations played a crucial part in the education of Ford staff members and in the development of Ford's feminist agenda. But like that of the ACLU, the foundation's agenda was also shaped to a considerable extent at the instigation and to fit the purposes of the national women's movement.

Ford Funding for Women's Projects

"If we are to continue our legal work . . . we are going to need money," wrote Faith Seidenberg to fellow members of NOW's board of directors in May 1970. "We cannot continue to take cases in the name of NOW unless we have, at the very least, case expenses." The Women's Equity Action League, the other national mainstream feminist organization, suffered similar financial deficiency. "So far . . . we do not have any money to speak of," Ellen Dresselhuis wrote apologetically to Laurine Fitzgerald in January 1973, informing Fitzgerald that she had just been elected treasurer of WEAL's Educational and Legal Defense Fund (WEAL Fund). Both organizations, along with other feminist groups, looked to the Ford Foundation for financial support. And their requests spurred the women employed at Ford to demand that feminist causes be funded.[51]

The National Organization for Women exerted the bluntest form of pressure during congressional hearings on tax reform in April 1973. Testifying on behalf of NOW, Fran P. Hosken urged members of the House Ways and Means Committee to terminate the tax-exempt status of foundations and universities that continued to practice discrimination. Hosken presented the results of a survey she had conducted of Ford and other large foundations, noting how few women there were in policymaking positions and how small the funds were that Ford had expended on women's programs. She criticized the "arrogant administrations . . . of the enormously wealthy powerful foundations led by the Ford Foundation," which used their power to "willfully subvert equal employment legislation of the land." Finally, she called for foundations to "police their grants" so that funds did not go to organizations that practiced discrimination—a proposal that had already been made by staff women at Ford and that was finally implemented in 1974.[52]

Some at NOW found a kid-gloves approach more productive than Hosken's bludgeon. Mary Jean Tully was president of NOW's Legal Defense and Education Fund (LDEF), a small body that was more conservative than the organization itself and dominated by lawyers used to working within the establishment. Tully understood the need to pressure foundations and the efficacy of collective action. In the summer of 1974 she called together representatives of feminist organizations to discuss ways of getting greater foundation support for the women's movement. When an economic recession forced cuts in philanthropic spending, Tully spearheaded a letter-writing campaign by this informal network. A draft letter used by network members urged the foundations to exempt feminist projects as much as possible from any cuts caused by the economic crisis. Tully made the same appeal to Ford, but she altered the letter to commend that foundation for its "serious commitment" to feminist projects.[53]

Tully resumed the pressure on foundations as well as the praise for Ford in an article, "Funding the Feminists," published in *Foundation News* in March 1975. Although critical of foundations in general for failing to respond positively to the women's movement, she noted one exception: "Among the giants, only the Ford Foundation has moved in all the appropriate ways to meet the needs of feminists." At the same time she distinguished between quality and quantity, pointing out that expenditures on women's

projects constituted only a small proportion of the total disburse-
ments. Tully's singling out of Ford for being "light-years ahead of
the other major foundations" reflected in part her organization's
receipt of its first Ford grant in summer 1974. But it was also a
fair assessment; and she exploited the situation to flatter the foundation into more support and to challenge other foundations to
catch up.[54]

In spite of the efforts of NOW and WEAL to obtain support
for extensive litigation efforts, Ford chose to target its considerable funding for litigation projects elsewhere. But it did support
two law-related projects of NOW and WEAL; in both cases, the
timing, size, and nature of that support were crucial. The first
NOW LDEF grant came in 1974 to underwrite its Project on
Equal Education Rights, a program that monitored enforcement
of anti–sex-discrimination legislation. Providing $91,500 for a
one-year period at a time when the total NOW LDEF income
was $260,000, the grant gave a boost to the organization itself.
But Ford support had wider ramifications. The project helped
shape the regulation for enforcement of Title IX, and its director,
Holly Knox, organized a network of feminists that eventually became the influential National Coalition for Women and Girls in
Education, which represented fifty-five organizations. The project
published a quarterly newsletter, sent out information on educational equity policy, and served as a watchdog on federal agencies
responsible for enforcement. By 1978, Ford had subsidized NOW
LDEF to the tune of $675,000.[55]

The WEAL Fund was no more successful than NOW LDEF
in obtaining Ford money for litigation, but it too benefited from
grants in law-related areas. Bernice Sandler, a WEAL Fund board
member and one of the first outsiders to confer with Ford staff on
women in November 1971, used her contacts at the foundation to
ease the way. Beginning in 1976, Ford underwrote an intern program that subsidized staff salaries and office rent in Washington
while providing human labor for a number of WEAL projects.

While the NOW project focused on elementary and secondary education, the WEAL Fund's project concentrated on higher education. It also made opportunities in the military and equity in sports prime target areas and built on Ford support to capture federal funds for a national information bureau on discrimination in sports. The organization that had only $900 when Fitzgerald became treasurer in 1973 landed a Ford grant of $150,000 in 1976 and would receive more than half a million dollars more over the next seven years.[56]

Women's rights litigation was an early and sustained emphasis of Ford's feminist agenda. The foundation had already made a name for itself in civil rights litigation with sizable grants to the NAACP Legal Defense and Education Fund (NAACP LDF), the Mexican American Legal Defense and Education Fund (MALDEF), and the Native American Rights Fund. Women staff members at Ford called for the creation of a program on women and the law as early as October 1971, pointing to the civil rights precedents as explicit models and to proposals for women's rights law firms that had come into National Affairs.[57]

Ford began negotiations for a litigation grant with Jane M. Picker, a Cleveland State University law professor who represented the WEAL Fund. When Picker's WEAL colleagues objected to taking a case dealing with pregnancy discrimination, she left WEAL, taking with her Ford's interest and eventually obtaining $140,000 of its money to start the Women's Law Fund (WLF). One of its first cases was *Cleveland Board of Education v. LaFleur* (1974), which Picker argued on behalf of Jo Carol LaFleur and Ann Elizabeth Nelson, two junior high school teachers challenging a school board rule that pregnant teachers had to take unpaid maternity leave five months in advance of their due dates. The rule also restricted their return to teaching and did not guarantee reemployment. In one of its first rulings against sex discrimination in employment, the Supreme Court found mandatory maternity leave unconstitutional under the Fourteenth Amendment.

The only WLF case to reach the Supreme Court, *LaFleur* was its most visible accomplishment. But with Ford assistance amounting to more than $1 million over the decade, the WLF enjoyed such other successes as securing the right of pregnant women to unemployment compensation and ending restrictions on women police officers.[58]

Ford soon extended support for litigation to other organizations. First, in April 1973 it funded a meeting convened by Ruth Bader Ginsburg, at that time the coordinator of the ACLU's Women's Rights Project, and Sylvia Roberts, president of NOW LDEF. They invited some thirty feminist lawyers, including representatives from NOW, WEAL, and the WLF; government employees responsible for equal opportunity policy; women in private practice who handled feminist litigation; and individuals like Pauli Murray, Ruth Weyand, and Sarah Weddington, the lawyer who won *Roe v. Wade*. The meeting reflected Ford's interest in increasing communication among feminist lawyers, identifying critical priorities for women, and encouraging the development of a coherent and orderly strategy for challenging sex discrimination.[59]

Soon a number of other organizations became Ford beneficiaries as well. The foundation granted more than half a million dollars to the NAACP LDF and MALDEF for projects concerning African American and Mexican American women. Another $570,000 enabled the Washington, D.C.–based Women's Rights Project of the Center for Law and Social Policy to represent WEAL and other feminist groups in compelling federal agencies to enforce antidiscrimination policy. By 1980, Ford had allocated $1 million to the Women's Rights Project of the ACLU, which, as we have seen, served as leader in the feminist advocacy movement. In the 1970s alone, Ford-supported organizations sponsored or filed amicus curiae briefs in more than twenty sex-discrimination cases that reached the Supreme Court. Although feminist advocates never convinced the Court to declare sex a suspect classification, as it had done with race, their efforts profoundly transformed women's status under the law.[60]

Sheila Tobias, who had helped found the women's studies program at Cornell University before becoming associate provost at Wesleyan University, was one of the first feminist academics to capture the ears of Ford Foundation staff. In March 1971, she met with Elinor Barber, Mariam Chamberlain, and Gail Spangenberg. According to Spangenberg, who wrote up the meeting for the files, Tobias "presented her case for Women's Studies in a way that was entertaining, informed, and compelling," despite her tendency "to view Kate Millett's *Sexual Politics* with adoration." Notwithstanding Tobias' impressive presentation, the foundation representatives discouraged any hopes that Ford would fund women's studies programs, primarily because such programs were "springing up all around the country without foundation help." Undaunted, Tobias talked with foundation staff again in August, a meeting that led to the November 1971 gathering of academic feminists that was attended by the top brass at the foundation.[61]

Although Chamberlain did not recommend support for Tobias' project, Tobias had clearly decreased her skepticism about women's studies. Under Chamberlain's leadership, support for research on women claimed the largest single share of Ford's program for women in higher education. That support began in 1972 with faculty research and doctoral dissertation fellowships for individuals conducting research on women. Amounting to more than $1 million by 1975, the 122 fellowships supported pathbreaking work among the first generation of women's studies scholars, including anthropologist Nancy Tanner; sociologists Ava Baron, Rae Blumberg, and Leonore Weitzman; historians Nancy Schrom Dye, Ellen C. Dubois, William R. Leach, Elaine Tyler May, and Kathryn Kish Sklar; and political scientist Susan J. Pharr. The fellowship programs conferred legitimacy on the work of these young scholars at a time when they were struggling for acceptance of their subject area, and it gave them opportunities for career advancement. Moreover, although the Woodrow Wilson Foundation administered the dissertation fellowships program, Ford staff handled the faculty program; in reviewing more than two hundred proposals each year, foundation staff gained further knowledge and awareness of women's issues.[62]

At mid-decade, the Ford Foundation's interest in women's studies shifted to concentration on research programs and centers at universities. By 1980 the foundation had helped pay for research centers at Stanford University, Radcliffe College, Columbia University, the University of California, Berkeley, Wellesley College, and the University of Arizona, among others. The Carnegie Corporation initially funded the Wellesley center, but in most instances Ford provided crucial seed money—averaging more than $200,000 for a two-year period—that paid for administrative services, individual research projects, newsletters, and the like. Equally important, the foundation's support signaled to university administrators the importance of research on women. In making these grants, Ford demanded a firm commitment from the institution and pressured it to increase its own support and prepare to eventually assume full responsibility for funding the center. Moreover, Ford's assistance to the Center for the American Woman and Politics at Rutgers University not only promoted research on the political participation of women but also underwrote a number of projects designed to bring more women into the political sphere. To director Ruth Mandel, Ford's support was "vital" in creating the center and an enormous help in attracting other funding.[63]

The third aspect of Ford assistance to women's studies in the 1970s involved a series of small grants for the creation and sustenance of the kind of supplementary institutions that are critical to emerging scholarly fields. In 1974 foundation support facilitated communication among pioneers in the field by enabling the Feminist Press to publish *Who's Who and Where in Women's Studies*. Two years later, Ford helped lay the groundwork for a national professional organization by funding planning activities for the National Women's Studies Association. And it invested seed money for *Signs: Journal of Women in Culture and Society*, which quickly became the premier interdisciplinary journal in women's studies. Nor did the foundation's influence stop there. Chamberlain made it a practice to fill her office bookshelves with women's studies publications, drawing attention to them whenever educational leaders visited, regardless of the purpose of their call. Like Howe, Saario, and others, Chamberlain used the influence that attended her position to speak on behalf of women's concerns to the world outside.[64]

The decision Chamberlain and Spangenberg made in 1971 not to push for funding of women's studies programs accorded with their professional culture. Foundation executives and trustees gave highest priority to areas where grants could make a difference, not simply replicate projects already in existence. And, as Chamberlain and Spangenberg noted, women's studies courses and programs were in fact springing up everywhere without foundation support; research centers were not. Yet the decision to focus on research centers rather than on women's studies programs left a heavy burden on advocates for the programs at most colleges and universities, where women—often untenured—struggled to build these programs without compensation or approval, in addition to their regular responsibilities. The alternative that Ford took— to concentrate on promoting research—gave a tremendous boost to scholarship about women but primarily benefited elite institutions and faculty.[65]

In the 1980s, however, the foundation expanded its approach in two directions. It funded new centers at Spelman College and Memphis State University that concentrated on women of color and working-class women. And although its women's studies focus continued to be research, Ford invested $1.6 million in a project to integrate minority women's studies into the general undergraduate curriculum.

The Ford Foundation's agenda deviated most sharply from that of liberal feminism in its attention to women of color and poor and working-class women. Although mainstream feminists often acknowledged the white middle-class bias of their concerns, they rarely prioritized the needs of other women. Poor and minority women did benefit from efforts to attack sex discrimination in a general way, and they profited from legislation-monitoring and litigation programs supported by both Ford and feminist organizations. But the foundation went beyond liberal feminism in specifically targeting disadvantaged women for assistance.

The National Affairs division led in the creation of foundation projects for poor, working-class, and minority women. Mitchell Sviridoff's background lay in labor union activism and antipoverty work, and the division had concentrated on programs for disadvantaged groups throughout the 1960s. Even before the foundation turned its attention to women, N.A. had supported the National Committee on Household Employment in its efforts to organize and upgrade the skills of domestic workers. Soon the staff at N.A. would realize that its goal of extending economic security to poor families depended on addressing the needs of women.

As we have seen, the staff women who organized Concerned Minority Women at Ford pushed N.A. farther in that direction. Sviridoff specifically cited the group's recommendations in 1972 when he ranked women's programs as second only to assisting community development corporations in a list of new program areas. In spite of some "overall progress for minorities and the poor in the 1960s," he wrote, "there was backward movement among what appears to be the most intractable part of the poverty program—that of the minority female-headed household." Sviridoff recognized that while the women's movement had generated a vast amount of information about women's status, "the discrimination experienced by some important groups of women has not yet been seriously addressed." These included single mothers, employed working-class women, and elderly unemployed or widowed women. Sviridoff then invited outside experts to meet with foundation staff and arranged for a series of research papers on these groups.[66]

National Affairs implemented its "central priority" to improve "the economic security of disadvantaged women" in several ways. To alleviate a burden that affected all employed women but weighed especially heavy on low-income women, Ford expended the largest amount of funds on day-care projects. After a presidential veto killed prospects for a federal day-care initiative in 1972, the foundation spent more than $3 million, one-third of which went to the Black Child Development Institute. It focused on the worst-paid and most exploited category of women workers with grants of more than a million dollars to the National Committee on Household Employment by 1977. In Bedford-Stuyvesant, in Brooklyn, the Sisterhood of Black Single Mothers used foundation funds to help teenage mothers obtain education and jobs and develop childrearing skills; similar projects in St. Louis and Chicago won grants, and in 1980, Ford appropriated $500,000 for additional efforts. Even larger amounts were used to support experimental programs to help women move from the welfare rolls to jobs. Making an exception to its general refusal to involve itself with public policy on abortion, Ford supported a study of how poor women fared when the Hyde Amendment restricted the use of Medicaid funds for abortions.[67]

Foundation-supported projects also targeted women in blue- and pink-collar jobs. One of Ford's first grants to women's projects went to Cornell University's School of Industrial and Labor Relations. With more than half a million dollars from Ford between 1972 and 1979, the project investigated female participation in trade union leadership and provided training and education for women union members. To help women move into jobs formerly monopolized by men, Ford supported projects to attack bias in vocational education and in the distribution of jobs under the Comprehensive Employment Training Act. Women attempting to enter the predominantly male field of coal mining could obtain training, legal support, and information from the Coal Employment Project, another example of Ford's programs for blue-collar women. The foundation aimed at pink-collar women with grants to the National Association of Office Workers to organize and train clerical workers in monitoring sex-discrimination complaints and with support for the project sponsored by the Center for Women in Government at the State University of New York, Albany, to help women break down sex segregation in civil service jobs.[68]

In spite of the Ford Foundation's historic commitment to projects around the world, its International Division came late to women's programming, after both external and internal pressures impelled it to develop funding for women abroad. In 1972 Elise Boulding pointed out to the Task Force on Women how development projects not only ignored women but frequently eroded their traditional status, power, and access to resources. As the task force encouraged the International Division to initiate women's programming, Elinor Barber and Adrienne Germain worked within the division on the same goal. Employed in the division's Population Office, Germain exploited the foundation's longstanding support of population planning, arguing that the elevation of the status of women would tend to decrease fertility. But while she maintained that achieving population goals depended upon increasing opportunities for women, she also insisted that Ford should promote women's well-being as an end in itself, not just as an instrument of population policy.[69]

Outside the foundation, the United Nations called attention to women during International Population Year (1974) and then designated 1975 International Women's Year. In the United States, scholars in the development field began to organize around issues concerning women in developing nations. In 1973 the group helped pass the so-called Percy Amendment to the Foreign Assistance Act, requiring federal agencies to examine the implications for women in foreign aid programs. In 1972, Elinor Barber began to canvas field offices around the world about their program activities concerning women. And in 1974 the International Division formed its own Committee on Women, with a commitment to develop programs to promote social justice for women as an end in itself as well as a means of furthering development by utilizing women's resources fully.[70]

Early foundation activities in the international realm concentrated on information gathering because of circumstances specific to many developing countries: previous inattention to women as a group; absence of the kind of strong and diverse women's organizations that existed in the United States; values associated with traditional gender roles; and foundation agents' desire to avoid cultural imperialism. Although virtually every field office devoted its initial attention to research, several moved quickly into such activities as conferences and publications designed to promote awareness of women's issues, and thence to supporting experimental programs.[71]

Foundation activities in Bangladesh were exceptional in their range and depth, but they can illustrate the kinds of efforts undertaken by other field offices. In 1974 the Bangladesh office made women's issues visible with small grants for research, seminars, and reports. Recognizing women's age-old and vital role in food production, Ford helped establish a pilot project for rural women's cooperatives, which would enable women to operate more effectively and improve their skills as agricultural producers. And it prodded the Bangladeshi government to take women into account in policy planning by offering a $220,000 grant for a research unit on women in agriculture. Another grant of $120,000 provided training for women to encourage their participation in research and policy formation relating to rural development, population, and education. As it did in other countries, the foundation's New York office provided considerable assistance: Germain spent several weeks in Bangladesh consulting with Ford staff as well as with Bangladeshi men and women outside the foundation.[72]

Research, training women for leadership and policymaking, and experimental projects to improve women's economic status formed the major emphases of foundation efforts in other countries. In Brazil, Ford provided $100,000 for research on women's education and employment; Beirut University College received $250,000 for its Institute for Women's Studies in the Arab World. Grants totaling $160,000 enabled the African Training and Research Centre for Women to study women's legal and economic status and to train women in food production and small-business management. Opportunities for Tanzanian women to pursue postgraduate education came with Ford grants of more than $200,000 to the University of Dar es Salaam. As the International Division's programming for women matured, it appropriated more funds to encourage development strategies that would be responsive to women's concerns, making special efforts to organize poor women and increase their opportunities for earning income.[73]

Mary Jean Tully exaggerated when she wrote that the Ford Foundation had "moved in all the appropriate ways" to meet feminist aspirations. The foundation was, after all, an established institution and tended to focus on high-priority issues for mainstream feminists. Ford did not, for example, address issues of specific concern to lesbians, nor did it provide any significant support for key priorities of radical feminists, such as violence against women. In 1973, Susan Berresford was struck by the number of inquiries to the foundation about proposals for projects on rape. Women's groups reported to Berresford that they could not "get even the most cursory hearing and people treat them as if they are crazy." In spite of Berresford's sympathy for these groups, Ford expended little money to reduce violence against women, and nearly all of those funds were spent on projects in developing nations.

The foundation did assist such organizations as the ACLU that identified reproductive freedom as a major priority, but it provided little direct funding in the area of abortion rights. Thanks considerably to the efforts of Concerned Minority Women at Ford, the foundation concentrated on issues critical to disadvantaged women to a much larger extent than did mainstream feminism. Yet it could point to far less progress in those areas than it could in matters of rights and access for more privileged women. The combination of sexism with racism and economic exploitation put minority and low-income women's problems beyond the means of foundation remedies to alleviate in a substantial way.[74]

Within these limitations, by the mid-1970s women's programming occupied a firm position in each of the major divisions and had captured about $9.5 million of foundation spending. In contrast to 1972, when the foundation employed few female program officers, by 1976 nearly a dozen women had work responsibilities that included grants furthering a feminist agenda. But advocates for women's programming did not stop there. When in 1976 the board of trustees embarked on planning for the 1980s, Esther Schacter protested the "apparent lack of concern for equity and fairness as it affects women" in the papers prepared for the trustees. After the trustees had included women's programs among their priorities, Schacter urged stronger language to describe the barriers confronting women. Along with Berresford and Chamberlain, she pressed to expand the women's program and make it a high priority for the 1980s.[75]

Perhaps to leave a clean slate for his successor, McGeorge Bundy terminated the foundation-wide Coordinating Committee on Women's Programs in 1978, noting that the major foundation divisions had "well-developed and well-staffed programs and projects on behalf of women." Recognizing that "our work on behalf of women is not complete," he assumed that it would "go forward within the regular offices of the Foundation." Women's programming did go forward—and then some—when Franklin A. Thomas took over in 1979.[76]

An attorney, Thomas had served as president of the Bedford-Stuyvesant Restoration Corporation, as a Ford trustee, and on the board of directors' executive committee of the Women's Action Alliance. One of his first objectives at Ford was restructuring the organization. He ended the separation between domestic and international programs, combining them into a single program division with six key emphases that included poverty, human rights and social justice, and education. Along with the integration of domestic and overseas programs, Thomas also moved to integrate women's programming more tightly throughout the foundation. Funding for women's projects shot up.[77]

In 1980 the trustees approved an increase in women's programming of more than 100 percent, allocating $19.3 million, 10 percent of total spending, to women-specific projects for the years 1980 and 1981. Thomas also restored a foundation-wide mechanism for overseeing and reviewing women's programs. He created a Women's Program Group with Berresford as chair; Barber, Chamberlain, Germain, and Saario were among the members, thereby maintaining continuity with past feminist organizations. The group proved even more active than its predecessor, the coordinating committee. Berresford and other members reviewed every grant recommended for approval and prepared a statement to the president about the proposed grant's relationship to women's concerns. Group members also commented on staff papers dealing with such subjects as migrants and refugees, rural America, and the military and society. Although the strategy of reviewing all proposed grants rarely influenced a particular application, the group's efforts on grants and staff papers emphasized women's concerns for staff members. In addition, Berresford interviewed most of the final candidates for all professional staff positions.[78]

In the course of reorganization several of the most active advocates for women—notably Mariam Chamberlain, Elinor Barber, Terry Saario, and Harold Howe—left the foundation. But others remained. Thomas appointed Berresford vice president in charge of U.S. and International Affairs programs; he thus filled one of the foundation's most powerful positions with a woman who throughout the 1970s had stood in the forefront of the movement to make the foundation embrace feminism. Berresford's rise to the vice presidency symbolized Ford's efforts at internal affirmative action, its commitment to furthering key goals of the women's movement, and its respect for staff members who promoted those goals. When Thomas retired in 1996, the board of directors appointed Berresford president of the foundation.[79]

Harold Howe once attempted to explain why the American Council on Education lagged behind other organizations in addressing sexism in education. He suggested that the council did not have "the lively characters on its staff who can be found in National Education Association [Shirley McCune] or in the American Association of Colleges [Bernice Sandler]." Howe, of course, had experienced firsthand the feminist passion of McCune and Sandler during the in-house sessions on women's issues. Yet in analyzing why an organization was or was not receptive to issues raised by the women's movement, he might just as well have been thinking about the "lively characters" in his own institution.[80]

To be sure, a number of circumstances made it likely that Ford would support at least some women's programs. The leadership envisioned the foundation as being on the cutting edge of social change and could hardly ignore either the sizable women's movement or the momentous changes taking place in women's social and economic roles. Moreover, the foundation's commitment to promoting civil rights and alleviating poverty at home and abroad guaranteed that staff and trustees would entertain ideas about women's stake in those objectives. In addition, feminists in education and other professions had begun to pressure the foundation for support even before it initiated a women's program. Yet, above all, it was feminists within the foundation—initially largely independent of the feminist movement and without an internal power base—who raised the issues and shaped them into a comprehensive program. Their efforts succeeded in part because feminists on the outside targeted the foundation as a potential supporter of movement aims and in part because men like Bundy, Howe, Sviridoff, and later Thomas possessed power as well as open minds and a willingness to be educated. In the end, however, staff women were the "lively characters" who played the key role in allying the Ford Foundation with the women's movement.

CHAPTER SIX

Closing Gaps in Civil Rights and Women's Rights

Black Women and Feminism

Because black women have an equal stake in women's liberation
and black liberation, they are key figures at the juncture of these
two movements. . . . By asserting a leadership role in the growing
feminist movement, the black woman can help to keep it allied to
the objectives of black liberation while simultaneously advancing
the interests of all women. —Pauli Murray

The white middle-class face of liberal feminism in the
1960s and 1970s was the image that appeared both in
contemporary commentary about the movement and
in later scholarship. Frances M. Beal, Toni Morrison,
Ida Lewis, and Linda La Rue, all critics of liberal feminism in
its early years, as well as such scholars as Paula Giddings, bell
hooks, and Jacqueline Jones in the 1980s, focused on the race-
and class-based limitations of the new women's movement.
They wrote about the hypocrisy of white women seeking to
recruit black women to feminist organizations while adopting
agendas that ignored their particular needs. They charged that
white feminists exploited laws and precedents that were won
by the struggle and blood of African Americans to serve their
own narrow interests. They decried what they saw as the igno-

rance and racism that led white middle-class women to compare their status to that of poor blacks. And they objected to the failure of white feminists to appreciate that black women needed to express solidarity with black men in the struggle against racism.[1]

These and other scholars argued that rejection of the white-dominated women's movement did not necessarily mean dismissal of feminist ideas. "For every black anti-feminist article," said bell hooks, "there existed a pro-feminist black female position." In writing *Black Feminist Thought,* Patricia Hill Collins drew on the work of a number of African American women writing in the 1960s and early 1970s. As Paula Giddings pointed out, several African American women were founders or early members of NOW, including Aileen Hernandez, Pauli Murray, Addie L. Wyatt, and Anna Arnold Hedgeman. The National Women's Political Caucus claimed Shirley Chisholm, Myrlie B. Evers, Marian Wright Edelman, Dorothy Height, Eleanor Holmes Norton, and Johnnie Tillmon as founding members. And public opinion polls routinely showed and continue to show substantially greater support among black women than among white women for "efforts to strengthen or change women's status in society" and for "efforts of women's liberation groups."[2]

Pauli Murray was not alone in insisting that black women had a stake in both women's liberation and black liberation. By shifting our focus away from the independent women's movement, we can observe the feminism of black women taking shape in other ways. Organizations like the American Civil Liberties Union, the National Council of Churches, and the Ford Foundation proved more hospitable to African American feminists than NOW and other explicitly feminist groups. The activities of women in these liberal organizations in the 1960s and 1970s complicate the truism that the women's movement piggybacked on the civil rights movement. White feminists indeed exploited the moral environment and legal precedents created by that struggle, and they

Thelma Stevens (left) and Pauli Murray examine Murray's *States' Laws on Race and Color* (Courtesy of the Schlesinger Library, Radcliffe College).

borrowed organizational strategies from civil rights activism. And black women used men's understanding of racism to drive home points about sexism. Betty Witherspoon Webb, speaking for the NCC women's caucus in 1972, challenged sexist language by comparing "the traditional use of male 'generic' terms" to "the experience of Black invisibility in the history of this country." But more often, African American feminists reinterpreted civil rights: they defined their interests in terms of their identities as blacks *and* as women, thus anticipating the academic theory about the interconnectedness of race, class, and gender that emerged in the 1980s. They gave life to Murray's vision of African American women as "key figures at the juncture" of women's rights and civil rights.[3]

A closer examination of the lives of women like Pauli Murray, Joan Martin, Eleanor Holmes Norton, and Beatrice Colebrook reveals the significant contributions that African American women made to the advancement of black and white feminist goals, contributions often obscured by scholars' concentration on the race and class bias of mainstream white feminism. In this chapter, I revisit those women as a group, explaining how certain African American women developed as feminists and how they exhibited their feminism in activism, pursuing feminist goals outside both the autonomous women's movement and the civil rights movement. I investigate the possibilities and limitations of interracial cooperation between women and explore the particular emphases and definitions that black women imparted to liberal feminist goals and activism; in Audre Lorde's words, "Black feminism is not white feminism in blackface."

Black Women's Paths to Feminism

The majority of African American women stood outside the mainstream women's movement; some actively criticized it. Those few who embraced it came to their position in various ways. Some confronted blatant sex discrimination in male-dominated professions like religion and the law. Some chafed at the male-centered nature of the black freedom struggle. Some found that the experience of racial oppression made them sensitive to other forms of discrimination and thus to the feminist ideas current in the late 1960s. Personal relationships with other feminists led some African American women to feminism. All of the women considered here had associations with liberal organizations whose historical purposes and more recent commitments to racial justice provided both inspiration and opportunities for feminism.

The sexism embedded in the legal profession was a bread-and-butter matter for Pauli Murray, a single woman trying to support herself as a lawyer. Having attended the all-female Hunter College and then worked in women's programs in the Works Progress Administration, Murray first became aware of sex discrimination when she began law school at Howard University in the early 1940s. There, she wrote, "the racial factor was removed . . . and the factor of gender was fully exposed." After her sole female classmate dropped out, Murray faced alone the experiences that were typical for women in professional schools at the time. The legal fraternity did not admit women, professors rarely called on her, and one teacher wondered aloud why women even came to law school.[4]

Murray continued her efforts for racial justice while she attended Howard, leading student sit-ins at segregated restaurants in the nation's capital. Yet she was disappointed to find that professors and other men whom she "deeply admired because of their dedication to civil rights, men who themselves had suffered racial indignities, could countenance exclusion of women from their professional association." The Howard experiences left Murray skeptical about male leaders and somewhat independent of them in her pursuit of racial justice. These men, she claimed, "aroused an incipient feminism in me long before I knew the meaning of the term 'feminism.'" As early as 1947, Murray documented what she called Jane Crowism in *Negro Digest* and challenged the black man to "accept the Negro female as his equal."[5]

Male control over the legal profession continued to be a problem; Murray's application to do graduate work at Harvard Law School came back with the announcement, "You are not of the sex entitled to be admitted." Even with a master's degree in law from the University of California (1945) and a doctorate from Yale University Law School (1965) Murray never prospered financially from the practice of law. Ever sensitive to the male monopoly of legal entitlements, she sent her contribution to the Lawyers Constitutional Defense Committee in 1967 with a note commenting that "the letter-head of LCDC is utterly void of representation of women attorneys." In addition, LCDC lawyers had incorporated a memorandum prepared by Murray and her collaborator into one of their briefs without crediting them. Sex discrimination thus had direct consequences for Murray, a member of "the class of unattached, self-supporting women for whom employment opportunities were necessary to survival . . . the ones most victimized by a still prevalent stereotype that men are the chief breadwinners."[6]

The problems Murray confronted challenged women in other

professions. Joan Martin was treated as an outsider at Princeton Theological Seminary on the basis of both her race and her sex. Entering professional school three decades after Murray, Martin had many female classmates, yet she found that "one's 'calling' as a woman was no more valid within the institutional church than [was] . . . Black theology." Like Murray, she insisted that minority women did not possess "the luxurious choice of which oppression to fight," and she devoted her ministry to the practice of "Black feminist theology" in the Presbyterian church and at the National Council of Churches. Likewise, Deborah Partridge Wolfe developed feminist leanings on her difficult path to ordination. An active member of Church Women United who served as the organization's observer at the United Nations, Wolfe reported, "I studied theology for 20 years before the American Baptist Church finally decided that I might be ordained." On the other hand, Katie Cannon, in 1974 the first African American woman ordained in the United Presbyterian Church, considered racism a more serious problem for black women than sexism. Nonetheless she, too, described the progress of black women in the church as "very slow, as if 'with all deliberate speed.' "[7]

African American women did not have to aspire to the ministry to develop a feminist perspective on women's place within the church. Theressa Hoover escaped overt sex discrimination in her profession because she served as an executive in the Women's Division of the United Methodist Church. When her job sent her traveling around the country from church to church, she "discovered that black women were truly the glue that held the churches together" but realized that their contributions found "little or no mention . . . in accounts of any black church or black theology." Hoover understood the century-old historical development of separate women's missionary groups as a reaction to the male clergy's control of mission work "to the point of the deliberate exclusion of women." She insisted that since "exclusion from main church channels still exist[ed]," so did the need for women's groups. Thus, Hoover participated actively in Church Women United and in the women's caucus of the National Council of Churches, in addition to serving on the NCC governing board.[8]

Although religion did not become Murray's profession until 1974, it formed a central core of her life from childhood on, and the disregard for women's needs or opinions by the male leadership increased her sense of frustration. In 1969, while devoting most of her feminist energies to the ACLU, Murray also worked on minority women's issues with CWU and took on her own denomination, the Protestant Episcopal Church, when it refused to extend voting rights to women at its national conventions. She declined an appeal from her bishop for contributions to a special fund because payment would constitute "taxation without representation." And she sent a nine-page memorandum to the national Episcopal leadership warning that women "will either share power *within* the Church or they will be outside of the Church as part of its most formidable opponents."[9]

Comparing Eleanor Holmes Norton's pathway to feminism with that of Murray shows the generational differences in the experiences of African American women even when they shared the same profession. Born in 1938 and nearly thirty years younger than Murray, Norton grew up in a middle-class family, attended the excellent (segregated) Dunbar High School in Washington, D.C., graduated from Antioch College, and entered law school at Yale University in 1960. She was not aware of sex discrimination at Antioch, and although she was just one of fourteen women in her class at Yale and heard male students assert that places there were "too valuable to go to women," she did not consider herself a feminist until years later. Nor did she experience sexism in the civil rights movement when she joined the Student Nonviolent Coordinating Committee and worked in Mississippi in 1963. Her legal skills and the dearth of civil rights lawyers willing to work with radicals, she believed, protected her from the sex discrimination that "many black girls did not escape."[10]

After receiving a law degree and a master's degree in American studies from Yale, Norton joined the legal staff of the American Civil Liberties Union in 1965, viewing the job as an opportunity to work on racial discrimination and First Amendment issues dealing with free speech and social protest. She first began to think of herself as a feminist during her years at the ACLU, from 1965 to 1970, a time that coincided with the rebirth of feminism generally as well as with the feminist efforts of Pauli Murray and Dorothy Kenyon in the ACLU. Norton had already come to admire Murray's "nerve and bravery" during their overlapping years at Yale, when she used Murray's personal papers as sources for a paper on World War II and the beginnings of nonviolent protest. Later Murray took credit for "exposing [Norton] to feminism . . . raising her consciousness a bit." The two joined the ACLU at about the same time, Norton as a staff member and Murray as a board member, and they collaborated in the effort to include women in federal civil rights legislation that banned racial discrimination in juries.[11]

While the feminism of such women as Murray, Martin, and Wolfe grew from their direct experience of discrimination, Norton remembered her conversion as being more intellectual. After several years of contact with Murray, Kenyon, and other women challenging sexism, Norton's awakening came when as ACLU counsel she represented women in a sex-discrimination charge against *Newsweek*. Because of her race, she understood "damn well that merit didn't determine who succeeded and who didn't." Thus, she recalled, "I could recognize when the *Newsweek* women, with their Phi Beta Kappa keys and study in London or Paris, were being ghettoized as researchers and not being allowed to move up into more important jobs." Norton often attributed her feminism to her race: "The connection to equality and its universality had been made to me through my experience as a black person, so to me the women's issue followed as night follows day."[12]

It was while working with Murray and other women to include a ban on sex discrimination in the federal bill prohibiting race discrimination in jury selection that Norton became aware of the invisibility of women to male civil rights leaders. At first, the chief sponsor of the bill, the Leadership Conference on Civil Rights (LCCR), refused to include the addendum. "They gave short shrift to women," Norton reported to Murray. Yet the feminist efforts eventually paid off when the LCCR not only testified in favor of the sex-discrimination provision but used arguments developed by Murray.[13]

In spite of this victory, Murray's frustrations with the male civil rights leadership ran considerably deeper than Norton's. On the eve of the 1963 March on Washington, Murray noted the exclusion of women from the list of the ten leaders of the march, even though women had directly pushed for the inclusion of presidents of black women's organizations. She also expressed dismay that march leaders had agreed to speak at the National Press Club luncheon, which barred women from membership and relegated the female reporters who were covering the speeches to the balcony. A year after the march, Murray pressed Whitney M. Young to explain why his organization, the Urban League, had never honored a woman with one of its awards. The absence of women from the speakers at the march and from the delegation that met with President Kennedy after the rally was not lost on Anna Arnold Hedgeman, who on behalf of the NCC had mobilized thousands of church members and leaders for the march. "Women, too," she reflected, "were not yet adequately included in man's journey toward humanity."[14]

Other African American women criticized the sexism expressed by male leaders. In a conversation with white and black women who worked at the National Council of Churches, African American women registered their dismay that black men were excluded from top positions in the NCC except for "the top black man in race relations." But they also resented the effect of such racism on black women. "The Negro male at this moment does not wish the woman to take the leadership," NCC staff member Olivia Stokes asserted, "because the society has emasculated the male." Black women who aspired to leadership did so "at a tremendous risk." Murray was appalled when former CORE leader James Farmer, whom she had "admired greatly over the years," campaigned against Shirley Chisholm by emphasizing the need for a "strong male image" and "a man's voice" in Congress, and she rallied other African American women behind Chisholm.[15]

The elevation of masculinity in the black power movement also strengthened feminism among some African American women. When Church Women United sponsored a meeting of black women in 1969, one participant criticized the black man who "wants to assert today his so-called masculinity" when the appropriate ideal was "really *personhood*—for both sexes." Another went farther, suggesting that women should "let the men have their power and status" and organize separately. Then, "when the men are ready for our help, they will have to bargain for it."[16]

Murray also bristled at the chauvinism in the black power movement. As a professor of African American studies at Brandeis University in 1968–69, she had painful confrontations with radical male students, an experience that led her to reject black militancy as "a bid of black males to share power with white males in a continuing patriarchal society." Only later did she recognize her inability to separate the cause of black militancy from the "crude sexism" of some of its leaders.[17]

Black Feminism and Liberal Institutions

The cultures and commitments of liberal organizations created environments that fostered—or at least did not hinder—the development of feminist perspectives and activism among African American women. Particularly in the Ford Foundation and the National Council of Churches, where staff women took feminist initiatives, the history of the organizations and their commitment to civil rights supported feminist efforts by black women. These organizations were relatively open to staff initiatives in general, and since the early 1960s they had made civil rights a priority. Moreover, because white men dominated these groups, African American women could make feminist claims without directly challenging their black brothers.

The racial justice agendas of these organizations meant that African American women were not forced to "choose" to combat one form of injustice over another. Their fight against sex discrimination would not have to come at the expense of the struggle against race discrimination. Murray stressed how "in many instances it was difficult to determine whether I was being discriminated against because of race or sex." Martin prized the part of her work at the NCC that allowed her to focus on "the relationship between racism and sexism."[18] They and other black women found it possible to work against both racism and sexism in their organizations. They could do so simultaneously by concentrating on issues that particularly affected minority women; and they could also shift the object of their concentration as their standpoints shifted.

At the Ford Foundation, black women furthered their interests despite their low standing in the organization, an achievement that was facilitated by the relative open-mindedness of foundation executives. The majority of African American women worked in support-staff positions: in the early 1970s only three minority women held professional staff positions (in contrast to more than fifty white women), while the support staff contained more than fifty women of color. At first, African American women pushed feminist claims as individuals or in conjunction with white women. Carmen Turay, a secretary to one of Ford's vice presidents, and Kathryn Mitchell, an administrative assistant, served on a committee established at the urging of a white woman to examine the role of women at the foundation. Mitchell also joined with nine white women in October 1971 in drafting a forty-page document offering recommendations for grant making to benefit women.[19] As individuals, a number of minority women signed a petition to McGeorge Bundy urging the foundation to adopt a policy requiring all grant recipients to practice affirmative action with regard to both race and gender.

The shift from individual efforts to collective action reflected the spread of feminism and the realization of the interconnection of race and gender. When Bundy asked some of the women who had signed the petition to meet with him, the three minority women who were invited—Turay, Bea Colebrook, and Beryl Jones—called together women of color from across the foundation. They wanted to be sure they represented the views of a larger group of women, and they hoped to establish an ongoing collective process to pursue their particular interests.[20]

The efforts by African American women to promote feminist change at the Ford Foundation grew out of several aspects of their experience there. Black women saw the disparity between their almost exclusive employment as clerical workers and the foundation's growing affirmation of the right of first African Americans and then women to equal opportunity. Consequently, while African American women pushed projects that focused on poor women, they also worked for changes from which they could benefit directly, including a pilot project at Ford to train clerical-level women for better jobs. In addition, a number of African American women heard the feminist ideas expressed by Eleanor Holmes Norton, Aileen Hernandez, Inez Reid, director of the Black Women's Community Development Foundation, and Elizabeth Koontz, when they came to the foundation to conduct the in-house educational sessions about women's issues in 1971 and 1972.[21]

Women of color at the Ford Foundation criticized the male-centricity of the foundation's projects dealing with racial justice. When Ford began to develop a long-range plan for future projects in 1972, the black women's group Concerned Minority Women at Ford insisted on broadening the approach. In a memo to Ford executives, the group protested that foundation efforts to cure "the social and economic ills indigenous to ghetto life . . . almost completely overlooked" minority women. Noting the high incidence of female-headed families and the high level of poverty among minority women, it asserted that "minority women need jobs as much or more than men" and recommended initiatives in the areas of education and job training, day care, and birth control.[22]

The environment at the National Council of Churches proved even more conducive than that of the secular organizations to feminism among African American women. A large number of black women worked at the NCC, and—in contrast to the Ford Foundation—several held middle-level administrative positions. Not as politically constrained as the foundation, the NCC displayed a more direct and outspoken commitment to the civil rights movement and to radical action in general; and its religious values allowed advocates of all forms of equality to take the moral high ground. Moreover, the long association of Church Women United with the NCC—and CWU's physical presence in the same building—provided a living example of independent, assertive womanhood as well as an institutional setting with a history of interracial cooperation among women.

In addition to nurturing gender consciousness among African American women, these liberal institutions frequently proved more convenient or congenial places to pursue feminist goals than did predominantly white feminist groups. Staff members at Ford and the NCC, for example, could act on their feminist beliefs without having to juggle demands after work. To be sure, they put in long hours, but they also enjoyed the opportunity to integrate their employment with their politics. As Martin put it, "My constituency reflects my own interests."[23] Moreover, black women in most of these groups were not tokens. They could count on joining with at least a handful of other women of color, and they could communicate their concerns to white colleagues and officials already accustomed to thinking about the connections among race, material deprivation, and human suffering.

For Pauli Murray, who did not receive a paycheck for her feminist labors, the ability to engage in feminist projects in volunteer organizations like the ACLU and CWU helped to compensate for the marginalization she experienced in the independent women's movement. That alienation was all the more striking in light of Murray's abundant contributions to the resurgence of feminism. Her work for the President's Commission on the Status of Women and her efforts on behalf of the sex-discrimination ban in Title VII of the Civil Rights Act of 1964 had laid the groundwork for the new women's movement. As early as 1964, in the course of strategizing to keep the sex-discrimination ban in the civil rights bill, she introduced the idea of a new feminist organization, "something a little more attuned to the Space Age than the NWP [the National Woman's Party, the only existing explicitly feminist group]."[24] As a founder of the National Organization for Women two years later, she helped create an organizational vehicle for the women's movement.

Yet just one year after NOW's founding, Murray came away from its national meeting deeply disillusioned. Part of her distress, which she shared with some white feminists, resulted from NOW's adoption of the Equal Rights Amendment as a primary objective. During her work with the PCSW, Murray had forged a compromise position, advocating an alternative to an equal rights amendment that involved attaining legal equality by means of the Fourteenth Amendment. She, along with some of her white feminist colleagues, felt that NOW was moving too fast to embrace the amendment, and they objected to what they saw as Betty Friedan's heavy-handedness and the "ferociousness and bloodletting" that accompanied the debate. As a woman who had done much to ignite the movement, Murray had anticipated the conference with "high hopes of being welcomed among my own."

She left feeling "like a stranger in my own household . . . passé, old [at 57], and declassed." [25]

But Murray's disaffection with NOW stemmed from more than seeing her views unappreciated and dismissed by younger feminists. Her "inability to be fragmented into Negro at one time, woman at another, or worker at another" required a women's movement that would fight for needs growing out of all those identities. She judged NOW sorely lacking in this respect. Moreover, instead of finding herself in the midst of a "widely representative organization," at the conference she beheld "no Catholic sisters, no women of ethnic minorities other than about five Negro women, and obviously no women who represent the poor." [26]

Murray's unsuccessful attempt to slow down NOW's support for the ERA reflected fears that a movement "confined almost solely to 'women's rights' without strong bonds with other movements toward human rights . . . might develop into a head-on collision" with black liberation initiatives, as had happened after the Civil War when some white feminists had advanced their claim to suffrage ahead of that of black men. For NOW to seize on the ERA in 1967, she warned, "would emphasize women's rights to the exclusion of other rights in an already inflamed and fragmented political climate, thus picking up little support and turning the spotlight of opposition upon us." Murray kept up her membership in a NOW chapter and served on the board of NOW's Legal Defense and Education Fund into the 1970s; and she maintained friendships with prominent white feminists, including WEAL founder Bernice (Bunny) Sandler and NOW leader Wilma Scott Heide. But she never again played a prominent role in any mainstream feminist national organization. "I am remaining aloof as to activity [in NOW] and finding other outlets for my feminism," she wrote in 1969 when she was promoting gender equity in the ACLU and in religious groups and inaugurating a women's studies course at Brandeis University. [27]

Murray was not alone in wanting NOW to practice a broader-based feminism. Anna Arnold Hedgeman, who served as director for ecumenical action and associate for racial justice at the National Council of Churches, pressed NOW to concentrate on poor women from its founding. In 1967 she called for NOW to plan "as quickly as possible for a national meeting geared primarily to the problems of women in poverty," which would focus on developing a plan of action. Although NOW's agenda had always included attention to women's poverty, and its leaders increasingly responded to the ideas of welfare rights activists, the organization's failure to mobilize its members behind a strong antipoverty movement lessened its appeal to Murray, Hedgeman, and other African American women, who were well aware of the unequal incidence of poverty among black and white women.[28] Much more than white women, these African Americans reached out across class lines and assigned high priority to issues that might not directly benefit them but were critical for large numbers of black women. And they found organizations like the IUE, the ACLU, the NCC, and the Ford Foundation more receptive to these issues than the explicitly feminist groups.

Foundations of Interracial Feminism

Disaffection from mainstream feminist organizations did not mean that black women would not work with white women for feminist goals. Some black women, in fact, noted the strategic necessity for interracial action. Theressa Hoover insisted on the need for black women to challenge both "her sisters in other denominations [white women in the ecumenical movement] and the clerical-male hierarchy in her own." Even while emphasizing the solidarity of African American women and men, Eleanor Holmes Norton called on black women to support feminism, because "every problem raised by white feminists has a disproportionately heavy impact on blacks." Black women should stop condemning "the white woman's struggle for being white," she insisted, "for it will only take on color if we who are black join it." [29]

Pauli Murray presented other strategic reasons for African Americans to line up with white women in the women's rights struggle. Her belief that white women generally proved more sympathetic to racial justice than did white men caused her to argue that empowering white women would promote racial justice. She claimed that "Southern women, and particularly white church women, have been a democratizing influence," most specifically in fighting lynching and supporting desegregation. And she believed that southern women both black and white had had a "humanizing effect" in the civil rights struggles of the 1950s and 1960s. Murray's assertions about the greater sympathy of white women for racial justice reflected her close relationships with white women who were relatively progressive on the issue of race and derived especially from her contacts with white church women.[30]

Murray also referred to history in arguing for the strategic imperative of combining women's rights and civil rights. She pointed to the breakup of the alliance between feminists and abolitionists during Reconstruction, contending that abandoning woman suffrage had hurt black men as well as both black and white women. "Whenever political expediency has dictated that the recognition of basic human rights be postponed," she maintained, "the resulting dissension and conflict has been aggravated." Because those in power always try to pit one dissident group against another, Murray warned, focusing on the rights of just one group might set in motion a backlash against "the gains which Negroes have made over the past few decades, meager as these gains may have been for the masses of blacks."[31]

Murray developed enduring relationships with white women when they had more than gender in common. In fact, she forged what was probably her deepest adult bond with a white woman, Irene Barlow. The relationship grew from their experiences together in a large New York law firm and solidified with their worship and feminist efforts within the Episcopal Church. Murray also developed close ties with several white feminists in the legal profession with whom she worked closely, including Mary O. Eastwood, Dorothy Kenyon, and Marguerite Rawalt. Murray met Eastwood, a Justice Department attorney, while working with the President's Commission on the Status of Women, and the two lawyers wrote a pathbreaking article, "Jane Crow and the Law: Sex Discrimination and Title VII," which they published in 1965. Many of Murray's closest feminist colleagues—including Eastwood, Kenyon, Catherine East, and Thelma Stevens—also shared her status as single or divorced women.[32]

In addition, Murray benefited professionally from the sponsorship and friendship of white women, among them Eleanor Roosevelt and the historian Caroline F. Ware. White women helped Murray financially when sex and racial discrimination made employment difficult for her. In the late 1940s, a two-year research project funded by the Women's Division of the United Methodist Church enabled her to keep her fledgling law office open. After leaving Yale in 1965, she was unable to secure a law school teaching post and relied for a year on another commission from the Methodist women, this time to write a history of human rights in the United States since 1948.[33]

Although Murray's interracial friendships were unusual in her era in their extent and depth, they suggest both the potential and and the risks of interracial collaboration. Murray's partial dependence on white women for employment and meaningful work, along with her own mixed racial heritage, probably inclined her to seek interracial friendships and collaborations. Conversely, white feminists would have seen in Murray a middle-class woman like themselves who shared cultural elements of their own racial background. White feminists may also have been drawn to Murray because a black woman offered stronger validation to their claim that they were being denied rights. But the fact that these white women were able to provide financial opportunities for Murray showed the unequal power configuration of their relationships, a bias that reflected racial discrimination. And the inherent hazards of co-optation for black women in those affiliations explain why Eleanor Holmes Norton and like-minded black women decided to create the National Black Feminist Organization in 1973.[34]

The element of Murray's interracial relationships that was most commonly found among black and white women was a strong religious bond. Of the organizations studied here, the National Council of Churches—and Church Women United, whose members overlapped with those of the council and whose practices informed women's activities within the NCC—boasted the most successful interracial feminist collaboration. In the NCC, African American women sometimes headed and often occupied important places in feminist projects, and those projects maintained a strong focus on the particular needs and interests of women of color.

As far back as the early nineteenth century, religion had mitigated the racism of white women and inspired them to work with and on behalf of black women. Religious commitment led many white women to oppose slavery and join the abolitionist movement, and it underlay the "unlikely sisterhood" that Evelyn Brooks Higginbotham found among black and white Baptist women at the end of the century. Similarly, Glenda Gilmore has related how temperance and missionary commitments called forth interracial work among North Carolina women in the 1880s and 1890s; this connection, however flawed, "represented a crack in the mortar of the foundation of white supremacy." Evangelical religion, according to Jacquelyn Dowd Hall, provided white women with the "rationale for seeking a female alliance across racial lines" to fight lynching in the South in the 1920s. And Susan Lynn has shown that religion played a large role in persuading white women to support black women's demands for racial justice in the Young Women's Christian Association.[35]

Pauli Murray discovered racial progressives within the Women's Division of the Methodist Church in the 1940s. Thelma Stevens, a white woman from Mississippi, proposed the research project on state laws dealing with racial segregation that paid Murray's bills for two years in the late 1940s. A lifelong activist on behalf of racial justice, Stevens "defied my racial stereotype of a white Mississippian," Murray said, expressing astonishment at finding that Stevens' dedication "to the demise of racial segregation was as unswerving as my own." [36]

Stevens belonged to the historical tradition of religion-based interracial alliances among women that manifested itself also in Church Women United, whose emphasis on racial justice reached back to the 1940s. In 1960, before civil rights emerged as a major national issue, CWU inaugurated a three-year project called Assignment Race. Not content to confine civil rights action to the national leadership, CWU leaders insisted to rank-and-file members that racial justice was "*their* effort, not something they could watch or receive as a report from the national office." To this end, the organization sent interracial pairs of women to visit local CWU groups throughout the nation to exemplify interracial cooperation and to train local churchwomen in antiracist action. Black and white women talked frankly to one another, an unusual occurrence for many. In Nashville an African American woman noted that previous interracial meetings had felt to her like "visiting day for Negroes" and another protested the exclusion of black women from leadership positions. White women who had taken pride in their relationships with black women "were incredulous and upset and said so." At the end of the project CWU could point to considerable growth in black women's participation, the integration of several dozen local councils, and the election of minority women as presidents of councils in Pittsburgh, Detroit, Denver, and other cities. [37]

Such efforts drew African American women like Clare Collins Harvey into Church Women United. A businesswoman in Jackson, Mississippi, Harvey established Womenpower United, an underground movement that helped support Freedom Riders and others who were in need of help because of their involvement in civil rights struggles. While working on behalf of these activists, she met Jane Schutt, head of CWU in Jackson, who organized an interracial prayer group in a black Baptist church when her own Episcopal church remained closed to African Americans. Through Schutt, Harvey became involved in CWU, the only integrated women's organization in Jackson. In 1971 she was elected national president of CWU.[38]

Other black women recognized religion as a potential vehicle for mutually beneficial alliances with white women. As an active member of CWU, Anna Arnold Hedgeman experienced first-hand the organization's "long history of interracial workshops." When the NCC's Commission on Religion and Race cast about for skilled negotiators to work in civil rights initiatives in 1963, Hedgeman reminded the commissioners of the extensive efforts of CWU "both as women in the church and as pioneers in the field of race relations since the early 1940s," and she recommended specific women, black and white, for the tasks at hand.[39]

Moreover, in the late 1960s, as CWU increasingly embraced goals that paralleled those of secular feminism, it challenged the tendency evident in the mainstream women's movement to iden-tify needs and interests of white middle-class women as the needs and interests of all women. Staff at CWU named a new feminist project of 1969 the Commission on Woman in Today's World, but they simultaneously contested the notion of a universal Woman. Prominent on the agenda of the commission's first meeting were the questions: "Who are the disadvantaged and deprived women? In what ways and why?"[40] This awareness that race and class shaped gender both reflected the involvement of African Ameri-can women in creating CWU's agenda and facilitated further interracial feminist efforts.

White women often entered into these interracial efforts with complex, and not necessarily altruistic, motives. It was difficult to overcome what Higginbotham calls the "racist paternalism and cultural imperialism" that often attended such relationships. Black women risked having their struggle appropriated and transformed by white feminists; in addition, they had to guard against exchanging their self-esteem and self-determination for access to the resources that white women could offer. They frequently maintained a separate organization, therefore, even while they joined white women in common projects. In the United Presbyterian Church, women of color belonged both to the Third World Women's Coordinating Committee and the predominantly white Council on Women and the Church.[41]

Structures and Theory in Black Feminism

Where interracial collaboration lacked the cement of religious commitment, African American women found it all the more necessary to combine such alliances with independent organization, as they did at the Ford Foundation. Moreover, their workplace activism differed significantly from that of white women: white feminists at the foundation operated within a relatively small, informal network that consisted largely of professional staff and that had no formal mechanism for gathering the views of the rest of the women employed there. In contrast, some thirty-five women, roughly two-thirds of all the women of color who worked there, signed up to join Concerned Minority Women at Ford. Furthermore, the concentration of women of color in support-staff jobs led them to develop a more representative political style that accommodated differences in class and status.[42]

In her work at the National Council of Churches, Joan Martin also created a political style that contrasted sharply with the top-down process and disregard for opposing views that so dismayed Pauli Murray at the NOW conference in 1967. As head of the Justice for Women program and later the women's caucus of the NCC governing board, Martin promoted "a collective feminist style" whose objective was to reach consensus. Although Martin's wording resembled that of predominantly white women's groups, the style she was promoting was based on "the understanding that this is a racially diverse group—and that we bring different cultural styles as well as gender and bureaucratic styles." [43]

Just as black women promoted different forms of feminism, they also infused feminism with a broader and deeper content in such organizations as the NCC and Ford Foundation. Before scholars theorized about linkages between gender and race or class, some of these women were articulating the multiple interlocking aspects of their identities. After succeeding in amending Title VII of the Civil Rights Act of 1964 to include sex discrimination, Pauli Murray declared herself "overjoyed . . . as a Negro woman" to see both race and sex addressed. In fact, Murray insisted that "the Negro woman has suffered more than the mere addition of sex discrimination to race discrimination. She has suffered the *conjunction* of these twin immoralities." [44]

In the 1970s, Murray's discussion of multiple oppressions reflected the strong influence of liberation theology, with its commitment to the struggle against all forms of exploitation, as did the ideas of Katie Cannon, Jacquelyn Grant, and other African American feminists. In theology school in the early 1970s, Joan Martin "looked for ways of talking about God and doing ministry from my perspective of growing up as both Black and as a woman." She shaped her job at the NCC so that it entailed "a special focus on the relationship between racism and sexism," in contrast to the "majority of white women [who] refuse a holistic analysis." [45]

Although few of the African American women in these liberal organizations explicitly theorized about their interlocking identities as black women, their actions clearly demonstrated an understanding that, as Elsa Barkley Brown has put it, "all women do not have the same gender." In practice, African American women insisted that projects to advance racial justice were incomplete if they did not embrace an attack on sex discrimination and that feminist projects were deficient if they did not contain an antiracist component.

As early as 1963, Murray worried that as the civil rights movement was progressing, black women were losing the "second class equality" that they shared with black men. They were "frozen out" of the leadership of the movement, yet those leaders did not "understand or appreciate either the problems or aspirations of Negro women."[46] But although she occasionally criticized the civil rights leadership, Murray was particularly concerned about black women falling through the cracks of civil rights legislation. She argued that including sex discrimination in Title VII was for black women a matter of "sheer survival." Murray stressed the unbalanced ratio of men to women in the black population, which meant that a black woman "cannot assume . . . that her economic support will come through marriage." In March 1966 she wrote to the head of the Equal Employment Opportunity Commission challenging an official statement that the commission proceeded slowly on sex discrimination because it did not want to hinder "its main concern, racial discrimination." With such an approach, Murray charged, "only half of the Negro population is protected." Repeating that black women had a greater need than white women to support themselves and their children, she insisted, "the sex provision becomes crucial to their employment opportunities."[47]

African American women at Ford also exposed the lacunae in efforts to alleviate racial and economic injustice and pushed the foundation to close the gaps. Kathryn Mitchell's hand was visible in recommendations for women's programming that included a detailed examination of various Ford-funded educational and training programs for minorities. The recommendations pointed out that of nearly three hundred opportunities provided through these grants, women of color benefited from fewer than fifty. Similarly, Concerned Minority Women at Ford criticized the neglect of minority women in projects aimed at the social and economic ills of inner cities. "The problems faced by minority women," they claimed, "are of critical dimensions and in a real and tangible way affect the total lifestyle of the ghetto." Like Pauli Murray, they insisted that black women "need jobs as much or more than men." [48]

Focusing on the foundation's community development program, Concerned Minority Women at Ford recommended a broad array of programs that reflected the distinctive cast of African American feminism. The group emphasized the importance of job-training programs and day care; efforts to reduce teen pregnancy and keep teenage mothers in school; and expansion of drug programs to include counseling for wives and mothers of addicts. The long-range plans recommended by Mitchell Sviridoff, head of the Division of National Affairs, in 1972, demonstrated the influence of the group. He enclosed the group's statement in his report to the president and ranked development of a program for minority women second only to sustaining community development corporations among projects for disadvantaged groups. [49]

In 1969, African American churchwomen too addressed the neglect of women in male-designed projects to alleviate poverty. When the National Council of Churches and member churches responded to occupation of their headquarters by black activists demanding economic development projects, religious feminists noted at once the "missing dimensions" of the militants' program. Church Women United called together a consultation of minority women and issued a statement in conjunction with denominational women's organizations. In it, the women emphasized the critical gap in the churches' plans for economic justice, that is, the lack of "any great concern for the fact that among those most disadvantaged are woman, many of whom are heads of families." Black women's influence also appeared in the churchwomen's call for attention to local projects where "people directly concerned could participate realistically in their solutions." Relying on the advice of black women, CWU created its own Commission on Economic Justice, with Coretta Scott King as the head. [50]

Making Feminism More Inclusive

As African American women sought to redefine the civil rights projects of the Ford Foundation and the NCC to include feminism, they also labored to redefine feminist projects to accommodate racial and economic justice, fulfilling Eleanor Holmes Norton's warning that feminism "will only take on color if we who are black join it." The black women associated with CWU challenged white women to examine their own complicity in racial and economic injustice. Middle-class women should inspect "their own life styles to discover the degree to which they support economic patterns which are unjust," and they should consider "reallocating the corporate resources of women's organizations" and reassessing their priorities. Katie Cannon told an audience of church women that white women should "begin to understand the privileges of being white, and how those privileges can be used to fight oppression."[51]

Other black women simultaneously labored to make feminist projects more inclusive even as they pushed feminism into racial justice agendas. At the Ford Foundation, the efforts of Kathryn Mitchell and Carmen Turay to claim a place for minority women in feminist projects appeared in a staff committee report, "The Role of Women in the Ford Foundation." Listed third among thirteen items for immediate action was the imperative to intensify efforts to recruit minority women at all levels. At Jefferson and Turay's insistence the report called for people of color to "have the same opportunity as women generally to be promoted to or hired into upper grade level jobs." Their efforts bore fruit as the number of minority women in the professional category grew from three to eleven and from 5 to 13 percent of all women between 1972 and 1974.[52]

Black women realized that keeping attention on women of color in the Ford Foundation's developing program of feminist

funding required constant vigilance. When the foundation created its Task Force on Women in 1972, every one of the members
was white. Beatrice Colebrooke, a leader of Concerned Minority
Women, protested to the task force chair. Just because few minority women held positions at the professional level, she insisted,
they should not be unrepresented in the group responsible for
overseeing the development of women's programs. Subsequently,
at least one minority woman served on the task force and the
bodies that succeeded it. Yet black women could not count on
white feminists for more than token representation. White feminists at Ford understood the need for "minority representation"
on the bodies dealing with women, but they usually considered
that need satisfied by just one woman of color.[53]

Much of Pauli Murray's feminist work occurred in collaboration with white women, but she too endeavored to give voice and
influence to women of color. Returning from a conference cele-
brating the Women's Bureau's fiftieth anniversary, she expressed
frustration that not enough time was provided for "economic
minorities to have their problems considered visibly." When she
testified on the status of women at congressional hearings, she
urged the lawmakers to invite women from other minority groups
to speak. Lamenting that she was the only black woman on the
ACLU national board, in 1969 she tried to persuade Aileen Hernandez and Patricia Harris to accept nomination to that body. In
addition, Murray criticized the ACLU for neglecting "the broad
representation of other ethnic minorities" and proposed an assignment for Mexican American Grace Olivarez that could position
her for eventual election to the board.[54]

Black women used their executive positions in the National
Council of Churches to advance feminist goals and to expand the
ability of women of color to shape feminist projects. They also
created structures to institutionalize interracial work that had frequently depended on personal bonds like Murray's relationships
with white women. As head of the NCC Division of Education

and Ministry, Emily Gibbes established a Commission on Women in Ministry, which set as its goal 50 percent minority representation. That commitment, though not realized, focused attention on the importance of diverse voices and raised the participation of women of color above 25 percent. The commission also sponsored a Task Force on Ethnic Women in Ministry and hosted a conference for minority women ministers.[55]

Black feminists sought inclusion of black women's voices in feminist projects both within and outside of these liberal organizations. When Eleanor Holmes Norton left the ACLU in 1970 to become chair of the New York City Commission on Human Rights, one of her first projects was a five-day series of hearings on women's rights. Black women and other women of color testified in substantial numbers throughout the hearings, speaking not just on issues that were closely associated with the particular experiences of women of their race but also for women's concerns generally. Thus, while Beulah Sanders spoke on welfare mothers and Patricia Jones on household employment, Ophelia DeVore testified about businesswomen, Shirley Chisholm spoke about women in politics, Faith Ringgold represented artists, and Pauli Murray examined the legal status of women. These and other women addressed topics of concern to all women but in ways that accounted for their variable meanings across racial and ethnic categories.[56]

The projects that developed from African American women's initiatives reflected the needs and interests of black women in two ways. They gave priority to issues other than those stressed by white feminists, and they cast issues affecting all women in terms that highlighted their particular bearing on black women's lives. For example, Joan Martin supported such key goals of the white-dominated independent feminist movement as abortion rights and the Equal Rights Amendment, but her Justice for Women program targeted domestic violence, sterilization abuse, and other issues in which women of color had a particularly strong stake. While acknowledging that domestic violence and rape crossed class and racial lines, Martin explained the unique vulnerability of black women who were victims of violence. Police often ignored or responded slowly to calls for help coming from predominantly black communities, she maintained, and "the woman is likely to be insulted if the police do show."[57]

Black women repeatedly refined generalizations about the economic status of women by pointing out that women of color earned considerably less than white women and occupied the lowest rungs on the occupational scale. In 1968, while NOW focused its attention on the ERA and abortion, Murray emphasized the need for health and labor standards to apply to all workers, inclusion of domestic workers in the national minimum wage, and a national child-care program. Church Women United likewise promoted structural change, advocating a minimum wage for household workers and mobilizing women in local communities to work against discrimination in housing and public services.[58]

Testifying before a congressional committee on the economic status of women, Frankie Freeman cast the issue of sex discrimination in the credit business in terms of its distinctive effects on black women. Financial institutions typically refused to count a wife's income when determining a family's loanworthiness, a practice that discriminated against all women. But because a greater proportion of black families than white depended on the wife's income, black families experienced credit discrimination more severely.[59]

In the years before and just after Congress passed the ERA, Murray articulated the distinctive perspectives of black women on the amendment. First, to those who opposed the ERA because it would invalidate protective labor legislation for women, she pointed out that such measures had "very little meaning for a large sector of the Negro female working population." Most black women worked in occupations that were untouched by protective laws. Nor, she reminded the opponents of ERA, had black women experienced the "the idealizations of 'womanhood' and 'motherhood'" that conservatives insisted were threatened by the ERA. Above all, Murray pointed to the symbolic import of the ERA. If rights were meant to guarantee human dignity, then black women had the greatest need for the constitutional protections of the ERA, for those women "historically have suffered the most violent invasions of that personal dignity and privacy which the law seeks to protect."[60]

"I have one foot in each camp and cannot split myself apart," remarked Murray about her dual identity as a black and as a woman. Although the African American women who advanced feminist goals in liberal organizations may not have agreed with Murray that they had "an *equal* stake in women's liberation and black liberation," they could no more easily split themselves apart than could she. Instead, they effected critical linkages between civil rights and feminist issues. Women like Murray, Martin, Hoover, and Kathryn Mitchell used the authority of their identities and experiences as black women to fill two critical gaps—the gap in racial justice efforts that left out women, and the gap in feminist projects that neglected women of color.[61]

These women found the ACLU, the NCC, and the Ford Foundation more convenient or more congenial places than mainstream feminist groups to pursue feminist aspirations. Consequently, if the independent women's movement mirrored the predominantly white middle-class aims of its leaders, the feminism constructed in the other organizations bore the mark of the African American women who educated white women about racism and helped shape agendas that addressed the needs of diverse groups of women.

To be sure, the impact of these efforts was limited. There were not enough organizations like these, where attention was already focused on racial justice, to give black women a place to raise their voices. And not enough white feminists either on the inside or the outside proved able or willing to examine gender issues in terms that encompassed race and class. Consequently, Murray's vision of a "feminist movement . . . allied to the objectives of black liberation while simultaneously advancing the interests of all women" has yet to be realized. Yet she and other African American women did succeed in constructing feminist projects based on the recognition that women's experiences and needs derived from intertwined strands of gender, race, and economic status. In struggling to shape a more inclusive feminism, they began a dialogue between feminists, black and white, that continues to enrich feminist thought and challenge feminist activists.

CHAPTER SEVEN

Conclusion

*Institutionalization and the
Persistence of Feminist Change*

In 1960 it was legal to pay women in the United States less than men for the same work, to confine women to "women's" jobs that inevitably fell below pay scales for "men's" jobs, or to fire women when they became pregnant. It was accepted practice to discriminate against female students and teachers; and no scholarly journal or research center focused on women's issues. Abortion was a crime in every state, and disadvantaged women were routinely sterilized without their informed consent. Language made women invisible by covering them with such words as "he" and "man"; and women were neither the recipients nor the decision makers in foreign aid programs for developing countries. Wife battering lay beyond public scrutiny and rarely resulted in prosecution.

In the space of two decades many of these conditions and practices had been banned, demolished, rendered unthinkable, or at least besieged by challenges. Nor was that all. Public opinion polls showed dramatic shifts in how people viewed the status of women and the principles of feminism. During the 1970s the percentage of respondents favoring "most of the efforts to strengthen and change women's status" shot up from 40 to 64 percent. That figure continued to climb, to 77 percent in 1990, during a decade when political conservatism also

Attorneys Jane Picker, director of the Women's Law Fund, (center) and Rita Page Reuss (right) sign a Law Fund brief for a case involving sex discrimination in the Cleveland Police Department. The Women's Law Fund was supported by the Ford Foundation (Copyright © Ford Foundation, 1974).

rose. Even support for "women's liberation" attracted a majority of responses by the end of the 1970s. And since the 1980s, between 30 and 40 percent of American women have called themselves feminists—about the same percentage as people who identify themselves as Democrats or Republicans.[1]

To be sure, these changes have ushered in no feminist utopia. The time limit for ratification of the Equal Rights Amendment was reached in 1982, leaving American women without a constitutional guarantee of their rights. Numerous restrictions on abortion encumber the ability of women to control their reproductive lives. Women have not approached parity with men in the economic sphere. There are proportionately more women than men below the poverty line. Just as women began gaining access to better-paying industrial jobs, corporations began moving production abroad. Nor have rape, wife battering, and other forms of violence against women diminished significantly. Nonetheless, in a political culture characterized by incremental, piecemeal change, the transformations wrought by feminism have been remarkable.

Explicitly feminist individuals and groups within the independent women's movement, of course, drove the engines of change. Rich in energy, imagination, and determination, they were nonetheless short of money, audience, and legitimacy, particularly in the early years. Established liberal organizations supplied that need by furnishing the women's movement with access to two critical arenas: public opinion and government. Not until the mid-1970s did membership in all feminist groups combined surpass 100,000. So the ability of activists alone to influence women beyond their membership rolls depended on the media, whose initial response to feminism was at best mixed.

As Susan Douglas has shown, television network news, popular news magazines, and major newspapers reported seriously on economic discrimination against women (even while failing to acknowledge the tremendous advantages that men would have to abandon if women were to achieve real equity). Yet these same media were hard-pressed to report on feminism itself without resorting to wisecracks, condescension, and ridicule. Leading news venues focused on the physical appearance of individual feminists, described feminists as abrasive, humorless, and self-hating, or pitted feminists and nonfeminists against one another. When the House of Representatives passed the Equal Rights Amendment in 1970, the *New York Times* entitled its editorial opposing the amendment "The Henpecked House." [2]

Fortunately for feminists, another way lay open to gain adherents, one unmediated by the derision that marked early reporting on the movement. When liberal organizations embraced feminist principles, they helped legitimate those ideas for their hundreds of thousands of members. Each organization interpreted or framed feminist principles in terms that were compatible with an agenda to which members were already attached. Thus, feminism was incorporated into the framework of class in the IUE, of rights in the ACLU, of Christian values in the NCC, and of social-justice philanthropy in the Ford Foundation. In this way, these organizations provided means by which members and employees could incorporate feminist values into their existing mindsets.[3]

In the International Union of Electrical Workers, the only organization where much of the feminist change depended on a top-down process, the legitimization of feminism was particularly significant. Although some women workers aggressively filed sex discrimination charges, for the most part, as Mary Callahan recalled, women "didn't realize . . . what was discrimination" and saw different jobs and rates of pay for men and women as "the way of life."[4] Thus the ability of officials and staff to demonstrate that gender equity formed part of the union's mission was especially important.

Particularly in the movement's infancy, these liberal organizations also provided an important bridge between the movement and policymakers. Mainstream and even radical feminists routinely appeared before congressional committees, but their testimony was significantly augmented and validated by appeals from male and female labor leaders, education experts, and public-interest lawyers, who were all long accustomed to partaking in policymaking and whose words commanded respect in government circles.

Moreover, these organizations contributed directly to the resurgence of the women's movement itself by providing their employees and members places in which to promote feminist principles before the movement existed. The ACLU enabled Dorothy Kenyon and Pauli Murray to begin shaping a legal strategy for gender equity in 1964; and Kenyon and Harriet Pilpel put the ACLU in the vanguard on abortion rights while the independent women's movement still lacked organization and money. Winn Newman and Ruth Weyand defined the issue of equal pay for work of comparable worth in the IUE; only later did NOW and other feminist groups make the issue their own. Church Women United struggled to foster interracial cooperation years before most mainstream feminists confronted the white middle-class bias of their movement. These and other actions both developed issues for subsequent action by official feminism and helped prepare the public to accept those issues.

The feminist reshaping of American society in the 1960s and 1970s was multidimensional. It depended not only on the well-known work of the President's Commission on the Status of Women but also on the efforts of Murray and other African American women in male-dominated organizations who amplified the notion of civil rights to include women's rights. It involved not just the consciousness-raising undertaken in radical women's liberation groups and NOW chapters but also the struggle of women in the National Council of Churches to eliminate gender-biased language from Scripture. It hinged not only on the work of the National Abortion Rights Action League but also on the ACLU's efforts to protect women from sterilization abuse. And feminist change required not only the ability of NOW and radical feminist groups to capture media attention with demonstrations but also the willingness of union workers to file sex-discrimination grievances.

Although the diversity of the organizations considered here precludes simple generalizations about how male-dominated groups were reoriented to feminist purposes, it is possible to discern common patterns. Activists exploited the particular structures available in their organizations: they pushed feminists into positions of power; they formed networks for mutual sustenance and influence; and they appealed to external authorities to rally support for feminist goals.

The most crucial element of the structure exploited by feminists were the commitments made to the black freedom struggle by each of these organizations in the early 1960s. The independent women's movement relied heavily on precedents won by the civil rights movement in its policymaking efforts. Such women's groups as NOW lobbied to expand civil rights policy to include women: they petitioned President Lyndon Johnson, for example, to add sex as a criterion to his executive order mandating affirmative action by federal contractors. In the early 1970s, Congresswoman Bella Abzug framed a standard clause banning sex discrimination to be attached to every civil rights bill.[5]

Parallel processes served the advance of feminism in civil society, where feminists incorporated attention to women's rights into civil rights projects already under way in their organizations. The ACLU's Southern Regional Office, with its focus on black civil rights, provided a precedent for the ACLU's Women's Rights Project. Black and white feminists at the Ford Foundation demanded that women's needs be incorporated into projects that targeted African American poverty. Similarly, Church Women United pressured the National Council of Churches to make women a part of the economic-justice project it established in 1969. As work on civil rights projects heightened sensitivity to racism within these organizations, feminists could more easily drive home their message about sexism. Moreover, the antiracist commitment of these groups made them relatively hospitable to African American women, who played crucial roles in reframing civil rights agendas to accommodate women's rights.

Feminists also made use of particular elements of their organizations' structures or practices. They seized on the decentralized structure of the National Council of Churches to concentrate feminist activity within the council's two most sympathetic divisions. There they advanced feminist goals, such as ordination of women and the support of lesbians, that the organization's central policymaking board would not abide. Conversely, the centralized structure of the IUE contributed to the clout that Winn Newman needed to convince local unions to implement antidiscrimination policy. Drawing on an established practice at the Ford Foundation, feminists called in experts on education, government, and social policy to enlighten male officials about the conditions and needs of women in these areas and to bolster their own efforts.

One opportunity for feminist change that feminists themselves helped to create was the presence of women in leadership positions. Among the first demands of women at the ACLU, the NCC, and the Ford Foundation was that the organizations abandon the male monopoly on authority and decision making. Feminists helped elevate Claire Randall to the highest management position in the National Council of Churches, and she in turn used her power to nourish feminism within the organization and to position the council behind woman-centered public policy like the ERA and abortion rights. Feminists won an internal affirmative action program at the ACLU, and women substantially increased their presence on the national board, on national committees, and at national conventions. Similarly, the Ford Foundation established an affirmative action plan, and women moved into staff positions, where they enjoyed considerable influence over funding decisions. The movement of women into policymaking positions in liberal organizations helped to sustain feminism in the United States even after a sizable backlash arose.

Activists in all four organizations created feminist networks, formal and informal, internal and external. In both the ACLU and the NCC, women's caucuses enabled feminists to plan strategy and reach out to more women. White feminists at Ford exchanged information and strategized informally over lunch, while black women created a formal organization, Concerned Minority Women at Ford. Gloria Johnson and other IUE women were active in an external network, the Coalition of Labor Union Women; so were Susan Berresford and the Ford colleagues who helped her create the group Women in Foundations. In a network focused on a single issue, Ruth Weyand of the IUE and Susan Deller Ross of the ACLU headed a broad feminist coalition to fight for a federal ban on discrimination against pregnant workers. Through these various networks, feminists exchanged information, orchestrated strategy, distributed tasks, and provided moral support for one another—even, when needed, a shoulder to cry on.

Legal staff and officers at the IUE employed a strategy that was unique among the organizations considered here. Chief counsel Newman held federal laws against sex discrimination—which the IUE had helped pass—as a hammer over the heads of national officers and local leaders to make them enforce the union's antidiscrimination program. Failure to do so, he warned, would render the union legally liable and gravely threaten its treasury.

All of these strategies worked to institutionalize feminism within these liberal organizations and to re-create the institutions as advocates for sex equity in the arenas of law, government, and public opinion. Their influence was such that virtually every institution in the United States that has adopted any level of feminist policy bears the mark of one or more of these organizations. Ruth Bader Ginsburg and the ACLU Women's Rights Project stood at the center of the legal transformation of the status of women. Women in the United States who are now entitled to medical benefits for pregnancy and assured of their jobs after childbirth owe thanks to the IUE, whose members and officers initiated the legal challenge and subsequently helped mobilize the legislative campaign. The hands of Mariam Chamberlain and others at the Ford Foundation are visible in the multitude of women's studies programs, feminist scholarly journals, and research on women in various disciplines throughout the country. The growing acceptance in mainstream churches of homosexuality, at however glacial a pace, was nudged along by the NCC Commission on Women in Ministry and its Justice for Women project. Harriet Pilpel's labors through the ACLU are visible in federal guidelines protecting poor and undereducated women against sterilization abuse. Women whose employers—primarily state and local governments—have revamped salary structures to provide equal pay for work of comparable worth are indebted to Newman's pioneering efforts in the IUE. And U.S. foreign aid programs that recognize women's role in production and attend to women's specific needs bear the mark of feminists at the Ford Foundation.

The development of feminist footholds in these organizations meant that American society experienced a broader feminist change than that emphasized by the predominantly white and middle-class independent women's movement. Feminism was institutionalized in organizations whose missions had originated with or been modified according to other priorities—meeting the needs of blue-collar workers, poor people, and racial and ethnic minorities. Consequently, when activists sought to introduce feminist principles into these organizations, they connected them to these priorities and produced an agenda that stood not just for the interests of relatively privileged women but also for those of working-class, poor, and minority women.

In contrast to the independent women's movement, these organizations promoted changes in a way that was generally undramatic and therefore usually ignored by the media. Yet they made life better for women. And they provided opportunities for feminist activism to women—notably African American women—who were put off by explicitly feminist organizations. The histories of these institutions demonstrate the efficacy of merging gender interests with those of class, race, and sexual orientation, explain the persistence of feminism, and suggest venues in which to accelerate the momentum of further feminist change.

NOTES

Chapter 1: Introduction

1. The International Union of Electrical, Radio and Machine Workers (AFL-CIO-CLC) was the union's name during most of the period of this study, and it will be referred to as the International Union of Electrical Workers or IUE. The National Council of the Churches of Christ in the U.S.A. will be referred to as the National Council of Churches or NCC.

2. The following important studies examine explicitly feminist groups: Steven M. Buechler, *Women's Movements in the United States: Woman Suffrage, Equal Rights, and Beyond* (New Brunswick, N.J.: Rutgers University Press, 1990); Anne N. Costain, *Inviting Women's Rebellion: A Political-Process Interpretation of the Women's Movement* (Baltimore: Johns Hopkins University Press, 1992); Flora Davis, *Moving the Mountain: The Women's Movement Since 1960* (New York: Simon and Schuster, 1991); Jo Freeman, *The Politics of Women's Liberation: A Case Study of an Emerging Social Movement and Its Relation to the Policy Process* (New York: David McKay, 1975); Sara Evans, *Personal Politics: The Roots of Women's Liberation in the Civil Rights Movement and the New Left* (New York: Vintage Books, 1979); Alice Echols, *Daring to Be Bad: Radical Feminism in America, 1967–1975* (Minneapolis: University of Minnesota Press, 1989); Myra Marx Ferree and Beth Hess, *Controversy and Coalition: The New Feminist Movement* (rev. ed.; Boston: Twayne Publishers, 1994); Joyce Gelb and Marion Lief Palley, *Women and Public Policies* (Princeton, N.J.: Princeton University Press, 1982); Cynthia Harrison, *On Account of Sex: The Politics of Women's Issues, 1945–1968* (Berkeley: University of California Press, 1988); Donald G. Mathews and Jane Sherron De Hart, *Sex, Gender, and the Politics of ERA: A State and the Nation* (New York: Oxford University Press, 1990); Leila Rupp and Verta

Taylor, *Survival in the Doldrums: The American Women's Rights Movement, 1945 to the 1960s* (New York: Oxford University Press, 1987); Winifred D. Wandersee, *On the Move: American Women in the 1970s* (Boston: Twayne Publishers, 1988). Mary Fainsod Katzenstein has studied feminism in male-dominated organizations, but she deals with conservative institutions, such as the Catholic Church and the U.S. military, and a much later time period. See her "Feminism Within American Institutions: Unobtrusive Mobilization in the 1980s," *Signs* 16 (Autumn 1990): 27–54, and "Discursive Politics and Feminist Activism in the Catholic Church," in Myra Marx Ferree and Patricia Yancey Martin, *Feminist Organizations: Harvest of the New Women's Movement* (Philadelphia: Temple University Press, 1995), 35–52.

3. Alice Walker defines "womanism" in *In Search of Our Mothers' Gardens* (New York: Harcourt Brace Jovanovich, 1983), xi. For a discussion of the meaning of the term "feminism," see Nancy F. Cott, "What's in a Name? The Limits of 'Social Feminism'; or, Expanding the Vocabulary of Women's History," *Journal of American History* 76 (December 1989): 809–29.

4. Freeman, *Politics of Women's Liberation,* 28–31; Ethel Klein, *Gender Politics: From Consciousness to Mass Politics* (Cambridge: Harvard University Press, 1984), 1–80.

5. See, for example, Buechler, *Women's Movements in the United States,* 23–35; Davis, *Moving the Mountain,* 34–55, 70–77; Harrison, *On Account of Sex,* 207–09; Echols, *Daring to Be Bad,* 23–50; Evans, *Personal Politics,* 83–192; Freeman, *Politics of Women's Liberation,* 44–102.

6. Dorothy Sue Cobble, "Recapturing Working-Class Feminism: Union Women in the Postwar Era," in Joanne Meyerowitz, *Not June Cleaver: Women and Gender in Postwar America, 1945–1960* (Philadelphia: Temple University Press, 1994), 57–83; Nancy Gabin, *Feminism in the Labor Movement: Women Workers and the United Auto Workers, 1935–1975* (Ithaca, N.Y.: Cornell University Press, 1990); Ruth Milkman, *Gender at Work: The Dynamics of Job Segregation by Sex During World War II* (Urbana: University of Illinois Press, 1987); Susan Lynn, *Progressive Women in Conservative Times: Racial Justice, Peace, and Feminism, 1945 to the 1960s* (New Brunswick, N.J.: Rutgers University Press, 1992); Harrison, *On Account of Sex;* Rupp and Taylor, *Survival in the Doldrums.* See also Dennis A. Deslippe, " 'We Had an Awful Time with Our Women': Iowa's Packinghouse Workers of America, 1945–1975," *Journal of Women's History* 4 (Spring 1993): 10–32.

7. For studies in which white middle-class women emerge as the key

feminist advocates and activists, see, for example, Sara Evans, *Born for Liberty: A History of Women in America* (New York: Free Press, 1989), 296–300; Freeman, *Politics of Women's Liberation*, 37–43; Buechler, *Women's Movements in the United States*, 150–58.

8. Mary Callahan, "Forty Years I'm Secretary-Treasurer of the Local," in Brigid O'Farrell and Joyce L. Kornbluh, *Rocking the Boat: Union Women's Voices, 1915–1975* (New Brunswick, N.J.: Rutgers University Press, 1996), 132.

9. Maren Lockwood Carden, *Feminism in the Mid-1970s: A Report to the Ford Foundation* (New York: Ford Foundation, 1977), 7. For membership figures, see Joyce Gelb and Marian Lief Palley, *Women and Public Policies* (Princeton, N.J.: Princeton University Press, 1982), 28; and Costain, *Inviting Women's Rebellion*, xi–xvii. Costain notes the relatively meager resources of the independent feminist movement and acknowledges the assistance it received from traditional women's groups and liberal organizations. She focuses, however, on the relationship between the grassroots movement and the federal government, arguing that the movement "created the wedge" that allowed the small women's lobby to gain access to policymakers and that it was the political uncertainty stemming from the disruption of the New Deal coalition that made policymakers receptive.

10. J. Craig Jenkins, "Resource Mobilization Theory and the Study of Social Movements," *Annual Reviews in Sociology* 9 (1983): 527–53; Doug McAdam, *Political Process and the Development of Black Insurgency, 1930–1970* (Chicago: University of Chicago Press, 1982), 20–59; Charles Tilly, *From Mobilization to Revolution* (Reading, Mass.: Addison-Wesley, 1978), 52; Bert Useem and Mayer N. Zald, "From Pressure Group to Social Movement: Efforts to Promote Use of Nuclear Power," in Mayer N. Zald and John D. McCarthy, *Social Movements in an Organizational Society: Collected Essays* (New Brunswick, N.J.: Transaction Books, 1987), 273; John D. McCarthy and Mark Woodson, "Consensus Movements, Conflict Movements, and the Cooptation of Civic and State Infrastructures," in Aldon D. Morris and Carol McClurg Mueller, *Frontiers in Social Movement Theory* (New Haven: Yale University Press, 1992), 280–87; Bert Klandermans' introduction to "Interorganizational Networks," part 4 of Klandermans, ed., *International Social Movement Research: A Research Annual* 2 (1989): 301–14. Klandermans argues that initially the women's movement was able to "succeed without developing a solid alliance system," a lack that "be-

came a liability" when opposition arose; not until feminism was thrown on the defensive did the women's movement begin to build new coalitions. I present evidence in this book that challenges Klandermans' argument, which focuses on the failure of ERA ratification and neglects other feminist goals.

Chapter 2: Implementing Feminist Policy

1. International Union of Electrical, Radio and Machine Workers, *Proceedings of the 18th Constitutional Convention, 1978* (Washington, D.C.: International Union of Electrical, Radio and Machine Workers, 1978), 322 [hereafter cited as IUE, *Proceedings, 19XX*]; IUE, *Proceedings, 1980*, 180; "Statement of IUE Before the U.S. Commission on Civil Rights on Affirmative Action in the 1980s," March 11, 1981, 4, papers in the possession of Winn Newman [hereafter cited as Newman papers]; International Union of Electrical Radio and Machine Workers, "Officers' Report," *Proceedings, 1976* (Washington, D.C.: International Union of Electrical, Radio and Machine Workers, 1976), 566 [hereafter cited as IUE, "Officers' Report," 19XX, or IUE, "President's Report," 19XX]; *IUE News*, February 1976, 7, July 1976, 7, June 1977, 10; *Affirmative Action in the 1980s: Dismantling the Process of Discrimination: A Statement of the United States Commission on Civil Rights* (Washington, D.C.: Government Printing Office, 1982), 33n9.

2. Donald Allen Robinson, "Two Movements in Pursuit of Equal Employment Opportunity," *Signs: Journal of Culture and Society* 4 (Spring 1979): 422, 430; Gary Bryner, "Congress, Courts, and Agencies: Equal Employment and the Limits of Policy Implementation," *Political Science Quarterly* 96 (1981): 418.

3. Mary Callahan, "Forty Years I'm Secretary-Treasurer of the Local," in Brigid O'Farrell and Joyce L. Kornbluh, *Rocking the Boat: Union Women's Voices, 1915–1975* (New Brunswick, N.J.: Rutgers University Press, 1996), 121.

4. Karen O'Connor and Lee Epstein, "The Importance of Interest Group Involvement in Employment Discrimination Litigation," *Howard Law Journal* 25 (1982): 710–11.

5. Callahan, "Forty Years I'm Secretary-Treasurer of the Local," 130. The United Packinghouse Workers of America, for example, moved minimally and grudgingly against sex discrimination, and then only after women filed

law suits charging discrimination by the union. See Dennis A. Deslippe, " 'We Had An Awful Time with Our Women': Iowa's Packinghouse Workers of America, 1945-1975," *Journal of Women's History* 4 (Spring 1993): 10–32. Nancy Gabin has provided an account of feminism in the United Auto Workers (UAW), which took a similarly progressive approach to women's issues. See Nancy Gabin, *Feminism in the Labor Movement: Women and the United Auto Workers, 1935-1975* (Ithaca, N.Y.: Cornell University Press, 1990).

6. See, for example, *IUE News,* February 29, 1960, 6, August 1, 1960, 8, November 7, 1960, 9.

7. For a history of the U.E., see Ronald W. Schatz, *The Electrical Workers: A History of Labor at General Electric and Westinghouse, 1923-1960* (Urbana: University of Illinois Press, 1983). For the U.E. and gender issues, see Ruth Milkman, *Gender at Work: The Dynamics of Job Segregation by Sex During World War II* (Urbana: University of Illinois Press, 1987); Lisa Kannenberg, "From World War to Cold War: Women Electrical Workers and Their Union, 1940-1955," M.A. thesis, University of North Carolina at Charlotte, 1990; and Lisa Kannenberg, "The Impact of the Cold War on Women's Trade Union Activism: The UE Experience," *Labor History* 34 (Summer 1993): 309-23. For a study of the Communist Party and gender issues in the 1940s, see Kate Weigand, "Vanguards of Women's Liberation: The Old Left and the Continuity of the Women's Movement in the United States, 1945-1970s," Ph.D. diss., Ohio State University, 1994. Gerald Zahavi describes a large U.E. local's struggles over race, gender, and communism in "Passionate Commitments: Race, Sex, and Communism at Schenectady General Electric, 1932-1954," *Journal of American History* 83 (September 1966): 514-48.

8. Terry Copp, *The IUE in Canada: A History* (Elora, Ont.: Cumnock Press, 1980), 96, 97; Peter B. Levy, *The New Left and Labor in the 1960s* (Urbana: University of Illinois Press, 1994), 12; Robert Zieger, *The CIO, 1935-1955* (Chapel Hill: University of North Carolina Press, 1995), 285, 363; Carey address to CIO Women's Auxiliaries, 1957, Records of the International Union of Electrical Workers [hereafter cited as IUE Records].

9. David Lasser Statement to the Equal Pay for Equal Work Conference, U.S. Department of Labor, March 31–April 1, 1952, IUE Records, box 2087, folder "Women's Auxiliaries, 1952"; Interview with Gloria Johnson, Washington, D.C., April 4, 1984; James B. Carey, "Statement on Equal

Pay Legislation," n.d. [ca. 1956], James B. Carey to David McDonald, February 2, 1956, James B. Carey to George Meany, February 3, 1956, and James B. Carey to William Schnitzler, March 19, 1956, IUE Records, box 46, folder "Legislation on Equal Pay, 1956." Carey's address to the CIO women's auxiliaries, cited above, has a long section referring to women's activism in the past.

10. Carey to Schnitzler, March 19, 1956. See Kim Blankenship, "Bringing Gender and Race In: U.S. Employment Discrimination Policy," *Gender and Society* 7 (June 1993): 204–26, for working men's interest in equal pay. Lasser Statement, Equal Pay for Equal Work Conference, 1952; Statement of James B. Carey, U.S. Congress, House, Committee on Education and Labor, Select Subcommittee on Labor, *Equal Pay for Equal Work,* 87th Cong., 2nd sess. (March 28, 1962), 169–83; James B. Carey to Alvine Krug, April 9, 1964, IUE Records, box 8, folder "Local 801." For an analysis of the discourse about equal pay legislation, see Alice Kessler-Harris, *A Woman's Wage: Historical Meanings and Social Consequences* (Lexington: University of Kentucky Press, 1990), 81–112.

11. Gabin, *Feminism in the Labor Movement,* 143–87; Frances Freeman Jolet, "Report on Women's Conference of IUE-AFL-CIO," Papers of the National Council of Churches of Christ, Presbyterian Historical Society, Philadelphia, Pa., record group 10, box 6.

12. IUE, *Proceedings, 1956,* 298–99; House, Committee on Education and Labor, *Equal Pay for Equal Work,* 183–89. For accounts of working-class feminism in the 1940s and 1950s, see Gabin, *Feminism in the Labor Movement;* Kannenberg, "Impact of the Cold War on Women's Trade Union Activism"; and Dorothy Sue Cobble, "Recapturing Working-Class Feminism: Union Women in the Postwar Era," in Joanne Meyerowitz, *Not June Cleaver: Women and Gender in Postwar America, 1945–1960* (Philadelphia: Temple University Press, 1994), 57–83.

13. Fitzgerald, quoted in Kannenberg, "Impact of the Cold War on Women's Trade Union Activism," 317; Mark McColloch, "The Shop-Floor Dimension of Union Rivalry: The Case of Westinghouse in the 1950s," in Steve Rosswurm, ed., *The CIO's Left-Led Unions* (New Brunswick, N.J.: Rutgers University Press, 1992), 195–99.

14. IUE, "Officers' Report," 1951, 398–400; IUE, *Proceedings, 1951,* 157; IUE, *Proceedings, 1954,* 354; *IUE News,* July 20, 1967, 6–7; IUE, "Officers' Report," 1956, 460–61; "IUE-CIO Leads the Fight for Women Workers,"

and "IUE-CIO's Fight for Women Workers Pays Off," Publications 161 and 162 of the IUE, March 1955, Department of Labor Library, Washington, D.C.; Kannenberg, "Impact of the Cold War on Women's Trade Union Activism," 318.

15. *IUE News,* June 20, 1960, 1, 2, 12, October 24, 1960, 1, 5, November 21, 1960, 1, 2; McColloch, "Shop-Floor Dimension of Union Rivalry," 195–96.

16. *Agreement Between Philco Corp., Sandusky, Ohio and International Union of Electrical, Radio and Machine Workers, AFL-CIO, Local 701,* 1960, 9–12, 23–24, 32, IUE Records, box 175, folder "701."

17. James Carey, Report to the International Executive Board, June 16–17, 1964, IUE Records, box 77; interview with Gloria Johnson, Washington, D.C., April 4, 1984; *IUE News,* April 5, 1962, 3, April 4, 1963, 3, May 30, 1963, 1, 9, June 24, 1965, 5.

18. *IUE News,* July 8, 1965, 2; "IUE Department of Social Action," July–August, 1975, 2–3, IUE Records, box 156, folder "Bill Gary"; Bill Gary to Paul Jennings, "Recommendations from Recent Women's Conference," October 27, 1967, IUE Records, box 6, folder "National IUE Women's Conference"; "Women in the IUE: A Preliminary Report Prepared for the Department of Social Action, 1969," IUE records in the possession of Ruth Weyand [hereafter cited as Weyand papers]; IUE, "President's Report," 1968, 344–45, 374–78.

19. Cobble, "Recapturing Working-Class Feminism;" Gabin, *Feminism in the Labor Movement;* R. J. Einbinder, "Leadership Is Not Limited to Male of IUE Species," *IUE News,* October 1979, 8; Margaret Mead and Frances Balgley Kaplan, eds., *American Women: The Report of the President's Commission on the Status of Women and Other Publications of the Commission* (New York: Charles Scribner's Sons, 1965); Jo Freeman, *The Politics of Women's Liberation: A Case Study of an Emerging Social Movement and Its Relation to the Policy Process* (New York: David McKay, 1975), 52, 67–68. Through the 1960s, Callahan served on the successor to the commission, the Citizens Advisory Council on the Status of Women, as well as on the IUE executive board.

20. Joseph T. Hawkins to Mr. Nelson, July 14, 1964, IUE Records, box 175, folder "Local 711"; Ruth Weyand to Winn Newman, May 23, 1972, IUE Records, box 242, folder "Pregnancy Bulletins"; *IUE News,* May 18, 1967, 8.

21. *IUE News,* May 18, 1967, 8, July 20, 1967, 11.

22. Steward Contact 373–1, December 19, 1965, and Steward Contacts 15–105 and 15–106, May 4, 1966, Weyand papers. Most often, women who had been in the plants for decades initiated grievances in these and other cases.

23. "Special Meeting with the Company," June 21, 1972, Bob Wire to Ruth Weyand, April 24, 1972, and Tom Willhelm and Bob Wire to Ruth Weyand, May 16, 1972, IUE Records, box 178, folder "Local 901."

24. Interview with Ruth Weyand, March 26, 1984; Winn Newman, "The Policy Issues: Presentation III," *Signs: Journal of Women in Culture and Society* 1 (Spring 1976): 268, 270; Winn Newman to Paul Jennings, November 11, 1974, IUE Records, box 25, untitled folder; Mary Callahan Interview II by Karen Budd, May 19, 1976, Twentieth-Century Trade Union Women, Oral History Project, Institute of Labor and Industrial Relations, University of Michigan/Wayne State University, 26. Nancy Gabin notes the attachment of some UAW women to the segregated work force; these women feared that they had more to lose than to gain from equal treatment. See Gabin, *Feminism in the Labor Movement,* 181–82. For the role of pay equity litigation in awareness of gender inequities and political mobilization, see Michael W. McCann, *Rights at Work: Pay Equity Reform and the Politics of Legal Mobilization* (Chicago: University of Chicago Press, 1994), 80.

25. Alma C. Dickensheets, Mary H. Ehren, and Margaret M. Craig to Paul Jennings, August 2, 1965, Margaret W. Call to Paul Jennings, September 20, 1965, and Dolores Fickert to Paul Jennings, February 21, 1965, and December 6, 1965, all in IUE Records, box 8, folder "Local 801."

26. Miss Julia Kuc v Westinghouse Electric Corporation and International Union of Electrical, Radio & Machine Workers—Local 601, Case No. 5–10–2103, November 17, 1965, IUE Records, box 246, folder "Local 601 v Westinghouse."

27. McGarr quoted in Copp, *IUE in Canada,* 108; IUE, *Proceedings, 1970,* 231–34; IUE, *Proceedings, 1972,* 191.

28. Interview with Mae Massie Eberhardt, November 5, 1979, in Ruth Edmonds Hill, ed., *The Black Women Oral History Project,* vol. 3 (Westport, Conn.: Meckler, 1991), 239–40.

29. Decision, Kuc v Westinghouse and IUE, Case No. 5–10–2103; Commissioner Decision, *Delores Fickert et al. v General Motors: Frigidaire Division, Dayton, Ohio and Local 801, International Union of Electrical,*

Radio & and Machine Workers, Case No. 5-11-2563, IUE Records, box 295, folder "Sex Decisions."

30. Commissioner Decision, Delores Fickert et al. v General Motors; Kuc v Westinghouse and IUE; Barbara Allen Babcock et al., *Sex Discrimination and the Law: Causes and Remedies* (Boston: Little, Brown, 1975), 261–77. EEOC Commissioner Aileen C. Hernandez referred specifically to the Dayton case in pressing the commission for closer scrutiny of the relationship between protective laws and Title VII. Aileen C. Hernandez to Commissioners, March 8, 1966, IUE Records, box 295, folder "Sex Decisions." See Gabin, *Feminism in the Labor Movement,* for the issue of protective laws in the UAW.

31. *IUE News,* November 2, 1967, 8, April 10, 1969, 10.

32. IUE, *Keeping up with the Law,* October 1971, 187–89; *IUE News,* April 4, 1967, 8, November 2, 1967, 7, April 18, 1968, 8, April 10, 1969, 10, June 25, 1970, 5, September 1971, 6.

33. *IUE News,* April 8, 1971, 3; author interview with Winn Newman, August 4, 1984; IUE, *Proceedings, 1972,* 87; IUE, "President's Report," 1972, 322–25, 461–63. Some IUE women apparently broke ranks with official policy on the ERA as early as September 1970. The *New York Times,* on September 15, 1970, reported that IUE women had joined women from other unions at a news conference announcing their support for the amendment. The *Times* did not name the women.

34. IUE, *Proceedings, 1972,* 189; IUE, "Officers' Report," 1974, 415; IUE, *Proceedings, 1974,* 65; Janet K. Boles, *The Politics of the Equal Rights Amendment: Conflict and the Decision Process* (New York: Longman, 1979), 51, 63; *IUE News,* November 1973, 3; "Equal Rights Amendment," n.d., Records of ERAmerica, box 148, Library of Congress, Washington, D.C.

35. *IUE News,* September 1977, 5, February 1978, 2; IUE, "Officers' Report," 1978, 54; "Organizational Contributions at December 31, 1979," Minutes of ERAmerica Corporate Board, box 6, July 15, 1977; Records of ERAmerica, box 5, Library of Congress, Washington, D.C. Paul Jennings succeeded James Carey as union president in 1964. The bitterly contested election had no apparent effect on the union's approach to women's rights. During the struggle to ratify the ERA, NOW called for a boycott of all states that had not ratified the amendment, urging organizations of every kind to hold their national meetings and conventions only in states that had ratified it.

36. Callahan, "Forty Years I'm Secretary-Treasurer of the Local," 130; author interview with Winn Newman, August 4, 1984. Some details of Newman's earlier career are in IUE Records, box 195. Newman's commitment to and expertise in civil rights was apparent in much of his work in the area of women's rights. For example, he translated the Supreme Court's reasoning in *Brown v Board of Education* that separating the races applied the stigma of inferiority to blacks into his arguments for pay equity for women. See Winn Newman and Jeanne M. Vonhof, " 'Separate but Equal' — Job Segregation and Pay Equity in the Wake of *Gunther*," *University of Illinois Law Review* (1981): 269–331.

37. Interviews with Ruth Weyand, March 26, 1984, and August 2, 1984; *IUE News,* April 8, 1971, 3, July 1977, 10; Mary McLeod Bethune to Director, May 18, 1948, Papers of the National Council of Negro Women, Washington, D.C., Series 5, folder 168.

38. IUE, "Officers' Report," 1976, 558–67. A study of unions and racial discrimination that was prepared during the early years of the compliance program noted that the IUE stood out among unions with its "forward-looking and unique stance on problems of hiring discrimination" and that it was "rapidly moving toward the best" position in terms of opening skilled trades to minorities. See William B. Gould, *Black Workers in White Unions: Job Discrimination in the United States* (Ithaca, N.Y.: Cornell University Press, 1977), 405–6.

39. Paul Jennings to All IUE Local Unions, March 16, 1973, IUE Records, box 25, unmarked folder; Paul Jennings and David J. Fitzmaurice, July 26, 1974, Weyand papers; "IUE Policy — Title VII, Civil Rights Act, Equal Pay Act," July 1974, Weyand papers. A number of memos from Newman to Jennings and other union officials demonstrate Newman's zeal in demanding local compliance. See IUE Records, box 25, unmarked folder. See also M. Hoyman, "Alternative Models of Policy Compliance by Unions with Civil Rights Legislation," *Law and Policy* 8 (January 1986): 77–103.

40. "Revised Title VII Program," January 15, 1979, Newman papers; IUE, "Officers' Report," 1980, 173–75.

41. "Statement of Policy on the Basic Bargaining Goals of GE-Westinghouse Unions in 1973, Adopted by the Steering Committee of the Coordinated Bargaining Committee of GE-Westinghouse," n.d., Newman papers; IUE, "Officers' Report," 1976, 562–64.

42. Ruth Weyand to Winn Newman, May 23, 1972, IUE Records, box

241, folder "Pregnancy Bulletins"; "Some Highlights of Recent IUE Anti-Discrimination Efforts," IUE Records, box 244, folder *Gilbert v General Electric*—Judge Merhige"; draft, "Ten Years of Litigation: Highlights of IUE Affirmative Fair Employment Litigation and Related Efforts, 1970–1980," 1–2, Newman papers.

43. Draft, "Ten Years of Litigation: Highlights of IUE Affirmative Fair Employment Litigation and Related Efforts, 1970–1980," 1–3, Newman papers; Joy Ann Grune, ed., *Manual on Pay Equity: Raising Wages for Women's Work* (Washington, D.C.: Committee on Pay Equity, Conference on Alternative State and Local Policies, 1981), 81; *New York Times,* January 1, 1984, III, 1 and 15. The lawsuit *IUE v Westinghouse Electric Corporation* began when five women working in a lamp plant in Trenton, New Jersey, filed sex-discrimination charges. See Frances C. Hutner, *Equal Pay for Comparable Worth: The Working Woman's Issue of the Eighties* (New York: Praeger, 1986), 99–120.

44. McCann, *Rights at Work,* 61; *IUE News,* September 1972, 12; Newman, "Policy Issues," 265–66; Grune, *Manual on Pay Equity,* 79–86.

45. *IUE News,* September 1975, 5–9.

46. Ruth Weyand to Jane Picker, December 10, 1973, IUE Records, box 25, untitled folder; *IUE News,* September 1979, 12, September 1976, 3; "Some Highlights of Recent IUE Anti-Discrimination Efforts," IUE Records, box 244, folder *"Gilbert v General Electric*—Judge Merhige."

47. Winn Newman to Paul Jennings and David J. Fitzmaurice, December 6, 1974, and "IUE Statement on Pre-Hire Seniority," IUE Records, box 25, untitled folder; Winn Newman to David Copus, January 14, 1975, Winn Newman and Ruth Weyand to Paul Jennings et al., September 9, 1975, IUE Records, box 156, folder "Newman"; Winn Newman and Carole W. Wilson, "The Union Role in Affirmative Action," *Labor Law Journal* 32 (June 1981): 323–42.

48. IUE organizing brochure, n.d., ca. 1973, IUE Records, box 255, folder *"Gilbert v General Electric*—Judge Merhige"; Winn Newman to Paul Jennings and David J. Fitzmaurice, July 6, 1973, IUE Records, box 25, folder "Title VII"; "Draft of Winn Newman Report" [probably to the IUE Executive Board], July 27, 1975, 6–7, IUE Records, box 156, folder "Newman."

49. "Draft of Newman Report," 1–2, 10.

50. Interview with Newman; Ruth Weyand to Winn Newman, Au-

gust 13, 1973, Winn Newman to Paul Jennings, August 13, 1973, Winn Newman to Paul Jennings and James D. Compton, September 14, 1973, IUE Records, box 25, untitled folder; Ruth Weyand to Paul Jennings, January 31, 1975, IUE Records, box 156, folder "Newman."

51. Extensive correspondence on the union liability issue exists in IUE records. See, for example, Winn Newman to Paul Jennings and David J. Fitzmaurice, October 1, 1973, box 246, folder "EEOC—General"; Ruth Weyand to Eugene V. Nelson, September 26, 1975, box 246, folder *"Local 627 v Westinghouse"*; Winn Newman to Paul Jennings and David Fitzmaurice, June 27, 1973, Winn Newman to Paul Jennings, April 11, 1974, May 30, 1974, Winn Newman and Mel Warshaw to Paul Jennings, November 12, 1974, box 25, untitled folder; Winn Newman to Paul Jennings and David J. Fitzmaurice, box 25, folder "Title VII"; Winn Newman to Paul Jennings, September 18, 1975, March 16, 1976, Winn Newman to Paul Jennings and David J. Fitzmaurice, January 23, 1975, December 8, 1975, box 156, folder "Newman." The complete IUE case against union liability is set forth in its statement before the Equal Employment Opportunity Commission with respect to its charge no. TNP4C-2000 against General Electric and charge no. TNP4C-2001 against IUE, box 281.

52. IUE, "Officers' Report," 1980, 173.

53. Winn Newman to Paul Jennings and David J. Fitzmaurice, October 1, 1973, IUE Records, box 246, folder "EEOC—General"; Winn Newman to Paul Jennings, August 26, 1975, IUE Records, box 156, folder "Newman."

54. *Keeping up with the Law,* April 1969, 88–89; *IUE News,* July 24, 1969, 9; "History of IUE-Westinghouse Negotiations Relating to IUE Efforts to Eliminate Sex Discrimination," n.d., 20, 23, 31, 34, Weyand papers; IUE, "Officers' Report," 1976, 577–79. Ruth Weyand noted, "I had to struggle for sixteen months to get 100 employees on obviously and grossly unequal pay to sign authorizations to sue, but was overwhelmed with as many as 350 charges with EEOC in one weekend after one local learned of the EEOC ruling in sickness and accident benefits for disabilities arising from pregnancy." Weyand to Edith Ann Ardissone, March 20, 1973, Papers of Pauli Murray, Schlesinger Library, Radcliffe College, box 123, folder 2200.

55. *IUE News,* March 1972, 9; *Keeping up with the Law,* April 1969, 88–89, May–June 1971, 117–18, January 1972, 13–24; Testimony of Robert

Gordon Delano in *Martha Gilbert, IUE, et al. v General Electric,* No. 74–1590, Appendix, I:436–42, Weyand papers. Extensive correspondence with local unions on the pregnancy issue can be found in IUE Records, box 245, folder "Pregnancy Letters."

56. Joyce Gelb and Marian Lief Palley, *Women and Public Policies* (Princeton, N.J.: Princeton University Press, 1982), 158–66; *IUE News,* April 1977, 3, November 1978, 2, May 1979, 5; U.S. Congress, Senate Subcommittee on Labor of the Committee on Human Resources, *Discrimination on the Basis of Pregnancy, 1977: Hearings,* 95th Cong., 1st sess. (April 26, 27, and 29, 1977), 222–53; David J. Fitzmaurice to All IUE Local Unions, July 28, 1977, IUE Records, box 242, folder "Pregnancy Bulletins, Letters, etc."

57. David J. Fitzmaurice to Carl D. Perkins, November 8, 1977, IUE Records, box 245, folder *"Gilbert v General Electric,* Correspondence, Vol. II."

58. Ruth Weyand to Winn Newman, March 27, 1972, IUE Records, box 242, folder "Pregnancy Bulletins."

59. Ruth Weyand to Judith Lonnquist, September 26, 1974, Papers of the National Organization for Women, Schlesinger Library, Radcliffe College, 72-75-79-M262, carton 26, folder "Legal VP"; Ruth Weyand to Irving Abramson, August 7, 1973, IUE Records, box 244, folder "LaFleur"; Karen O'Connor, *Women's Organizations' Use of the Courts* (Lexington, Mass.: D. C. Heath, 1980), 114.

60. *A Chronology of the IUE's Social Action Programs,* Publication 273 of the International Union of Electrical, Radio and Machine Workers, revised, 1981, 27; *IUE News,* March 1974, 5, April 1974, 11, September 1975, 5, October 1975, 5–9, July 1976, 7, January 1978, 11; IUE, *Proceedings, 1974,* 183, 193–99; IUE, *Proceedings, 1978,* 321–25; IUE, *Proceedings, 1980,* 179–85.

61. Gabin, *Feminism in the Labor Movement,* 232.

62. Callahan Interview III by Karen Budd, May 26, 1976, Twentieth-Century Trade Union Women, Oral History Project, 45; Eberhardt interview in Hill, *Black Women Oral History Project,* 269.

63. Winn Newman testimony, *Hearings Before the United States Equal Employment Opportunity Commission on Job Segregation and Wage Discrimination,* Washington, D.C., April 28–30, 1980 (Washington, D.C.: EEOC, 1980), 21–22; Linda M. Blum, *Between Feminism and Labor: The Signifi-*

cance of the Comparable Worth Movement (Berkeley: University of California Press, 1991), 41–46, 192–202.

64. Callahan Interview III by Karen Budd, May 26, 1976, Twentieth-Century Trade Union Women, Oral History Project, 8–10.

65. *IUE News,* July 1976, 7.

66. Gabin, *Feminism in the Labor Movement,* provides the fullest account of the UAW's Women's Department.

67. For a discussion about the respective roles of leadership and rank and file in promoting racial justice, see Bruce Nelson, "Class, Race and Democracy in the CIO: The 'New' Labor History Meets the 'Wages of Whiteness,'" *International Review of Social History* 41 (December 1996): 351–74.

68. Marcia Hams, "Women Taking Leadership in Male-Dominated Locals," *Women's Rights Law Reporter* 8 (Winter 1984): 71–82; Alex Brown and Laurie Sheridan, "Pioneering Women's Committee Struggles with Hard Times," *Labor Research Review* 7 (Spring 1988): 63–77; Susan R. Strauss, "Strategy for Failure: Affirmative Action in a Mass Production Context," in Glenn Adler and Doris Suarez, *Union Voices: Labor's Responses to Crisis* (Albany: State University of New York Press, 1993), 151–70.

Chapter 3: Litigating Feminist Principles

1. Samuel Walker, *In Defense of American Liberties: A History of the ACLU* (New York: Oxford University Press, 1990), 168, 237, 267.

2. Kenyon and Murray to Board, September 24, 1970, Papers of Pauli Murray, Schlesinger Library, Radcliffe College, Cambridge, Mass. [hereafter cited as Murray papers], box 55, folder 956. Harriet Pilpel joined the ACLU board in 1962, but her feminist efforts focused nearly exclusively on reproductive rights.

3. Pauli Murray, *Song in a Weary Throat: An American Pilgrimage* (New York: Harper and Row, 1987), 347–57.

4. Author telephone interview with Suzanne Post, August 17, 1995.

5. Jo Freeman, "Resource Mobilization and Strategy: A Model for Analyzing Social Movement Organization Actions," in Mayer N. Zald and John D. McCarthy, eds., *The Dynamics of Social Movements* (Cambridge, Mass.: Winthrop, 1979), 175.

6. Memorandum by Roger Baldwin on the Origins of the ACLU,

November 8, 1973, Microfilm Records of the American Civil Liberties Union [hereafter cited as ACLU Records], reel 96.

7. ACLU Annual Reports, April 1925, 24–25, 38, June 1929, 25; Board of Directors Meeting, November 27, 1933, ACLU Records, reel 4; David Garrow, *Liberty and Sexuality: The Right to Privacy and the Making of Roe v. Wade* (New York: Macmillan, 1994), 41–44.

8. ACLU Annual Report, 1939, 45–46; Walker, *In Defense of American Liberties,* 167.

9. Dorothy Kenyon to Fellow Board Member, February 21, 1967, Murray papers, box 114, folder 2042.

10. Susan M. Hartmann, "Dorothy Kenyon," in Barbara Sicherman, ed., *Notable American Women: The Modern Period* (Cambridge: Harvard University Press, 1980), 395–97; Dorothy Kenyon interview with Jacqueline Van Voris, June 14, 1971, Smith Centennial Study, Oral History Project, Sophia Smith Collection.

11. Kenyon interview, June 14, 1971.

12. Walker, *In Defense of American Liberties,* 167; Memorandum on Women's Rights Adopted by the Board of Directors, July 1945, John Haynes Holmes papers, Library of Congress, box 82; ACLU Annual Reports, No. 24 (July 1946), 19, 58, No. 25 (August 1947), 18, 45, No. 26 (August 1948), 59; ACLU press release, "Testimony of Dorothy Kenyon on Equal Pay Bills," April 27, 1962, ACLU Records, reel 16; "Statement by the American Civil Liberties Union on H.R. 3861," March 26, 1963, ACLU Records, reel 16. The Committee on Discrimination Against Women in Employment later became the Committee on Women's Rights, and after 1955 its work was subsumed within the Due Process and Equality Committee.

13. See, e.g., Dorothy Kenyon, "Is the Law Unfair to Women?" *Woman's Day* (August 1943), 27, 40, 62; "Equal Rights: A Debate," *New York Times Magazine,* May 7, 1944, 14, 36–37; Dorothy Kenyon, "The Woman's Charter: A Charter of Liberties for Women and Society," speech manuscript, n.d., Papers of Dorothy Kenyon, Sophia Smith Collection, Smith College, Northampton, Mass. [hereafter cited as Kenyon papers], box 23, folder 242; Kenyon, "Equal Rights," speech manuscript, May 4, 1935, Kenyon papers, box 18, folder 180.

14. National Committee to Defeat the Unequal Rights Amendment, Minutes of Meeting, September 28, 1944, Records of the National Consumers' League, C-16, Library of Congress; National Committee on the

Status of Women, Release, February 18, 1947, Records of the National Consumers' League, C–16, Library of Congress; ACLU Annual Report, No. 32 (June 1956), 78–79. Minutes, Board of Directors, June 20, 1955, ACLU Records, reel 14. Correspondence between ACLU staff and Kenyon on women's rights cases can be found in Kenyon papers, box 44.

15. Ruth Barrett, "Rights of Women a Judge's Frontier," *Trade Union Courier,* July 13, 1957; ACLU Board of Directors minutes, June 22, 1959, ACLU Records, reel 15.

16. Barbara Allen Babcock, Ann E. Freedman, Eleanor Holmes Norton, and Susan C. Ross, *Sex Discrimination and the Law: Causes and Remedies* (Boston: Little, Brown, 1975), 97–104; ACLU press release, August 28, 1961, ACLU Records, reel 16.

17. Dorothy Kenyon to Pauli Murray, January 30, 1963, Murray papers, box 49, folder 878; ACLU pamphlet, "Goals for the 1960s with Highlights from the Past 40 Years," ACLU Records, reel 95.

18. Murray, *Song in a Weary Throat,* provides details of Murray's life and the quote (p. 271). See also Rosalind Rosenberg, "Pauli Murray and the Killing of Jane Crow," in Susan Ware, ed., *Forgotten Heroes from America's Past* (New York: Free Press, 1998).

19. Cynthia Harrison, *On Account of Sex: The Politics of Women's Issues, 1945–1968* (Berkeley: University of California Press, 1988), 111; Margaret Mead and Frances Balgley Kaplan, eds., *American Women: The Report of the President's Commission on the Status of Women and Other Publications of the Commission* (New York: Charles Scribner's Sons, 1965), 149; Katherine P. Ellickson to Pauli Murray, June 26, 1962, Edith Green to Pauli Murray, August 11, 1962, Pauli Murray to Edith Green, August 19, 1962, Murray papers, box 49, folder 875; Dorothy Kenyon to Pauli Murray, January 30, 1963, Murray papers, folder 878; Dorothy Kenyon to the Board of Directors, March 28, 1963, Kenyon papers, box 45, folder 447; Alan Reitman to Dorothy Kenyon, April 10, 1964, Kenyon papers, box 45, folder 447; Board of Directors minutes, April 1, 1963, ACLU Records, reel 16; Alan Reitman to Pauli Murray, April 3, 1963, Murray papers, box 49, folder 878; ACLU press release, February 21, 1964, ACLU Records, reel 17.

20. Murray, *Song in a Weary Throat,* 356–57; Minutes, Board of Directors, February 17, 1964, ACLU Records, reel 17.

21. Marguerite Rawalt to Pauli Murray, October 2, 1964, Murray papers, box 94, folder 1644; Pauli Murray and Mary O. Eastwood, "Jane Crow and

the Law: Sex Discrimination and Title VII," *George Washington Law Review* 34 (December 1965): 232–56.

22. Dorothy Kenyon to Charles T. Duncan, March 17, 1966, Kenyon papers, box 44, folder 430; Dorothy Kenyon to Esther Peterson, February 28, 1966 and April 6, 1966, Kenyon papers, folder 426; ACLU News Release, October 4, 1965, ACLU Records, reel 17. When the court made its favorable ruling in February 1966, ACLU officials presented the issue of women's exclusion as an important element of the case. See ACLU News Release, February 8, 1966, ACLU Records, reel 19. I am grateful to Rosalind Rosenberg for her insights into the case.

23. ACLU Bulletin No. 2258, February 28, 1966, ACLU Records, reel 18.

24. Walker, *In Defense of American Liberties,* 269–70; Judith Paterson, *Be Somebody: A Biography of Marguerite Rawalt* (Austin: Eakin Press, 1986), 161–63. See also Esther Peterson to Pauli Murray, February 9, 1966, Murray papers, box 59, folder 999; Mary Dublin Keyserling to Dorothy Kenyon, March 22, 1966, Kenyon papers, box 44, folder 429. At the national Conference of Commissions on the Status of Women in June 1966, Kenyon, Murray, and Morgan of the ACLU were the only non-governmental panelists on a session on sex discrimination. "Program Highlights," Conference of Commissions on the Status of Women, June 28, 29, 30, 1966, Washington, D.C., Kenyon papers, box 14, folder 139.

25. Minutes of the Board of Directors meeting, January 29–30, 1966, 20–21, ACLU Records, reel 17; ACLU News Release, March 4, 1966, ACLU Records, reel 19; ACLU News Release, July 14, 1966, Statement of Lawrence Speiser on Senate Civil Rights Act of 1966, ACLU Records, reel 18. See chapter 6 for a discussion of Murray's arguments about the connections between women's rights and the rights of minorities.

26. Eleanor Holmes Norton to Pauli [Murray], January 31, 1966, Pauli Murray to Marguerite [Rawalt], February 2, 1966, February 16, 1966, Murray papers, box 59, folder 999; Susan M. Hartmann, "Women's Issues and the Johnson Administration," in Robert A. Divine, ed., *The Johnson Years: LBJ at Home and Abroad* (Lawrence: University of Kansas Press, 1994), 63–65; Karen O'Connor, *Women's Organizations' Use of the Courts* (Lexington, Mass.: Lexington Books, 1980), 125.

27. ACLU lawyers first made the right to privacy argument in an amicus curiae brief in a birth control case heard by the Supreme Court in 1961. A

majority of the Court affirmed that right in the *Griswold* birth control case of 1965. Harriet F. Pilpel, "A Right Is Born: Privacy as a Civil Liberty," *Civil Liberties* 231 (November 1965), 2.

28. Dorothy Kenyon, "Nullification or Repeal," *Birth Control Review* (October 1930): 278–80; Garrow, *Liberty and Sexuality,* 276; The Office to the Board of Directors, February 8, 1967, ACLU Records, reel 25.

29. Draft of speech, "The Legal Concept of Equality," 4/2/59, 6–7, Kenyon papers, box 23, folder 227. Documents accompanying this speech indicate Kenyon's attention to legal and medical discussions of abortion law reform.

30. Judge Dorothy Kenyon, "Women of the U.S.A., Awake!" *New York Americans for Democratic Action Bulletin,* March, 1967, 3, Kenyon papers, box 14, folder 139.

31. For Ernst and Pilpel's work with Planned Parenthood, see Garrow, *Liberty and Sexuality,* chapters 1–4; Ben Gerson, "Renaissance Woman: A Feminist Pioneer's Trail of Achievements," *National Law Journal,* September 27, 1982, 1, 24–25.

32. Pilpel quoted in Gerson, "Renaissance Woman"; Harriet Pilpel to Theodore S. Kenyon, February 22, 1972, Kenyon papers, box 1, folder 9.

33. Paper by Harriet Pilpel presented at "Civil Liberties and the War on Crime" workshop at the ACLU Biennial Conference, June 21–24, 1964, ACLU Records, reel 29, 7–8; Summary Report of 1964 ACLU Biennial Conference, July 9, 1964, ACLU Records, reel 29, 7–8; The Office to the Board of Directors, February 8, 1967, ACLU Records, reel 25.

34. Susan Staggenborg, *The Pro-Choice Movement: Organization and Activism in the Abortion Conflict* (New York: Oxford University Press, 1991), 23; Testimony of Harriet F. Pilpel before the Committee on Health and Codes, New York State Assembly, February 3, 1967, ACLU Records, reel 25.

35. The Office to the Board of Directors, February 9, 1967, ACLU Records, reel 25; Alan Reitman and Trudy Hayden to Board of Directors, October 31, 1967, ACLU Records, reel 25; *Civil Liberties* 246 (May 1967): 4.

36. Minutes, Board of Directors, February 14, 1967, Murray papers, box 114, folder 2042; Lois G. Forer to Dorothy Kenyon, February 27, 1967, Kenyon papers, box 45, folder 436; Dorothy Kenyon to Harriet Pilpel, April 25, 1967, Kenyon papers, box 44, folder 431; Dorothy Kenyon to John

de J. Pemberton, Jr., April 29, 1969, Kenyon papers, folder 433; Dorothy Kenyon and George Soll to the Board, June 9, 1967, ACLU Records, reel 25. Pauli Murray did not engage in the abortion issue. Among Kenyon's tiny band of allies were Lois Forer, a Philadelphia lawyer, and George Soll, one of Kenyon's longtime colleagues.

37. The Office to Board, June 12, 1967, The Office to Board of Directors, September 1, 1967, Alan Reitman and Trudy Hayden to Board of Directors, October 31, 1967, ACLU Records, reel 25; Minutes, Board of Directors, December 2–3, 1967, Kenyon papers, box 45, folder 438; Jack Pemberton to Board of Directors, December 21, 1967, Kenyon papers, folder 436; Minutes, Board of Directors, January 25, 1968, ACLU Records, reel 19; Policy No. 247, "Abortion," Kenyon papers, box 35, folder 313.

38. Susan Staggenborg, *Pro-Choice Movement*, 20–21; *Inside ACLU*, January 13, 1969, 3, March 31, 1969, 2.

39. *New York Times*, February 17, 1969; Women's Rights Cases, February 1971, attached to letter from Aryeh Neier to Dorothy Kenyon, February 1, 1971, Kenyon papers, box 44, folder 435; Women's Rights Project Legal Docket, January 1973, ACLU Records, reel 28; Rosalind Pollack Petchesky, *Abortion and Woman's Choice: The State, Sexuality, and Reproductive Freedom* (Boston: Northeastern University Press, 1985), 103, 113.

40. *Women's Role in Contemporary Society: The Report of the New York City Commission on Human Rights, September 21–25, 1970* (New York: Avon Books, 1972), 615–17; Pauli Murray and Mary O. Eastwood, "Jane Crow and the Law."

41. Pauli Murray to Mary Eastwood, January 25, 1968, Eastwood to Murray, February 5, 1968, Murray to Eastwood, February 10, 1968, The Office to Equality Committee, February 15, 1968, Murray papers, box 55, folder 957; Alan Reitman and Susan Goldstein to the Board, September 16, 1968, ACLU Records, reel 26.

42. Minutes, Equality Committee, April 26, 1966, December 28, 1967, Murray papers, box 54, folder 943; Minutes, Equality Committee, April 1, 1970, Murray papers, box 54, folder 944.

43. Minutes, Equality Committee, April 26, 1966, Murray papers, box 54, folder 943; The Office to the Board of Directors, October 3, 1968, ACLU of Michigan Statement, ACLU Records, reel 26; The Office to the Board, December 12, 1968, Howard Samuel's Comments, ACLU Records, reel 26.

44. Norman Dorsen to ACLU Executive Committee, December 23, 1968, Murray papers, box 55, folder 959; Louise Noun to Pauli Murray, November 4, 1969, Murray papers, box 105, folder 1895; Minutes, Equality Committee, April 1, 1970, Murray papers, box 54, folder 944; Minutes, Equality Committee, November 30, 1967, Murray papers, folder 943; Pauli Murray to the Board of Directors, December 1, 1968, Dorothy Kenyon to the Board, December 12, 1968, ACLU Records, reel 26.

45. Minutes, ACLU Board, December 14–15, 1968, Kenyon papers, box 45, folder 438; Dorothy Kenyon to Board Member of A.C.L.U., December 23, 1968, Kenyon papers, box 44, folder 432; Telephone interview with Suzanne Post, August 17, 1995. One of Kenyon's colleagues responded to her remarks by asserting that she had received "shabby treatment" from the board and that she owed no apologies. David Carliner to Dorothy Kenyon, January 13, 1969, Kenyon papers, box 44, folder 433.

46. Susan Deller Ross to the Equality Committee, Murray papers, box 54, folder 958.

47. Nancy Van Vuuren to Pauli [Murray], July 22, 1970, Murray papers, box 105, folder 1895; Karen DeCrow to Alan Reitman, December 5, 1968, Alan Reitman to Pauli Murray, December 24, 1968, Murray papers, box 55, folder 959; Reitman to Murray, January 17, 1969, Murray papers, box 59, folder 1002; Reitman to Murray, March 10, 1970, Murray to Reitman, June 20, 1970, Murray papers, box 59, folder 1003.

48. Walker, *In Defense of American Liberties,* 316–18. The crimes connected with Watergate also contributed substantially to the swelling of ACLU membership rolls.

49. Pauli Murray to Norman Dorsen, September 12, 1969, Murray papers, box 59, folder 1002; *Inside ACLU,* November 17, 1969, 3–4.

50. ACLU, "Women's Rights Audit," June 1974, 5, ACLU Records, reel 30; ACLU press release, April 27, 1970, ACLU Records, reel 19; author telephone interview with Suzanne Post, August 17, 1995; author telephone interview with Faith Seidenberg, September 1, 1995; Barbara Allen Babcock et al., *Sex Discrimination and the Law: Causes and Remedies* (Boston: Little, Brown, 1975) 1038–47.

51. "ACLU 1970 Biennial Conference, New York University, NYC," June 4, 1970, Murray papers, box 54, folder 944.

52. The Office to Board of Directors, November 20, 1970, ACLU Records, reel 27.

53. "Report of the 1970 ACLU Biennial Conference," ACLU Records, reel 30; author interview with Seidenberg, September 1, 1995.

54. Jack Pemberton to Members of the National and Affiliate Boards et al., July 9, 1970, Murray papers, box 55, folder 951.

55. Murray to Jack Pemberton, July 16, 1970, Murray papers, box 55, folder 951; Murray to Aileen Hernandez, September 18, 1969, Murray papers, box 105, folder 1895.

56. Suzy [Post] to Pauli Murray, October 5, 1970, Murray papers, box 59, folder 1003; Suzy Post to Pauli Murray, February 5, 1973, Murray papers, box 56, folder 965; author interview with Post, August 17, 1995. Post recalled that Harriet Pilpel rarely attended the caucus meetings, but "when push came to shove she was always with us."

57. ACLU, "Policy 316a: ACLU Internal Organization," reel 27.

58. Report of the ACLU Biennial Conference of 1972, ACLU Records, reel 30, 24–26; Ruth Bader Ginsburg et al. to Advisory Committee Members, Women's Rights Project, July 11, 1972, Murray papers, box 56, folder 961; George Slaff, Chairperson, and Ad Hoc Committee for Implementation of Policy No. 316A to Members of the Board of Directors et al., September 12, 1972, ACLU Records, reel 27.

59. Pauli [Murray] to Suzy Post, February 1, 1973, Post to Murray, February 5, 1973, Murray papers, box 56, folder 965; Pauli Murray to Board of Directors, February 9, 1973, ACLU Records, reel 28; Alan Reitman to Board of Directors, March 1, 1973, ACLU Records, reel 28; Women's Rights Audit, prepared for the June 13–16, 1974, Biennial Conference, 1, 3–5, ACLU Records, reel 30.

60. Pauli Murray to Equality Committee, March 30, 1970, Murray papers, box 55, folder 959; Dorothy Kenyon to Betsy Nolan, June 29, 1970, Kenyon papers, box 44, folder 434; Kenyon quoted in Marilyn Bender, "Liberation Yesterday—The Roots of the Feminist Movement," *New York Times,* August 21, 1970.

61. U.S. Congress, Senate Committee on the Judiciary, *Equal Rights 1970: Hearings on S.J. Res. 61 and S.J. Res. 231,* 91st Cong., 2d sess. (September 15, 1970), 312–26, 427–33; Dorothy Kenyon and Pauli Murray to Board, September 24, 1970, Murray papers, box 55, folder 956.

62. Minutes, Board of Directors, September 26–27, 1970, ACLU Records, reel 19.

63. ACLU, Board of Directors Meeting, October 2–3, 1971, 12–13,

ACLU Records, reel 20; "Sexual Equality: This Is the Law," ACLU Records, reel 95.

64. Minutes of the Equality Committee, October 14, 1971, November 11, 1971, December 9, 1971, Murray papers, box 54, folder 945; Edward J. Ennis to Dorothy Kenyon, December 7, 1971, Kenyon papers, box 44, folder 435; ACLU board minutes, 1/18/71, 9, Kenyon papers, box 45, folder 438; "ACLU Activity Report," February 1972–March 1972, ACLU Records, reel 27; Ruth B. Cowan, "Women's Rights Through Litigation: An Examination of the American Civil Liberties Union Women's Rights Project, 1971–1976," *Columbia Human Rights Law Review* 8 (1977): 385; Jo Freeman, *The Politics of Women's Liberation: A Case Study of an Emerging Social Movement and Its Relation to the Policy Process* (New York: David McKay, 1975), 154; Brenda Feigan Fasteau testimony, U.S. Congress, Senate Committee on the Judiciary, *The "Equal Rights" Amendment: Hearings Before the Subcommittee on Constitutional Amendments of the Committee on the Judiciary*, 91st Cong., 2d sess. (May 5–7, 1970), 57–59.

65. Cowan, "Women's Rights Through Litigation," 384; David Von Drehle, "The Quiet Revolutionary," *Washington Post National Weekly Edition,* July 26–August 1, 1993, 6–9.

66. Von Drehle, "Quiet Revolutionary," 8; Cowan, "Women's Rights Through Litigation," 378; "Ruth Bader Ginsburg," in Lynn Gilbert and Gaylen Moore, eds., *Particular Passions: Talks with Women Who Have Shaped Our Times* (New York: Clarkson N. Potter, 1981), 153, 156.

67. Cowan, "Women's Rights Through Litigation," 383, 387; Deborah L. Markowitz, "In Pursuit of Equality: One Woman's Work to Change the Law," *Women's Rights Law Reporter* 11 (Summer 1989): 79; Ginsburg to Murray, June 5, 1974, Murray papers, box 60, folder 1011.

68. Women's Rights Project, "Status of the Equal Rights Amendment," February 8, 1973, ACLU Records, reel 28; Minutes, ACLU Board, April 14–15, 1973, 8, ACLU Records, reel 21; Women's Rights Audit, June 1974, 12, ACLU Records, reel 30; Patricia Beyea to Martha West, December 20, 1976, ERAmerica Records, Library of Congress, box 113; "Organization Financial Contributions," October 26, 1977, "Board of Directors," December 1977, ERAmerica Records, Library of Congress, box 5; Patricia Beyea to Arlie Scott and Sheila Greenwald, March 13, 1978, ERAmerica Records, Library of Congress, box 113.

69. ACLU press release, May 4, 1979, ACLU Records, reel 19; *Inside*

ACLU, March 23, 1970, 1, May 4, 1970, 3, September 7, 1970, 1–2, ACLU Records, reel 20; O'Connor, *Women's Organizations' Use of the Courts,* 123–30.

70. Ruth Bader Ginsburg to Pauli Murray, February 28, 1973, Murray papers, box 123, folder 2199; "Women's Law Program: Litigation and Monitoring Strategy Paper," July 1975, Ford Foundation Archives, New York City, Report No. 003176; O'Connor, *Women's Organizations' Use of the Courts,* 123–30.

71. O'Connor, *Women's Organizations' Use of the Courts,* 96–98, 118–20, 128.

72. Ruth Bader Ginsburg, "Gender in the Supreme Court: The 1973 and 1974 Terms," in Philip Kurland, ed., *The Supreme Court Review* (Chicago: University of Chicago Press, 1976), 1–24; Von Drehle, "Quiet Revolutionary," 8–9.

73. Walker, *In Defense of American Liberties,* 313; "Women's Rights Project Legal Docket," January, 1973, ACLU Records, reel 28; O'Connor, *Women's Organizations' Use of the Courts,* 98; "With Liberty and Justice for Women: The ACLU's Contributions to Ten Years of Struggle for Equal Rights," December 1982, 4, 7–8, 16, 17, manuscript in ACLU national office, New York.

74. Walker, *In Defense of American Liberties,* 301, 312; *Civil Liberties,* November 1982, 7. In the 1980s the ACLU established the Gay and Lesbian Rights Project.

75. Harriet F. Pilpel, "The Crazy Quilt of Our Birth Control Laws," *Journal of Sex Research* 1 (July 1965): 135–42; Minutes, Board of Directors, November 29, 1965, 2–4, January 19, 1966, 5–6, February 14, 1966, 3–4, ACLU Records, reel 17; John de J. Pemberton to Sargent Shriver, March 24, 1966, ACLU Records, reel 19; ACLU press release, March 30, 1966, ACLU Records, reel 19.

76. U.S. Congress, Senate Subcommittee on Employment, Manpower, and Poverty, Committee on Labor and Public Welfare, *Family Planning Program: Hearings on S. 2993,* 89th Cong., 2d sess. (May 10, 1966), 100–103; Harriet F. Pilpel, "The Challenge of Privacy," in Alan Reitman, ed., *The Price of Liberty* (New York: Norton, 1968), 20, 31; Harriet F. Pilpel, "Birth Control and a New Birth of Freedom," *Ohio State Law Journal* 27 (1966): 682, 688; Testimony of Harriet F. Pilpel for the New York Civil Liberties Union, Committee on Health and Codes, New York State As-

sembly, February 3, 1967, ACLU Records, reel 25. Pilpel stood arguments for population control on their heads. To those calling for disincentives to childbearing, ranging from reducing welfare benefits to compulsory sterilization, she suggested that until people actually enjoyed freedom of choice, including the right to abortion, it made no sense to move to coercion. See Harriet F. Pilpel, "The Civil Liberties Aspects of Human Reproduction," a paper prepared for the June 3–7 Biennial Conference, ACLU Records, reel 30.

77. *New York Times,* July 4, 1970, August 29, 1971; Philip R. Reilly, *The Surgical Solution: A History of Involuntary Sterilization in the United States* (Baltimore: Johns Hopkins University Press, 1991), 146–47; Board of Directors, February 15–16, 1969, ACLU Records, reel 19; Women's Rights, a paper prepared for discussion at the June 13–16, 1974, Biennial Conference, ACLU Records, reel 30; ACLU press release, "Forced Sterilization in North Carolina," July 12, 1973, ACLU Records, reel 30; "Right Not to Be Sterilized," *Civil Liberties* (July 1974): 8.

78. ACLU to Assistant Secretary for Health, October 23, 1973, ACLU Records, reel 21; Thomas M. Shapiro, *Population Control Politics: Women, Sterilization and Reproductive Choice* (Philadelphia: Temple University Press, 1985), 137–40.

79. Women's Rights, a paper prepared for discussion at the June 13–16, 1974, Biennial Conference, ACLU Records, reel 30.

80. "With Liberty and Justice for Women," 21. In 1978, ACLU funding for women's rights (at $275,000) and reproductive freedom ($200,000) stood second and third only to its Prisoner's Rights Project ($368,000). Together, they received the majority of the ACLU Foundation budget. Jim Mann, "Hard Times for the ACLU," *New Republic,* April 15, 1978, 14.

81. Jo Freeman, "Resource Mobilization and Strategy," 175.

Chapter 4: Establishing Feminism's Moral Authority

1. The organization known as Church Women United began in 1941 as the United Council of Church Women. For clarity, I have used Church Women United, the name it adopted in 1966, throughout this study. I refer to the National Council of Churches of Christ as the NCC; it also goes by the acronym NCCC.

2. Report of Consultation, Committee on the Changing Role of

Women, October 13, 1965, 1, Records of the National Council of Churches of Christ in the U.S.A., Presbyterian Historical Society, Philadelphia, Pa. [hereafter cited as NCC Records, PHS], record group 10, box 1.

3. Claire Randall, "Women as Church Decision-Makers," *Tempo* 2 (October 1, 1970): 2. For an overview of women's challenges to religious institutions in the 1960s see Blanche Linden-Ward and Carol Hurd Green, *American Women in the 1960s: Changing the Future* (New York: Twayne, 1993), 173–93. See also Virginia Brereton, "United and Slighted: Women as Subordinated Insiders," in William R. Hutchison, ed., *Between the Times: The Travail of the Protestant Establishment in America, 1900–1960* (Cambridge: Cambridge University Press, 1989), 162. For an examination of feminism in the Catholic Church, see Mary Jo Weaver, *New Catholic Women: A Contemporary Challenge to Traditional Church Authority* (New York: Harper and Row, 1996). Mary Fainsod Katzenstein, "Discursive Politics and Feminist Activism in the Catholic Church," in Myra Marx Ferree and Patricia Yancey Martin, *Feminist Organization: Harvest of the New Women's Movement* (Philadelphia: Temple University Press, 1995), 35–52, deals with a later period but has influenced my approach to feminism in the NCC.

4. Henry J. Pratt, *The Liberalization of American Protestantism: A Case Study in Complex Organizations* (Detroit: Wayne State University Press, 1972), 13–16, 120, 160–64; James F. Findlay, Jr., *Church People in the Struggle: The National Council of Churches and the Black Freedom Movement, 1950–1970* (New York: Oxford University Press, 1993), 6, 173, 178; A. James Reichley, *Religion in American Public Life* (Washington, D.C.: Brookings Institution, 1985), 245, 247, 251–53, 257–67.

5. Pratt, *Liberalization of American Protestantism,* 112–20, 160–99.

6. *Tempo* 1 (July 1, 1969): 6–9.

7. Findlay, *Church People in the Struggle,* 49.

8. Findlay, *Church People in the Struggle,* 49–50; Brereton, "United and Slighted," 154. Brereton points out (p. 156) that CWU women "prided themselves on taking . . . . unorthodox social, political, and economic stances." Ruth Weber, "The New President," *Church Woman* 37 (June–July 1971): 18–24. See chapter 6 for more detail on the antiracist work of CWU.

9. Mary Ely Lyman, "Goals, and Some Steps to Take," September 29, 1953, NCC Records, PHS, record group 3, box 13; "Questions for Research and Survey: Some Questions from a Meeting of the Secretarial Conference,"

December 16, 1960, NCC Records, PHS, record group 14, box 9; "Notes from the General Policy and Strategy Committee Concerning a Letter to Heads of Member Communions About a Study of Men and Women in the Churches," June 6, 1962, NCC Records, PHS, record group 4, box 28; "Cooperation of Men and Women," 1962, NCC Records, PHS, record group 14, box 9; "Suggested Criteria for Organizational Participation of Councils of Church Women in State and Local Councils of Churches," August 2, 1954, NCC Records, PHS, record group 4, box 9.

10. Cynthia Wedel, *Employed Women and the Church* (New York: National Council of Churches of Christ in the U.S.A., 1959); Board of Managers, United Church Women, "Christian Social Relations Resolution on Equal Pay," May 2, 1962, NCC Records, PHS, record group 4, box 28; Department of Church and Economic Life, "Proposed Resolution on Equal Pay for Equal Work for Presentation to the General Board, February 25–March 1, 1963," NCC Records, PHS, record group 6, box 41; Statement presented to the Select Labor Sub-Committee of the House Committee on Education and Labor Relating to the subject of Equal Pay for Equal Work, March 15, 1963, by Rev. Huber Klemme, NCC Records, PHS, record group 6, box 41.

11. CWU, Committee on the Role of Women, "Reports and Recommendations," April 29, 1965, NCC Records, PHS, record group 10, box 1; Minutes, Committee on Laity and Cooperation of Men and Women, May 13, 1965, NCC Records, PHS, record group 10, box 1; Mrs. Theodore O. Wedel to Dr. Harvey Cox, October 1, 1965, NCC Records, PHS, record group 10, box 1; Report of Consultation, Committee on the Changing Role of Women, October 13, 1965, NCC Records, PHS, record group 10, box 1.

12. Brereton, "United and Slighted," 162–63; Margaret Shannon to Dr. [R. H. Edwin] Espy, August 29, 1968, NCC Records, PHS, record group 10, box 1; The Status of Women in the Church, May 9, 1969, 16–17, Papers of Pauli Murray, Schlesinger Library, Radcliffe College, Cambridge, Mass. [hereafter cited as Murray papers], box 139, folder 2536.

13. Shannon to Espy, August 29, 1968, NCC Records, PHS, record group 10, box 1; The Status of Women in the Church, May 9, 1969, 18, Murray papers, box 139, folder 2536.

14. Summary Report, Consultation on Recruiting, Training and Employing Women Professional Church Workers, February 26–27, 1969, NCC Records, PHS, record group 4, box 41; Minutes, General Secretariat, Sep-

tember 17, 1969, December 10, 1969, NCC Records, PHS, record group 4, box 41.

15. Margaret Shannon to Pauli Murray, August 15, 1969, Murray papers, box 119, folder 2136; Murray, "Some Queries," Murray papers, box 119, folder 2136; Church Women United, press release, September 26, 1969, NCC Records, PHS, record group 5, box 17; Margaret Shannon to Dr. R. H. Edwin Espy et al., October 3, 1969, NCC Records, PHS, record group 5, box 17.

16. Margaret Shannon to DCU [Division of Christian Unity] Cabinet, January 2, 1970, NCC Records, PHS, record group 10, box 7; Margaret Shannon to Mrs. Theodore O. Wedel, January 20, 1970, March 3, 1970, NCC Records, PHS, record group 4, box 37; "Response of the General Secretary to Church Women United on National Council of Churches–Church Women United Relationships," March 9, 1970, NCC Records, PHS, record group 4, box 37; *Church Woman* 36 (August–September 1970): 32–33.

17. Concerning Church Women United, November 19, 1969, Murray papers, box 119, folder 2132. Shannon, *Just Because,* 280–81.

18. Minutes, CWU board of managers, March 16–19, 1970, 18, Church Women United records in national office [hereafter cited as CWU-NO]; Mrs. James M. Dolbey to Dr. R. H. Edwin Espy, March 25, 1970, NCC Records, PHS, record group 4, box 37.

19. Claire Randall to Pauli Murray, November 19, 1969, Murray papers, box 119, folder 2135; Commission on Woman in Today's World [agenda], November 7, 1969, Murray papers, box 119, folder 2135; Thelma Stevens and Claire Randall to Members of the Commission on Woman in Today's World and Denominational Liaison Members, December 16, 1969, and "Statement of Women's Caucus," Murray papers, box 119, folder 2135.

20. Thelma Stevens and Claire Randall to Members of the Commission on Woman in Today's World and Denominational Liaison Members, December 16, 1969, Murray papers, box 119, folder 2135.

21. NCC press release, December 4, 1972, NCC Records, PHS, record group 2, box 5; Notes on Women's Meetings at the NCC Governing Board, October 11–12, 1974, Justice for Women file, Division of Church and Society, NCC national office [hereafter cited as NCC-NO]; Joan M. Martin to Members of PPEC, DCS, November 18, 1977, Justice for Women file, NCC-NO.

22. Mary Gene Boteler to Women of the NCC Governing Board, Feb-

ruary 5, 1982, Justice for Women files, NCC-NO; Joan Milton to Joan
Martin, May 4, 1979, October 23, 1979, Justice for Women files, NCC-
NO; Jorge Lara-Brand to Lacy Camp, November 16, 1978, Justice for
Women files, NCC-NO; "A Decade of Women's Issues in the NCCCUSA:
Next Steps," November 1979, Justice for Women files, NCC-NO; author
interview with Chris Cowap, October 15, 1984.

23. Joan M. Martin to NCC Governing Board, October 27, 1980, files
of the Division of Overseas Ministries, NCC-NO; author interview with
Cowap.

24. Author interview with Cowap; Joan M. Martin to Letty M. Russell,
draft, n.d. [1977], Justice for Women files, NCC-NO.

25. The Status of Women in the Church, May 9, 1969, 15–17, Murray
papers, box 139, folder 2536.

26. Study Commission on the Participation of Women in the United
Methodist Church, "The Status and Role of Women in Program and
Policy Making Channels of the United Methodist Church," June 1, 1972,
NCC Records, PHS, record group 5, box 20; report from the Task Force
on Women in Church and Society to the Executive Council and to the
Ninth General Synod of the United Church of Christ, March 8, 1973,
NCC Records, PHS, record group 5, box 20; United Presbyterian Church
in the U.S.A., "Report of the Interim Task Force on Women—1973,"
NCC Records, PHS, record group 5, box 20; Lois A. Boyd and R. Douglas
Breckenridge, *Presbyterian Women in America: Two Centuries of a Quest for
Status* (Westport, Conn.: Greenwood Press, 1983), 225–26; ibid. (2d ed.,
1996), 51–57. The Presbyterian Church of the United States, representing
southern Presbyterians, was much more conservative on women's issues
and critical of many of the liberal positions of the NCC. A restructuring
of the PCUS in 1972 disbanded the separate women's mission board; the
church established a women's advocacy group, the Committee on Women's
Concerns, in 1973 but failed to fund it adequately.

27. Minutes, National Council of Churches General Nominating
Committee, January 24, 1969, April 2, 1969, NCC Records, PHS, record
group 3, box 7; NCC press releases, December 2 and 4, 1969, NCC Records, PHS, record group 2, box 5. It is not clear whether all women, including African American women, supported Wedel against the black candidate.
CWU executive director Margaret Shannon reported that at a meeting be-

tween the two groups, called by the black caucus, that group had no women in its delegation, while black women comprised half of those brought by the women's caucus. Margaret Shannon, *Just Because: The Story of the National Movement of Church Women United in the U.S.A., 1941 through 1975* (Corte Madera, Calif.: Omega Books, 1977), 272–74.

28. "Cynthia Wedel: Woman with a Mission for the 70s," *Church Woman* 36 (March 1970): 3; The Status of Women in the Church, Murray papers, box 139, folder 2536; Cynthia C. Wedel, "Agenda for the Future," *Church Woman* 36 (May 1970): 20.

29. Pratt, *Liberalization of American Protestantism,* 106–8, 120. The *New York Times* is quoted in "Claire Randall Elected Top Administrator of NCC," *Church Woman* 40 (January 1974): 32.

30. "Claire Randall," October 1973, NCC Records, PHS, record group 5, box 18; "Claire Randall: NCC's New General Secretary-Elect," *Tempo* 3 (October 1973): 1, 4, 7; Randall, "Women in the World of Now," *Church Women* 36 (March 1970): 17; Minutes of the NCCC General Board, June 11–12, 1971, NCC Records, PHS, record group 3, box 4; Elizabeth Hambrick-Stowe, "A Conference on Women and Theology," *Church Woman* 39 (February 1973): 30–32.

31. Irene Tinker, ed., *Women in Washington: Advocates for Public Policy* (Beverly Hills, Calif.: Sage Publications, 1983), 305.

32. *NCCC Chronicles* 77 (Fall 1977): 2; *NCCC Chronicles* 78 (Fall 1978): 2; National Council of Churches of Christ in the U.S.A., *Report for the Triennium, 1976–1978* (New York: National Council of Churches of Christ in the U.S.A., 1979), 71.

33. Minutes of the NCC governing board, March 6, 1975, 29, 38–39, November 8–10, 1979, 10, February 25–28, 1974, 12, 25, 34, October 11–13, 1974, 11, 23, NCC-NO.

34. Minutes of the NCC governing board, October 11–13, 25, 26, November 10, 1977, May 5, 1977, May 12, 1978, November 8, 1980, NCC-NO.

35. Minutes of the NCC governing board, March 6, 1975; May 6, 1977; May 9, 1980, NCC-NO; Memo from Joan Martin to Arleon Kelley, June 16, 1980, Justice for Women files, NCC-NO.

36. Annual Program Report, Justice for Women Program Area, 1979, 1980, NCC-NO; Religious Committee for the ERA, press releases, Feb-

ruary 6, 1976, September 21, 1977, Records of ERAmerica, Library of Congress, Washington, D.C., boxes 120, 121; "ERA Means 'Equal Rights Amendment,'" *Church Woman* 42 (October 1976): 29.

37. Kay Leslie, "The Abortion Issue and the Churches," *Tempo* 4 (July–August 1972): 3–4; *Religious Newsweekly,* February 17, 1970, 2; Muriel S. Webb to Members of the General Board, NCC, NCC Records, PHS, record group 3, box 4; Minutes of the NCC General Board, February 11–14, 1972, NCC Records, PHS, record group 5, box 15.

38. "Proposed Policy Statement on Abortion," as presented to the Governing Board, December 8, 1972, NCC Records, PHS, record group 5, box 15.

39. Claire Randall to NCC Task Force on Abortion, December 14, 1972, NCC Records, PHS, record group 5, box 15; Claire Randall to NCC Task Force on Abortion, March 12, 1972, NCC Records, PHS, record group 5, box 15; General Planning and Program Committee, NCCC, *Program Budget Directions for 1971,* NCC Records, PHS, record group 3, box 12; *Capsule,* March 3, 1970, 5, February 1, 1972, 1, NCC Records, PHS, record group 15, box 1; Ed Luidens and Ann Patrick Ware to Christian Unity Section Staff Team, February 20, 1973, NCC Records, PHS, record group 5, box 14; Minutes of the NCC General Board, December 2, 1972, 12–13; NCC press release, March 1, 1973, NCC Records, PHS, record group 15, box 4.

40. Minutes of the NCC Governing Board, October 8–10, 1976, 43–44, NCC-NO.

41. Author interview with Cowap; minutes of the NCC Governing Board, November 11, 1977, NCC-NO; Claire Randall to Congressman Daniel J. Flood, November 16, 1977, Justice for Women files, NCC-NO; Minutes of the Division of Church and Society, Program Unit Committee, March 17–18, 1980, 9–21, Justice for Women files, NCC-NO; Thomas M. Shapiro, *Population Control Politics: Women, Sterilization and Reproductive Choice* (Philadelphia: Temple University Press, 1985), 137, 197–99.

42. Opponents of the NCC's liberal stance have criticized the subunits' lack of accountability to the general board. See K. L. Billingsley, *From Mainline to Sideline: The Social Witness of the National Council of Churches* (Washington, D.C.: Ethics and Public Policy Center, 1990).

43. Peggy Billings et al. to Sisters, April 16, 1975, Commission on Women in Ministry [hereafter cited as COWIM] files, NCC-NO; Peggy Billings, "Memorandum of Concern. Re: Harassment of Women's Move-

ment," April 14, 1975, COWIM files, NCC-NO; "Groups Hit 'Antiwomen' FBI Tactics," *Boston Globe,* May 4, 1975.

44. Minutes of the Unit Committee of the Division of Church and Society [hereafter cited as DCS], May 8, 1975, 4, NCC-NO; "Church Women, Feminists Fight FBI Harassment," *Minneapolis Tribune,* June 9, 1975; Susan Savell to Sisters and Brothers, July 10, 1975, COWIM files, NCC-NO; Richard Harris, "Annals of Law," *New Yorker,* April 19, 1976, 42–97.

45. Minutes of the Executive Committee, DCS, December 15, 1976, 2, Justice for Women file, NCC-NO.

46. Sara Maitland, *A Map of the New Country: Women and Christianity* (London: Routledge and Kegan Paul, 1983), 92–93; Joan Martin, "Speaking Out from a Black Perspective," *Church Woman* 44 (November 1978): 11–13.

47. Minutes, DCS Program Planning and Evaluation Council, November 21–22, 1977, Attachment D, Justice for Women files, NCC-NO; Joan M. Martin to Justice for Women Working Group Members, May 17, 1979, Justice for Women files, NCC-NO.

48. Justice for Women Program Area, Annual Program Reports to DCS Program Planning and Evaluating Council, July 1979, July 1980, Justice for Women files, NCC-NO.

49. *Boston Globe,* May 4, 1975.

50. NCC press release, June 9, 1972, NCC Records, PHS, record group 15, box 4; "Emily Gibbes Receives Award at New York University," *Church Woman* 44 (March 1978): 36.

51. Burnice Fjellman, "COWIM: How It All Began," July 1978, COWIM files, NCC-NO; Burnice Fjellman to Friend, October 29, 1973, COWIM files, NCC-NO; NCC, Professional Church Leadership, Commission on Women in Ministry, Proceedings, September 30–October 1, 1974, COWIM files, NCC-NO.

52. Organization for Commission on Women in Ministry, March 17, 1975, COWIM files, NCC-NO; Fjellman, "COWIM: How It All Began."

53. Summary of Proceedings, COWIM meeting, September 30–October 2, 1974, 7, 10, COWIM files, NCC-NO; Untitled announcement of Service in Celebration of Women in Ministry, October 27, 1974, COWIM files, NCC-NO; Minutes of the NCC Governing Board, March 4–6, 1975, NCC-NO.

54. Minutes of the NCC Governing Board, March 4–6, 1975, NCC-NO; Susan Savell to Sisters and Brothers, March 25, 1975, COWIM files, NCC-NO.

55. Minutes, Unit Committee, Division of Education and Ministry, October 10–11, 1974, 3, COWIM files, NCC-NO; Organization for Commission on Women in Ministry, March 17, 1975, COWIM files, NCC-NO; Summary of Proceedings, COWIM meeting, February 5–7, 1975, 3–4, and October 6–8, 1975, 3–4, 5, 10, COWIM files, NCC-NO.

56. "Event Will Assess Job Outlook for Minority Women in Ministry," *NCCC Chronicles* 78 (Spring 1978): 7; "Unique Event Gathers Minority Churchwomen," *NCCC Chronicles* 78 (Summer 1978): 7.

57. Report on COWIM meetings, October 6–8, 1975, 3–4, October 18–20, 1976, 2, COWIM files, NCC-NO; Susan Savell to Sisters and Brothers, March 15, 1975, COWIM files, NCC-NO.

58. Summary of COWIM meetings, February 5–7, 1975, 2, October 6–8, 1975, 4, 7, February 16–18, 1976, 3, 5, October 18–20, 1976, 1, 3, October 25–27, 1978, 5–7, March 21–23, 1979, COWIM files, NCC-NO.

59. Patricia E. Farris to Mai Gray, September 11, 1979, COWIM files, NCC-NO; Linda Brebner to Sisters, September 19, 1979, COWIM files, NCC-NO; summary of COWIM meeting, October 25–27, 1978, 5–7, COWIM files, NCC-NO.

60. COWIM, Summary of Meetings, October 18–20, 1976, 1–2, October 25–27, 1978, 3, COWIM files, NCC-NO; Burnice Fjellman to William Holladay, October 24, 1977, COWIM files, NCC-NO; COWIM Communicator, December 17, 1979, 1, COWIM files, NCC-NO.

61. COWIM, Summary of Meeting, July 16–17, 1976, 2, COWIM files, NCC-NO; COWIM Steering Committee, Meeting Notes, December 10–11, 1976, 1–4, COWIM files, NCC-NO; Mary E. Isaac to the Rev. Thomas E. Wood, February 2, 1977, COWIM files, NCC-NO; quote from Report of the Working Group on the Future of COWIM, March 1978, COWIM files, NCC-NO.

62. Letty M. Russell, ed., *The Liberating Word: A Guide to Nonsexist Interpretation of the Bible* (Philadelphia: Westminster Press, 1976), 89, 120.

63. "Sexism in Biblical Language," *Tempo* 4 (August–September 1974), 3; Notes from Discussions, Interim Executive Committee, Division of Education and Ministry [hereafter cited as DEM], May 9, 1974, DEM records,

NCC-NO; Minutes, Unit Committee, DEM, June 5–6, 1974, 9, DEM records, NCC-NO.

64. Statement of Members of the Task Force on Biblical Translation, June 12, 1980, 6, 7–8, 10, DEM records, NCC-NO.

65. Russell, *Liberating Word,* 107–8; Task Force on Sexism in the Bible, June 3–4, 1975, DEM records, NCC-NO; Phyllis Trible, "The Pilgrim Bible," in Sarah Cunningham, ed., *We Belong Together: Churches in Solidarity with Women* (New York: Friendship Press, 1992), 15–16. For other examples of the passion that Christian women felt about sexism in the Bible, see Maitland, *A Map of the New Country,* chap. 6; and Nelle Morton, *The Journey Is Home* (Boston: Beacon Press, 1985).

66. *NCCC Chronicles* 1 (Summer 1975), 7; Task Force on Sexism in the Bible, June 3–4, 1975, DEM records, NCC-NO.

67. Russell, *Liberating Word,* 15, 89–93; Minutes of the Unit Committee, DEM, December 8–9, 1976, 10–11, DEM records, NCC-NO; report, Task Force on Sexism in the Bible, June 1–2, 1977, DEM records, NCC-NO.

68. Report of the RSV Bible Committee to the meeting of the DEM Unit Committee, December 8–9, 1976, DEM records, NCC-NO; Minutes, Unit Committee, December 8–9, 1976, DEM records, NCC-NO.

69. Minutes, Unit Committee, DEM, June 1–2, 1977, 14–16, DEM records, NCC-NO.

70. COWIM Steering Committee, meeting notes, June 3, 1977, 8, COWIM files, NCC-NO; report of the Task Force on Issues of Biblical Translation, May 9, 1989, 1–3, DEM records, NCC-NO.

71. Report of the Task Force on Issues of Biblical Translation, May 9, 1989, 1–3, DEM records, NCC-NO, 6–8; Minutes of the Unit Committee, DEM, November 16, 1979, 3–7, DEM records, NCC-NO. In the late 1970s the RSVBC had just one female member.

72. Report of the Task Force on Issues of Biblical Translation, May 9, 1980, 8–10, DEM records, NCC-NO; Statement of Members of the Task Force on Biblical Translation, June 12, 1980, DEM records, NCC-NO; Minutes of Unit Committee, DEM, June 12, 1980, 14–19, DEM records, NCC-NO; Minutes of the Unit Committee, DEM, November 25, 1980, 8–20, DEM records, NCC-NO.

73. *NCCC Chronicles* 80 (Fall 1980), 1, 7; *New York Times,* October 16,

1983; The D. E. & M. Lectionary Project, n.d. [ca. early 1981], DEM records, NCC-NO; Questions and Answers on Inclusive Biblical Language, n.d., DEM records, NCC-NO; Inclusive Language Lectionary Committee, DEM records, NCC-NO.

74. *New York Times,* November 12, 1983, 24; UPI, December 2, 1983 (Lutherans); *Time,* October 24, 1983, 57 (Metzger).

75. UPI, December 2, 1983, July 13, 1984; Allen Kratz, "Inclusive Language Lectionary," *Nor'easter,* December 1983, 15.

76. *The Record,* April 25, 1987; *Los Angeles Times,* May 27, 1989.

77. *Church Woman* 49 (Winter 1983–84): 34.

78. "Mrs. Stewart's Farewell Address to Her Friends In the City of Boston. Delivered September 21, 1833," reprinted in Bert James Loewenberg and Ruth Bogin, eds., *Black Women in Nineteenth-Century American Life: Their Words, Their Thoughts, Their Feelings* (University Park: Pennsylvania State University Press, 1976), 198–200; Sarah Grimke, "Province of Women: The Pastoral Letter," *Liberator* 7 (October 6, 1837).

79. Stanton, quoted in Elisabeth Griffith, *In Her Own Right: The Life of Elizabeth Cady Stanton* (New York: Oxford University Press, 1984), 210; Frances E. Willard, *Glimpses of Fifty Years: The Autobiography of an American Woman* (Chicago: Woman's Temperance Publication Association, 1889), 465.

Chapter 5: Financing Feminism

1. Arthur D. Trottenberg to McGeorge Bundy, June 7, 1971, 5. Report No. 006316, Ford Foundation Archives [hereafter cited as FFA].

2. Interview with Susan Berresford, October 17, 1984. Susan Berresford's name was Susan Stein until 1974; to avoid confusion she is referred to as Berresford throughout. Mary Jean Tully, "Funding the Feminists," *Foundation News* 16 (March–April 1975): 25.

3. Waldemar A. Nielsen, *The Big Foundations* (New York: Columbia University Press, 1972), 78; *That 51 Per Cent: Ford Foundation Activities Related to Opportunities for Women* (New York: Ford Foundation, 1974), 4.

4. In addition, no African American sat on Ford's board of trustees until 1968.

5. J. Craig Jenkins, "Nonprofit Organizations and Policy Advocacy," in Walter W. Powell, ed., *The Nonprofit Sector: A Research Handbook* (New

Haven: Yale University Press, 1987), 312; Waldemar A. Nielsen, *The Golden Donors: A New Anatomy of the Great Foundations* (New York: E. P. Dutton, 1985), 63–69; Richard Magat, *The Ford Foundation at Work: Philanthropic Choices, Methods, and Styles* (New York: Plenum Press, 1979), 154.

6. David Halberstam, *The Best and the Brightest* (Greenwich, Conn.: Fawcett Publications, 1973), 68–69, 72–73, 759–60; Nielsen, *Golden Donors,* 61–73.

7. "An Interview with McGeorge Bundy," *Black Enterprise* (September 1975): 30; Ford Foundation, *Annual Report: 1971* (New York: Ford Foundation, 1971), 8, 15–27, 35–46, 63; Nielsen, *Big Foundations,* 356–57; *A Selected Chronology of the Ford Foundation* (New York: Ford Foundation, n.d. [ca. 1980]), 10–11.

8. *That 51 Per Cent,* 3, 11–16; Thomas M. Shapiro, *Population Control Politics: Women, Sterilization and Reproductive Choice* (Philadelphia: Temple University Press, 1985), 54–85.

9. Drake-Beam and Associates, "Attitude Survey Concerning the Role of Women at the Ford Foundation," December 1970. FFA, Report No. 006002; Elinor G. Barber to Arthur Trottenberg, March 16, 1971. FFA, Elinor G. Barber Files, RG 10, Series IIA, Box 8; Arthur D. Trottenberg to McGeorge Bundy, "Employment of Women and Minorities on the Professional Staff," April 20, 1972, 3, 5. FFA, Report No. 007788; Starry Krueger, "To Those Interested in Women's Issues," March 30, 1972, 7. FFA, PA72-326.

10. Krueger, "To Those Interested in Women's Issues," 1.

11. Krueger, "To Those Interested in Women's Issues," 1; author interview with Gail Spangenberg, October 18, 1984.

12. Krueger, "To Those Interested in Women's Issues," 2, 8; author interview with Spangenberg; Arthur D. Trottenberg to McGeorge Bundy, June 7, 1971, 6. FFA, Report No. 006316.

13. Author interview with Mariam Chamberlain, October 14, 1984; "Affirmative Action Program for the Employment of Women and Minorities on the Professional Staff of the Ford Foundation: A Review and Analysis," February 1974. FFA, Report No. 001984; letter to Patricia M. Wald from Harold Howe II, June 20, 1973. FFA, PA72-326.

14. "Affirmative Action Program," 3; *That 51 Per Cent,* 3–4; Krueger, "To Those Interested in Women's Issues," 3, 5, 8.

15. Arthur D. Trottenberg, "The Ford Foundation As an Affirmative

Action Employer," n.d. [ca. March 1973], 3–5. FFA, Report No. 008011; "Affirmative Action Program," 3–4, 9–10, 19–22.

16. Author telephone interview with Ruth Mandel, November 3, 1994.

17. "Affirmative Action Program," 3–4, 9–10, 19–22; Richard Magat, *Ford Foundation at Work,* 44.

18. "Recommendations for Women's Programs," October 1971, 23–27. FFA, Report No. 0026549. The names of the women making the recommendations are given in Krueger, "To Those Interested in Women's Issues," 6.

19. Krueger, "To Those Interested in Women's Issues," 7; McGeorge Bundy to the Staff, November 15, 1972. FFA, Report No. 001994; McGeorge Bundy to the Staff, October 12, 1973. FFA, PA74-816; Ford Foundation, *Annual Report: 1974* (New York: Ford Foundation, 1974), 59; Ford Foundation, "External Affirmative Action Program," October 6, 1975. FFA, Report No. 002196.

20. Krueger, "To Those Interested in Women's Issues," 7.

21. Gail Spangenberg to Marshall Robinson, December 14, 1970. FFA, L71-26.

22. Gail Spangenberg to File L71-26 (Women in Academe), January 6, 1971, February 25, 1971, March 1, 1971, March 26, 1971. FFA, L71-26; Gail Spangenberg to Marshall A. Robinson, June 18, 1971, FFA, L71-26; Mariam K. Chamberlain to Marshall A. Robinson, May 17, 1971, FFA, L71-26; author telephone interview with Sheila Tobias, November 10, 1994.

23. Susan Glauberman, "A Conversation with Mariam Chamberlain and Fred Crossland," *Change* 13 (1981): 32–37; Mariam K. Chamberlain to Marshall A. Robinson, May 17, 1971. FFA, L71-26; author interview with Chamberlain, October 14, 1984.

24. "Toward a Revised Program Emphasis for the Division of Education and Research of the Ford Foundation: An Information Paper for Discussion by the Trustees at the September 1971 Meeting," September 1971, 11–12. FFA, Report No. 002006; Harold Howe II to McGeorge Bundy, February 22, 1971, 2–3. FFA, Report No. 001461.

25. Sheila Tobias to Mariam Chamberlain, July 31, 1971. FFA, L71-26; Mariam K. Chamberlain to Harold Howe II, August 20, 1971, FFA, L71-26; Harold Howe II to McGeorge Bundy, October 8, 1971, FFA, L71-26; author interview with Chamberlain, October 14, 1984; author interview with Tobias, November 10, 1994.

26. "Elinor G. Barber Version of Meeting on Women in Higher Education," November 17, 1971. FFA, Report No. 007751.

27. "Elinor G. Barber Version of Meeting on Women in Higher Education"; for the follow-up letters, see, for example, Bernice Sandler to McGeorge Bundy, November 18, 1971. FFA, L71-26.

28. Trottenberg to Bundy, June 7, 1971, 1; Nielsen, *Big Foundations,* 354–56.

29. Trottenberg to Bundy, June 7, 1971, 1; "Recommendations for Women's Programs," October 1971.

30. "Recommendations for Women's Programs," October 1971, 27; "The Ford Foundation's Program in the Changing Role of Women," March 1973, A–1, A–3. FFA, Report No. 002255.

31. Esther Peterson, "Long Overdue—Full Partnership for Women in American Society," October 21, 1971, 2, 34–43. FFA, Report No. 001991; Krueger, "To Those Interested in Women's Issues," 5; "The Ford Foundation's Program on the Changing Role of Women."

32. Mitchell Sviridoff to McGeorge Bundy, February 23, 1972, 2–4. FFA, Report No. 002460.

33. Author interviews with Mariam Chamberlain, Susan Berresford, and Gail Spangenberg.

34. Avery Russell, "The Women's Movement and Foundations," *Foundation News* 13 (November–December 1972): 16–22.

35. "A Proposal to Inaugurate the Program of Women and Foundations/Corporate Philanthropy," June 2, 1978. FFA, PA-78-530; Susan Calhoun, "New Ways to Lead," *Foundation News* 28 (November–December 1987): 24–29.

36. McGeorge Bundy, "Memorandum to the Staff," January 14, 1972. FFA, L72-363; Harold Howe II to Marshall A. Robinson, May 22, 1972. FFA, L72-168.

37. Harold Howe II to McGeorge Bundy, February 22, 1972, 2–3, 9. FFA, Report No. 002461; Mitchell Sviridoff to McGeorge Bundy, February 23, 1972, 2–6, 10–12.

38. "New Girl in Town: The Changing Role of Women in United States Society," n.d. [ca. February 1972]. FFA, PA72-363.

39. Harold Howe II to McGeorge Bundy, April 28, 1972, and attachment from information paper to the trustees, March 1972, "Planning for the Foundation's Program in 1973 and Beyond." FFA, PA-72-326.

40. Beatrice Colebrooke to Harold Howe II, June 1, 1972. FFA, PA 72-326; Mariam K. Chamberlain to McGeorge Bundy, September 26, 1975. FFA, PA74-816.

41. Harold Howe II, Mitchell Sviridoff, and David E. Bell to McGeorge Bundy, July 10, 1972, 4. FFA, PA72-326; Elinor Barber to Mr. Howe, May 23, 1972. FFA, Report No. 007750; David E. Bell to Overseas Reps, June 23, 1972. FFA, PA72-326; Elinor G. Barber to Task Force on Women, November 28, 1973, FFA, PA72-326; Harold Howe II to David E. Bell, December 10, 1973, FFA, PA72-326; Elinor G. Barber and Adrienne Germain to POICs, Heads, and Overseas Reps, April 18, 1974. FFA, Report No. 00771.

42. "The Ford Foundation's Program in the Changing Role of Women."

43. Memos to the staff from McGeorge Bundy, December 26, 1973, and March 25, 1974. FFA, L72-363.

44. Coordinating Committee on Women's Programs, Reports of Meetings on June 18, 1975, January 29, 1976, June 17, 1976. FFA, PA74-816; Coordinating Committee on Women's Programs, "Inequality in Pension Benefits for Men and Women," an Interim Report, April 1977. FFA, Report No. 008111.

45. "The Ford Foundation's Program in the Changing Role of Women," May 7, 1973, A1–A5; transcript of meeting of Women's Task Force on July 13, 1972, with Shirley McCune of the National Education Association on Sex Bias in Elementary and Secondary Schools, p. 35. FFA, Report No. 007673.

46. Women's Task Force Meeting with Elizabeth Koontz, Director of the Women's Bureau of the U.S. Department of Labor, December 13, 1972, 16, 21. FFA, PA72-363; transcript of Women's Task Force Meeting with Elise Boulding, October 10, 1972, 39–40. FFA, Report No. 007884.

47. Transcript of Women's Task Force Meeting with Professor Lee Rainwater, Department of Sociology, Harvard University, October 25, 1972. FFA, Report No. 007885; Women's Task Force Meeting with Elise Boulding, 40; Women's Task Force Meeting with Elizabeth Koontz, 27.

48. Women's Task Force Meeting with Elise Boulding, 40–41.

49. Paul A. Strasburg to McGeorge Bundy, June 21, 1972, 4. FFA, L72-363; Women's Task Force Meeting with Elise Boulding, 10; Women's Task Force Meeting with Elizabeth Koontz, 31.

50. Terry N. Saario, Carol Nagy Jacklin, and Carol Kehr Tittle, "Sex

Role Stereotyping in the Public Schools," *Harvard Educational Review* 43 (August 1973): 386–416; Terry Saario, "Sex Discrimination: The Big New Problem for Boards," April 9, 1973. FFA, Report No. 007802; U.S. Congress, Senate Subcommittee on Education of the Committee on Labor and Public Welfare, *Women's Educational Equity Act of 1973,* 93rd Cong., 1st sess. (October 17, 1973), 14–21; Harold Howe II, "Sex, Sports, and Discrimination," *Chronicle of Higher Education,* June 18, 1979.

51. Faith Seidenberg to Members of the Board of Directors, May 1979, Papers of the National Organization for Women [hereafter NOW papers], 72-75-79-M262, carton 1, folder "Board," Schlesinger Library, Radcliffe College; Ellen Dresselhuis to Laurine E. Fitzgerald, January 25, 1973, Papers of the Women's Equity Action League [hereafter WEAL Fund papers], MC–311, box 2, folder 4, Schlesinger Library, Radcliffe College.

52. U.S. Congress, House, Committee on Ways and Means, *General Tax Reform, Part 16,* 93rd Cong., 1st sess. (April 13, 1973), 6424–57; National Organization for Women press release, April 13, 1973, NOW papers, NOW DONORS 72-8-83-M211, carton 8.

53. Marjorie Fine Knowles to Mary Jean Tully, July 2, 1974, NOW papers, NOW LDEF 84-M198, carton 3; draft letters to foundations, October 1974, NOW papers, NOW LDEF 84-M198, carton 3.

54. Mary Jean Tully, "Funding the Feminists," *Foundation News* 16 (March–April 1975): 24–33.

55. Annual Report, NOW Legal Defense and Education Fund, MJT Draft, 3/8/74, NOW papers, 72-75-79, carton 26; NOW LDEF Auditors' Report, December 31, 1974, 5, 7, NOW papers, 72-75-79-M262; 81-M106, box 15, folder "NOW LDEF, 1974"; Mary Ann Millsap, "Sex Equity in Education," in Irene Tinker, ed., *Women in Washington: Advocates for Public Policy* (Beverly Hills, Calif.: Sage Publications, 1983), 98–102, 108.

56. As will be seen below, Ford channeled its litigation support to organizations that already had substantial experience. WEAL Fund Board of Directors Minutes, September 9, 1973, and December 1, 1973, WEAL Fund papers, box 2, folder 3; Women's Equity Action League Educational and Legal Defense Fund, Inc., Grants, 1974–1976, WEAL Fund papers, box 2, folder 12; Ford Foundation, *Annual Reports,* 1978, 1980, 1983 (New York: Ford Foundation, 1978, 1980, 1983).

57. Jack Greenberg, *Crusaders in the Courts: How a Dedicated Band of Lawyers Fought for the Civil Rights Revolution* (New York: Basic Books,

1994), 371–72, 488; "Recommendations for Women's Programs," October 1971, 6–7; Robert B. McKay, *Nine for Equality Under Law: Civil Rights Litigation, a Report to the Ford Foundation* (New York: Ford Foundation, 1977), 11–22.

58. Karen O'Connor, *Women's Organizations' Use of the Courts* (Lexington, Mass.: D.C. Heath, 1980), 94, 106, 110; *Nine for Equality Under the Law*, 22–24; RGA to McGeorge Bundy from Mitchell Sviridoff, March 26, 1974. FFA, PA74-816.

59. Ruth Bader Ginsburg to Pauli Murray, February 28, 1973, Papers of Pauli Murray, Schlesinger Library, box 123, folder 2199; "Women's Law Program: Litigation and Monitoring Strategy Paper," July 1975. FFA, Report No. 003176.

60. O'Connor, *Women's Organizations' Use of the Courts*, 96–98; Margaret A. Berger, *Litigation on Behalf of Women: A Review for the Ford Foundation* (New York: Ford Foundation, 1980).

61. Gail Spangenberg to File L71-26, March 1, 1971. FFA, L71-26; Sheila Tobias to Marian [sic] Chamberlain, August 31, 1971, FFA, L71-26.

62. RGA to McGeorge Bundy from Harold Howe II, March 26, 1974. FFA, PA74-14; RGA to McGeorge Bundy from Harold Howe II, November 11, 1975. FFA, PA73-383; *That 51 Per Cent*, 29–31.

63. *That 51 Per Cent*, 29–31; Letter to Myra H. Strober from Mariam K. Chamberlain, March 3, 1978. FFA, PA73-383; Memo to Susan Berresford from Ruth B. Mandel, July 31, 1978. FFA, PA73-152; RGA to McGeorge Bundy from Mitchell Sviridoff, October 10, 1978, FFA, PA73-152. See also Mariam K. Chamberlain and Alison Bernstein, "Philanthropy and the Emergence of Women's Studies," *Teachers College Record* 93 (Spring 1992): 556–68.

64. Terry N. Saario and Mariam K. Chamberlain, "The Education and Research Division's Program on Sex Discrimination and Equality of Opportunity for Women," March 1978, 12. FFA, Report No. 004136; author interview with Chamberlain.

65. Chamberlain and Bernstein, "Philanthropy and the Emergence of Women's Studies," 560, 563; Caryn McTighe Musil and Ruby Sales, "Funding Women's Studies," in Johnella E. Butler and John C. Walter, eds., *Transforming the Curriculum: Ethnic Studies and Women's Studies* (Albany: SUNY Press, 1991), 25–26, 32. It is ironic that while women's studies pro-

grams—some of them at nonelite institutions—won grants for minority women's studies projects, the Ford initiative also benefited faculty members who did not integrate women of color into their teaching until presented with a material incentive.

66. Memo to McGeorge Bundy from Mitchell Sviridoff, February 23, 1972. FFA, Report No. 002460; memo from Sviridoff to Bundy, 8/20/73, 1. FFA, PA 73-818.

67. *Created Equal: A Report on Ford Foundation Women's Programs* (New York: Ford Foundation, 1986), 15, 18; "Women at Work," *Ford Foundation Letter* 3 (September 1, 1972): 1; "About Women," *Ford Foundation Letter* 5 (May 1, 1974); Ford Foundation, *Annual Report: 1978*, 8; Ford Foundation, *Annual Report: 1980*, 15–16; "Abortion: The Political Factor," *Ford Foundation Letter* 11 (August 1, 1980): 5.

68. RGA to McGeorge Bundy from Harold Howe II and Mitchell Sviridoff, February 15, 1972. FFA, PA72-361; *That 51 Per Cent . . . Plus: A Ford Foundation Report* (New York: Ford Foundation, 1979), 15, 22, 31; "Special Report: Sex Barriers in Job Training," *Ford Foundation Letter* 11 (December 1, 1980): 3; Ford Foundation, *Annual Report: 1979* (New York: Ford Foundation, 1979), 16–17.

69. "Women's Task Force Meeting with Elise Boulding," 7–10; memo to David E. Bell from Elinor G. Barber, September 30, 1974, 1–3. FFA, Report No. 007004.

70. Irene Tinker, "Women in Development," in Tinker, *Women in Washington*, 227–32; David E. Bell to Overseas Reps, June 23, 1972. FFA, PA72-326; Eleanor G. Barber and Adrienne Germain to POICs, Heads, and Overseas Reps, April 18, 1974. FFA, Report No. 00771.

71. Elinor G. Barber, "The International Division's Women's Program: Information Paper," January 1979, 7–8. FFA, Report No. 007889; "Interim Report on the Expanded Women's Program," February 1981, 8–9. FFA, Report No. 008008.

72. Barber, "The International Division's Women's Program," Appendix, 1–2, 5, 8; Ford Foundation, *Annual Report: 1975* (New York: Ford Foundation, 1975), 36; Adrienne Germain, "Women in Development: Final Consultancy Report," April 25, 1977. FFA, Report No. 007630.

73. Barber, "The International Division's Women's Program," Appendix, 5–6, 8–9; "Women of the World," *Ford Foundation Letter* 8 (April 1,

1977): 22; "Women Advancing at Different Rates," *Ford Foundation Letter* 10 (December 1, 1979): 1; "Interim Report on the Expanded Women's Program," 4–5, 9.

74. Transcript of Women's Task Force Meeting, May 31, 1973, 33, 40. FFA, Report No. 008146; *Created Equal,* 48.

75. Esther Roditti Schachter to Richard S. Sharpe and Harry Dodds, April 13, 1976. FFA, PA75-147; Esther Roditti Schachter, Susan Berresford, and Mariam Chamberlain, "Women—A Priority Area for the Ford Foundation in the 1980s," October 15, 1976, 1–3. FFA, Report No. 007888.

76. Memorandum for the Staff from McGeorge Bundy, January 24, 1978.

77. *Ford Foundation Letter* 12 (June 1, 1981): 1.

78. Susan Berresford to Franklin Thomas, July 24, 1980. FFA, Report No. 007013; author interview with Berresford.

79. Terry Saario went on to head the Northwest Area Foundation.

80. Harold Howe II to Edward J. Meade, July 25, 1972. FFA, L71-26.

Chapter 6: Civil Rights and Women's Rights

1. See, for example, Charlayne Hunter, "Many Blacks Wary of 'Women's Liberation' Movement," *New York Times,* November 17, 1970, 47, 60; Linda J. M. La Rue, "Black Liberation and Women's Lib," *Trans-Action* (November–December 1970): 59–64; Toni Morrison, "What the Black Woman Thinks About Women's Lib," *New York Times Magazine,* August 22, 1971, 15–16, 63–64, 66; Frances M. Beal, "Slave of a Slave No More: Black Women in Struggle," *Black Scholar* (March 1975): 2–10; Paula Giddings, *When and Where I Enter: The Impact of Black Women on Race and Sex in America* (New York: Bantam Books, 1985), 299–311; bell hooks, *Ain't I a Woman: Black Women and Feminism* (Boston: South End Press, 1981), 185–92; Jacqueline Jones, *Labor of Love, Labor of Sorrow: Black Women, Work, and the Family from Slavery to the Present* (New York: Basic Books, 1985, 314–19.

2. hooks, *Ain't I a Woman,* 187; Patricia Hill Collins, *Black Feminist Thought: Knowledge, Consciousness, and the Politics of Empowerment* (New York: Routledge, 1990); Giddings, *When and Where I Enter,* 303–4, 345.

3. Report of the Women's Caucus to the Assembly of the National

Council of Churches, December 6, 1972, 3, Records of Church Women United, General Commission on Archives and History, United Methodist Church, Drew University [hereafter CWU records], box 54, folder 34. Important works of theory about African American women, race, and gender are Collins, *Black Feminist Thought;* Deborah K. King, "Multiple Jeopardy, Multiple Consciousness: The Context of A Black Feminist Ideology," *Signs* 14 (Autumn 1988): 42–72; Elizabeth V. Spelman, *Inessential Woman: Problems of Exclusion in Feminist Thought* (Boston: Beacon Press, 1988); bell hooks, *Talking Back: Thinking Feminist, Thinking Black* (Boston: South End Press, 1989); Elsa Barkley Brown, " 'What Has Happened Here': The Politics of Difference in Women's History and Feminist Politics," and Nancy A. Hewitt, "Compounding Differences," *Feminist Studies* 18 (Summer 1992): 295–312, 313–26; Evelyn Brooks Higginbotham, "African-American History and the Metalanguage of Race," *Signs* 17 (Winter 1992): 251–74; Kimberle Crenshaw, "Whose Story Is it Anyway? Feminist and Antiracist Appropriations of Anita Hill," in Toni Morrison, ed., *Race-ing Justice, Engendering Power: Essays on Anita Hill, Clarence Thomas, and the Construction of Social Reality* (New York: Pantheon Books, 1992), 402–40.

4. Pauli Murray, *Song in a Weary Throat: An American Pilgrimage* (New York: Harper and Row, 1987), 183, 184.

5. Ibid.; Pauli Murray, "Why Negro Girls Stay Single," *Negro Digest,* July 1947, 4–8, excerpted in Mary Beth Norton and Ruth M. Alexander, eds., *Major Problems in American Women's History* (Lexington, Mass.: D.C. Heath, 2d ed., 1996), 404–7. Murray attributed sexism on the part of black men to the racism they experienced.

6. Murray, *Song in a Weary Throat,* 239, 360; Pauli Murray to Henry Schwarzchild, February 5, 1967, Papers of Dorothy Kenyon, Sophia Smith Collection, Smith College, Northampton, Mass., box 44, folder 431.

7. Sara Maitland, *A Map of the New Country: Women and Christianity* (London: Routledge and Kegan Paul, 1983), 92–93; Joan Martin, "Speaking Out from a Black Perspective," *Church Woman* 44 (November 1978): 11–13; Deborah Partridge Wolfe, "Women in the Church: The Crisis of Changing Identity and New Roles," *Church Woman* 41 (May 1975): 25; Katie Cannon, "When the Minister Is a Black Woman," *Church Woman* 44 (November 1978): 37 (her allusion is to the Supreme Court's decision on school desegregation). See also Jacquelyn Grant, "Black Women and the Church," in

Gloria T. Hull, Patricia Bell Scott, and Barbara Smith, eds., *All the Women Are White, All the Blacks Are Men, But Some of Us Are Brave: Black Women's Studies* (Old Westbury, N.Y.: Feminist Press, 1982), 141–52.

8. Theressa Hoover, "Black Women and the Churches: Triple Jeopardy," in Alice L. Hageman, ed., *Sexist Religion and Women in the Church: No More Silence!* (New York: Association Press, 1974), 63–69.

9. Pauli Murray to the Rt. Rev. Anson P. Stokes, October 19, 1969, Papers of Pauli Murray, Schlesinger Library, Radcliffe College, Cambridge, Mass. [hereafter Murray papers], box 122, folder 2185; Pauli Murray, Memorandum to the House of Bishops, the House of Deputies, Protestant Episcopal Church in the U.S., "Reflections on the Special General Convention, September 1969," 5, Murray papers, box 119, folder 2136.

10. " 'Some People Derive Their Energy from Struggle': Conversation with Eleanor Holmes Norton, New York City Human Rights Commissioner," *Civil Liberties Review* (Winter 1975): 92, 96.

11. Murray, *Song in a Weary Throat*, xx–xi, 229; Leila Rupp and Verta Taylor interview of Pauli Murray, June 16, 1983, 35, transcript in Leila Rupp's possession.

12. "Some People Derive Their Energy from Struggle," 96–97; Lynn Gilbert and Gaylen Moore, *Particular Passions: Talks with Women Who Have Shaped Our Times* (New York: Clarkson N. Potter, 1981), 145.

13. Eleanor Holmes Norton to Pauli [Murray], January 31, 1966, Murray papers, box 59, folder 999; Eleanor Holmes Norton to Pauli [Murray], April 1, 1966, Murray papers, folder 1000; Alan Reitman to Dorothy Kenyon, May 18, 1966, Murray papers, folder 1000.

14. "Memorandum: The Role of the Negro Women in the Civil Rights Revolution, August 27, 1963," Murray papers, box 94, folder 1644, 5, 6; Murray to Whitney M. Young, Jr., December 7, 1964, Murray papers, box 94, folder 1644, 5, 6; Anna Arnold Hedgeman, *The Gift of Chaos: Decades of American Discontent* (New York: Oxford University Press, 1977), 86.

15. "The Status of Women in the Church," May 9, 1969, Murray papers, box 139, folder 2536, 10; Pauli Murray, "Fair Play in the Shirley Chisholm Congressional Campaign," October 19, 1969, Anna Arnold Hedgeman to Pauli Murray, November 7, 1968, Aileen C. Hernandez to Shirley Chisholm, November 11, 1968, Murray papers, box 119, folder 2130.

16. Hoover, "Black Women and the Churches," 70.

17. Murray, *Song in a Weary Throat*, 397–416. See also Jean M. Humez, "Pauli Murray's Histories of Loyalty and Revolt," *Black American Literature Forum* 24 (Summer 1990): 324–26.

18. Murray, *Song in a Weary Throat*, 356; Maitland, *Map of the New Country*, 93.

19. Arthur D. Trottenberg to McGeorge Bundy, June 7, 1971, 5–6. Ford Foundation Archives [hereafter FFA], Report No. 006316; Affirmative Action Program for the Employment of Women and Minorities on the Professional Staff of the Ford Foundation: A Review and Analysis, February 1974, 9. FFA, Report No. 001984; "Recommendations for Women's Programs," October 1971. FFA, Report No. 002659; Starry Krueger "To Those Interested in Women's Issues," March 30, 1972, 2, 6. FFA, PA72-326.

20. Krueger, "To Those Interested in Women's Issues," March 30, 1972, 2, 6.

21. Concerned Minority Women at Ford, "New and Expanded Program for Minority Women," Memo from Mitchell Sviridoff to McGeorge Bundy, February 12, 1972, 2–4. FFA, Report No. 002460; "The Ford Foundation's Program in the Changing Role of Women: An Information Paper for the Trustees," March 7, 1973, A3–A4. FFA, Report No. 002255.

22. Concerned Minority Women at Ford, "New and Expanded Program for Minority Women," 2–3.

23. Maitland, *Map of the New Country*, 93.

24. Murray to Marguerite [Rawalt], April 14, 1964, Murray papers, box 135, folder 2456.

25. Pauli Murray to Kathryn Clarenbach, November 21, 1967, Murray papers, box 51, folder 899; Murray diary, November 21, 1967, and June 3, 1968, Murray papers, box 51, folder 899; Pauli Murray to Al [Reitman], November 24, 1971, Murray papers, box 2, folder 30V.

26. Murray to Clarenbach, November 21, 1967.

27. Murray to Clarenbach, November 21, 1967; Wilma [Scott Heide] to Pauli [Murray], July 20, 1970, Murray papers, box 51, folder 901; Bunny [Sandler] to Pauli Murray, October 15, 1970, and March 7, 1971, Murray papers, folders 2550, 2551; Pauli Murray to Aileen Hernandez, September 18, 1969, Murray papers, box 105, folder 1895; Pauli Murray to Elizabeth Duncan Koontz, September 22, 1969, Murray papers, box 97, folder 1725.

28. Anna Arnold Hedgeman to Kathryn Clarenbach and Betty Friedan,

September 13, 1967, Murray papers, box 51, folder 899; Martha F. Davis, "Welfare Rights and Women's Rights in the 1960s," *Journal of Policy History* 8 (1966), 144–65.

29. Hoover, "Black Women and the Churches," 74–75; "Some People Derive Energy from Their Struggle," 98; Eleanor Holmes Norton, "A Strategy for Change," in *Women's Role in Contemporary Society: The Report of the New York City Commission on Human Rights,* September 21–25, 1970 (New York: Avon Books, 1972), 60–61.

30. Pauli Murray to Marguerite Rawalt, February 2, 1966, Murray papers, box 59, folder 999; Pauli Murray testimony, U.S. Congress, House, Committee on Education and Labor, *Discrimination Against Women: Hearings Before the Special Subcommittee on Education of the Committee on Education and Labor,* 91st Cong., 2d sess. (June 19, 1970), 332.

31. Pauli Murray testimony, House, Committee on Education and Labor, *Discrimination Against Women,* 366–67; Pauli Murray to Richard Graham, March 28, 1966, Murray papers, box 55, folder 958; Pauli Murray to Thomas I. Emerson, February 1, 1966, Murray papers, box 59, folder 999; Pauli Murray, Memorandum to the House of Bishops, the House of Deputies, Protestant Episcopal Church in the U.S.A., "Reflections on the Special General Convention," September 1969, 2, 9, Murray papers, box 119, folder 2136.

32. Murray, *Song in a Weary Throat,* 314–17.

33. Murray, *Song in a Weary Throat,* 284–89, 360–61. The two projects supported by the Women's Division of the Methodist Church resulted in the publication of *States' Laws on Race and Color* in 1950 and *Human Rights U.S.A.: 1948–1966* in 1967.

34. Nell Irvin Painter explores the appropriation of a black woman by white feminists in *Sojourner Truth: A Life, a Symbol* (New York: W. W. Norton, 1996), 281–87. Glenda Elizabeth Gilmore, *Gender and Jim Crow: Women and the Politics of White Supremacy in North Carolina, 1896–1920* (Chapel Hill: University of North Carolina Press, 1996), 179–90, examines the life of Charlotte Hawkins Brown earlier in the twentieth century as "a parable of the possibilities and the personal costs of interracial cooperation."

35. Evelyn Brooks Higginbotham, *Righteous Discontent: The Women's Movement in the Black Baptist Church, 1880–1920* (Cambridge: Harvard University Press, 1993), 88–119; Gilmore, *Gender and Jim Crow,* 46–59, 170, 172; Jacquelyn Dowd Hall, *Revolt Against Chivalry: Jessie Daniel Ames and*

the *Women's Campaign Against Lynching* (New York: Columbia University Press, rev. ed., 1993), 66, 163; Susan Lynn, *Progressive Women in Conservative Times: Racial Justice, Peace, and Feminism, 1945 to the 1960s* (New Brunswick, N.J.: Rutgers University Press, 1992), 65.

36. Murray, *Song in a Weary Throat,* 285–86.

37. Margaret Shannon, *Just Because: The Story of the National Movement of Church Women United in the U.S.A., 1941 through 1975* (Corte Madera, Calif.: Omega Books, 1977), 116–37 (italics are mine); United Church Women, Executive Committee Minutes, October 1952, 11, CWU records, box 62, folder 1; Carrie E. Meares, "Three-Year Project: Assignment: Race 1961–1964," Confidential Reports I and II, CWU records, folder 6. See also James F. Findlay, Jr., *Church People in the Struggle: The National Council of Churches and the Black Freedom Movement, 1950–1970* (New York: Oxford University Press, 1993), 49–50; Virginia Brereton, "United and Slighted: Women as Subordinated Insiders," in William R. Hutchison, ed., *Between the Times: The Travail of the Protestant Establishment in America, 1900–1960* (Cambridge: Cambridge University Press, 1989), 154, 156.

38. Shannon, *Just Because,* 131–35; "Wednesdays in Mississippi, 1964–1965, Final Report," 25–26, CWU records, box 62, folder 15; Ruth Weber, "The New President," *Church Woman* (June–July 1971): 24.

39. Hedgeman, *Gift of Chaos,* 80, 101–2.

40. Commission on Woman in Today's World, Agenda, November 7, 1969, Murray papers, box 119, folder 2135.

41. Higginbotham, *Righteous Discontent,* 92; Lois A. Boyd and R. Douglas Brackenridge, *Presbyterian Women in America: Two Centuries of a Quest for Status* (Westport, Conn.: Greenwood Press, 2d ed., 1996), 55.

42. Author interviews with Susan Berresford, October 17, 1984, Mariam Chamberlain, October 14, 1984, and Gail Spangenberg, October 18, 1984; Krueger, "To Those Interested in Women's Issues," 7.

43. Maitland, *Map of the New Country,* 93.

44. For discussion of black women's construction of theory in their lives, see Elsa Barkley Brown, "Womanist Consciousness: Maggie Lena Walker and the Independent Order of Saint Luke," *Signs* 14 (Spring 1989): 631–32, and Collins, *Black Feminist Thought,* 15–16. Murray, *Song in a Weary Throat,* 356; U.S. Congress, Senate, Committee on the Judiciary, *Equal Rights 1970: Hearings before the Committee on the Judiciary,* 91st Cong., 2d sess. (September 9–15, 1970), 429.

45. Pauli Murray, "Black Theology and Feminist Theology," in Gayraud S. Wilmore and James H. Cone, eds., *Black Theology: A Documentary History, 1966–1979* (Maryknoll, N.Y.: Orbis Books, 1979), 398–417; Jacquelyn Grant, "Black Theology and the Black Woman," in *Black Theology*, 418–33; Katie Geneva Cannon, "The Emergence of Black Feminist Consciousness," in Letty M. Russell, ed. *Feminist Interpretation of the Bible* (Philadelphia: Westminster Press, 1985), 30–40; Martin, "Speaking Out from a Black Perspective," 13; Maitland, *A Map of the New Country*, 93.

46. Pauli Murray, "Memorandum: The Role of the Negro Women in the Civil Rights Revolution," August 27, 1963, Murray papers, box 94, folder 1644.

47. "Memorandum in Support of Retaining the Amendment to H.R. 7152," Murray papers, box 85, folder 1485; Pauli Murray to Richard Graham, March 28, 1966, Murray papers, box 55, folder 958; Office to the Equality Committee, April 13, 1966, Murray papers, box 55, folder 958.

48. Recommendations for Women's Programs, October 1971, 30–40. FFA, Report No. 0026549; Concerned Minority Women at Ford, "New and Expanded Program for Minority Women," 2.

49. Concerned Minority Women at Ford, "New and Expanded Program for Minority Women," 3; Mitchell Sviridoff to McGeorge Bundy, February 23, 1972, 2–4. FFA, Report No. 002460.

50. Margaret Shannon to Pauli Murray, August 15, 1969, Murray papers, box 119, folder 2136; Murray, "Some Queries," Murray papers, box 119, folder 2136; Church Women United, press release, September 26, 1969, NCC records, record group 5, box 17; Margaret Shannon to Dr. R. H. Edwin Espy et al., October 3, 1969, NCC records, record group 5, box 17.

51. CWU press release, September 26, 1969; Cannon, "When the Minister Is a Black Woman," 38. Again, it should be noted that these African American women anticipated theory subsequently developed by scholars about the importance of understanding the "relational nature" of differences among women. See Brown, " 'What Has Happened Here,' " 298–302.

52. Arthur D. Trottenberg to McGeorge Bundy, "The Role of Women in the Ford Foundation," June 7, 1971, 3, 6, 7. FFA, Report No. 006316; "Affirmative Action Program for the Employment of Women and Minorities on the Professional Staff of the Ford Foundation: A Review and Analysis," February 1974. FFA, Report 001984. Kathryn Mitchell was among the black women who moved into the professional ranks.

53. Beatrice Colebrooke to Harold Howe II, June 1, 1972. FFA, PA 72-326; Mariam Chamberlain to McGeorge Bundy, March 18, 1974. FFA, L73-418.

54. Pauli Murray to Alan Reitman, June 20, 1970, Murray papers, box 59, folder 1003; U.S. Congress, House, Committee on Education and Labor, *Discrimination Against Women,* Hearings Before the Special Subcommittee on Education, 91st Cong., 2d sess. (June 19, 1970, 365–66); Pauli Murray to Aileen [Hernandez], September 18, 1969, Murray papers, box 105, folder 1895; Pauli Murray to Norman Dorsen, September 12, 1969, Murray papers, box 59, folder 1002.

55. Gilmore, *Gender and Jim Crow,* 177, prompted my distinction between interracial work through personal connections and interracial work through institutional structures. Minutes, Unit Committee, Division of Education and Ministry, October 10–11, 1974, 3, Commission on Women in Ministry files, National Council of Churches, National Office [hereafter NCC-NO]; Organization for Commission on Women in Ministry, March 17, 1975, Commission on Women in Ministry files, NCC-NO; Summary of Proceedings, COWIM meeting, February 5–7, 1975, 3–4, and October 6–8, 1975, 3–4, 5, 10, Commission on Women in Ministry files, NCC-NO.

56. *Women's Role in Contemporary Society.*

57. Justice for Women Program Area, Annual Program Reports to DCS [Division of Church and Society] Program Planning and Evaluating Council, July 1979, July 1980, Justice for Women Files, NCC-NO; Martin, "Speaking Out from a Black Perspective," 13.

58. See, for example, Pauli Murray's testimony in Senate Committee on the Judiciary, *Equal Rights 1970,* 429, and Norton, "A Strategy for Change," 60. Pauli Murray to Sonia Pressman, August 12, 1968, Murray papers, box 128, folder 2332; Report of Church Women United to the General Board, June 6, 1968, CWU records, box 53, folder 32.

59. U.S. Congress, Joint Economic Committee, *Economic Problems of Women: Hearings Before the Joint Economic Committee, Part 3,* 93rd Cong., 1st sess. (1973), 548, 550.

60. Pauli Murray testimony, Senate, Committee on the Judiciary, *Equal Rights 1970,* 428–29. Murray's position on the ERA reflected her professional interest in legal change, her class position, and her relationships with white women for whom the ERA was important. For a discussion of the

ERA's failure to capture "a ground swell of Black support," see Giddings, *When and Where I Enter,* 340–88.

61. "Pauli Murray on Challenge to Structure," n.d. [ca. 1969], 2, CWU records, box 54, folder 20.

Chapter 7: Conclusion

1. Myra Marx Ferree and Beth B. Hess, *Controversy and Coalition: The New Feminist Movement Across Three Decades of Change* (New York: Twayne, 1994), 86–90.

2. Susan Douglas, *Where the Girls Are: Growing up Female with the Mass Media* (New York: Random House, 1994), 163–91; "The Henpecked House," *New York Times,* August 11, 1970.

3. See Bert Klandermans, "The Social Construction of Protest and Multiorganizational Fields," in Aldon D. Morris and Carol McClurg Mueller, eds., *Frontiers in Social Movement Theory* (New Haven: Yale University Press, 1992), 77–103.

4. Callahan, quoted in Brigid O'Farrell and Joyce L. Kornbluh, eds., *Rocking the Boat: Women, Unions, and Change, 1915–1975* (New Brunswick, N.J.: Rutgers University Press, 1996), 130.

5. Jo Freeman, *The Politics of Women's Liberation* (New York: David McKay, 1975), 204. Of course, Abzug's efforts, and those of sympathetic colleagues, were not always successful.

BIBLIOGRAPHY

Interviews

Berresford, Susan, conducted by author, October 17, 1984.

Callahan, Mary, conducted by Alice M. Hoffman and Karen Budd, May 7, 19, 26, 1976, Twentieth-Century Trade Union Woman: Vehicle for Social Change, Oral History Project, Institute of Labor and Industrial Relations, University of Michigan/Wayne State University.

Chamberlain, Mariam, conducted by author, October 14, 1984.

Cowap, Chris, conducted by author, October 15, 1984.

Eberhardt, Mae Massie, November 5, 1979, in Ruth Edmonds Hill, ed., *The Black Women Oral History Project,* vol. 3 (Westport, Conn.: Meckler, 1991), 229–75.

Johnson, Gloria, conducted by author, April 4, 1984.

Kenyon, Dorothy, June 14, 1971, Smith Centennial Study, Oral History Project, Sophia Smith Collection, Smith College, Northampton, Mass.

Mandel, Ruth, conducted by author, November 3, 1994.

Murray, Pauli, conducted by Leila Rupp and Verta Taylor, June 16, 1983, transcript in possession of Leila Rupp.

Newman, Winn, conducted by author, August 4, 1984.

Post, Suzanne, conducted by author, August 17, 1995.

Seidenberg, Faith, conducted by author, September 1, 1995.

Spangenberg, Gail, conducted by author, October 18, 1984.

Tobias, Sheila, conducted by author, November 10, 1994.

Weyand, Ruth, conducted by author, March 26, 1984, and August 2, 1984.

Manuscript Collections

American Civil Liberties Union Records and Publications, Microfilming Corporation of America, Sanford, N.C.

Church Women United records, General Commission on Archives and History, United Methodist Church, Drew University, Madison, N.J.

Church Women United records, national office, New York.

ERAmerica records, Library of Congress, Washington, D.C.

Ford Foundation Archives, New York.

International Union of Electrical Workers records, Special Collections and Archives, Rutgers University, New Brunswick, N.J.

National Consumers' League records, Library of Congress, Washington, D.C.

National Council of Churches of Christ in the U.S.A. records, national office, New York.

National Council of Churches of Christ in the U.S.A. records, Presbyterian Historical Society, Philadelphia.

National Council of Negro Women papers, National Archives for Black Women's History, Washington, D.C.

National Organization for Women papers, Schlesinger Library, Radcliffe College, Cambridge, Mass.

Papers of Dorothy Kenyon, Sophia Smith Collection, Smith College, Northampton, Mass.

Papers of Pauli Murray, Schlesinger Library, Radcliffe College, Cambridge, Mass.

Papers of Ruth Weyand, in possession of Ruth Weyand.

Papers of Winn Newman, in possession of Winn Newman.

Women's Equity Action League Fund papers, Schlesinger Library, Radcliffe College, Cambridge, Mass.

Periodical Publications of Organizations

American Civil Liberties Union, *Annual Report,* 1940–1980.

American Civil Liberties Union, *Civil Liberties,* 1965–1982.

Church Women United, *The Church Woman,* 1960–1980.

Ford Foundation, *Annual Report,* 1960–1985.

Ford Foundation, *Ford Foundation Letter,* 1970–1985.

International Union of Electrical Workers, Convention *Proceedings,* 1950–1980.

International Union of Electrical Workers, *IUE News,* 1960–1980.

National Council of the Churches of Christ, *NCCC Chronicles,* 1975–1985.

National Council of the Churches of Christ, *Triennial Reports,* 1960–1981.

Government Documents

Affirmative Action in the 1980s: Dismantling the Process of Discrimination; A Statement of the United States Commission on Civil Rights. Washington, D.C.: Government Printing Office, 1982.

Hearings Before the United States Equal Employment Opportunity Commission on Job Segregation and Wage Discrimination, April 28–30, 1980. Washington, D.C.: EEOC, 1980.

U.S. Congress. House. Committee on Education and Labor. Select Subcommittee on Labor. *Equal Pay for Equal Work.* 87th Cong., 2d sess., March 28, 1962.

U.S. Congress. House. Committee on Ways and Means. *General Tax Reform, Part 16.* 93rd Cong., 1st sess., April 13, 1973.

U.S. Congress. House. *Discrimination Against Women: Hearings Before the Special Subcommittee on Education of the Committee on Education and Labor.* 91st Cong., 2d sess., June 19, 1970.

U.S. Congress. Joint Economic Committee. *Economic Problems of Women: Hearings Before the Joint Economic Committee, Part 3.* 93rd Cong., 1st sess., 1973.

U.S. Congress. Senate. Committee on the Judiciary. *The "Equal Rights" Amendment: Hearings Before the Subcommittee on Constitutional Amendments of the Committee on the Judiciary.* 91st Cong., 2d sess., May 5–7, 1970.

U.S. Congress. Senate. Committee on the Judiciary. *Equal Rights 1970: Hearings on S.J. Res. 61 and S.J. Res. 231.* 91st Cong., 2d sess., September 15, 1970.

U.S. Congress. Senate. Subcommittee on Education of the Committee on Labor and Public Welfare. *Women's Educational Equity Act of 1973.* 93rd Cong., 1st sess., October 17, 1973.

U.S. Congress. Senate. Subcommittee on Labor of the Committee on

Human Resources. *Discrimination on the Basis of Pregnancy, 1977: Hearings.* 95th Cong., 1st sess., April 26–29, 1977.

Dissertations

Deslippe, Dennis Arthur. " 'Rights, Not Roses': Women, Industrial Unions, and the Law of Equality in the United States, 1945–80." Ph.D. diss., University of Iowa, 1984.

Kannenberg, Lisa. "From World War to Cold War: Women Electrical Workers and Their Union, 1940–1955." M.A. diss., University of North Carolina, Charlotte, 1990.

Weigand, Kate. "Vanguards of Women's Liberation: The Old Left and the Continuity of the Women's Movement in the United States, 1945–1970s." Ph.D. diss., Ohio State University, 1994.

Articles

Blankenship, Kim. "Bringing Gender and Race In: U.S. Employment Discrimination Policy." *Gender and Society* 7 (June 1993): 204–26.

Brereton, Virginia. "United and Slighted: Women as Subordinated Insiders." In *Between the Times: The Travail of the Protestant Establishment in America, 1900–1960,* ed. William R. Hutchison. Cambridge: Cambridge University Press, 1989.

Brown, Alex, and Laurie Sheridan. "Pioneering Women's Committee Struggles with Hard Times." *Labor Research Review* 7 (Spring 1988): 63–77.

Brown, Elsa Barkley. " 'What Has Happened Here': The Politics of Difference in Women's History and Feminist Politics." *Feminist Studies* 18 (Summer 1992): 295–312.

Bryner, Gary. "Congress, Courts, and Agencies: Equal Employment and the Limits of Policy Implementation." *Political Science Quarterly* 96 (1981): 411–30.

Calhoun, Susan. "New Ways to Lead." *Foundation News* 28 (November–December 1987): 24–29.

Cannon, Katie. "When the Minister Is a Black Woman." *Church Woman* 44 (November 1978): 36–38.

Cannon, Katie Geneva. "The Emergence of Black Feminist Consciousness."

In *Feminist Interpretation of the Bible,* ed. Letty M. Russell. Philadelphia: Westminster, 1985.

Chamberlain, Mariam K., and Alison Bernstein. "Philanthropy and the Emergence of Women's Studies." *Teachers College Record* 93 (Spring 1992): 556–68.

Cobble, Dorothy Sue. "Recapturing Working-Class Feminism: Union Women in the Postwar Era." In *Not June Cleaver: Women and Gender in Postwar America, 1945–1960,* ed. Joanne Meyerowitz. Philadelphia: Temple University Press, 1994.

Cowan, Ruth B. "Women's Rights Through Litigation: An Examination of the American Civil Liberties Union Women's Rights Project, 1971–1976." *Columbia Human Rights Law Review* 8 (1977): 373–412.

Crenshaw, Kimberle. "Whose Story Is it Anyway? Feminist and Antiracist Appropriations of Anita Hill." In *Race-ing Justice, En-gendering Power: Essays on Anita Hill, Clarence Thomas, and the Construction of Social Reality,* ed. Toni Morrison. New York: Pantheon, 1992.

Davis, Martha F. "Welfare Rights and Women's Rights in the 1960s." *Journal of Policy History* 8 (1966): 144–65.

Deslippe, Dennis A. " 'We Had an Awful Time with Our Women': Iowa's Packinghouse Workers of America, 1945–1975." *Journal of Women's History* 4 (Spring 1993): 10–32.

Freeman, Jo. "Resource Mobilization and Strategy: A Model for Analyzing Social Movement Organization Actions." In *The Dynamics of Social Movements,* ed. Mayer N. Zald and John D. McCarthy. Cambridge, Mass.: Winthrop, 1979.

Gerson, Ben. "Renaissance Woman: A Feminist Pioneer's Trail of Achievements." *National Law Journal,* September 27, 1982, 1, 24–25.

Ginsburg, Ruth Bader. "Gender in the Supreme Court: The 1973 and 1974 Terms." In *The Supreme Court Review,* ed. Philip Kurland. Chicago: University of Chicago Press, 1976.

Ginsburg, Ruth Bader. "The Status of Women." *American Journal of Comparative Law* 20 (1972): 585–91.

Glauberman, Susan. "A Conversation with Mariam Chamberlain and Fred Crossland." *Change* 13 (1981): 32–37.

Grant, Jacquelyn. "Black Theology and the Black Woman." In *Black Theology: A Documentary History, 1966–1979,* ed. Gayraud S. Wilmore and James H. Cone. Maryknoll, N.Y.: Orbis, 1979.

Grant, Jacquelyn. "Black Women and the Church." In *All the Women Are White, All the Blacks Are Men, But Some of Us Are Brave: Black Women's Studies,* ed. Gloria T. Hull, Patricia Bell Scott, and Barbara Smith. Old Westbury, N.Y.: Feminist Press, 1982.

Hams, Marcia. "Women Taking Leadership in Male-Dominated Locals." *Women's Rights Law Reporter* 8 (Winter 1984): 71–82.

Harris, Richard. "Annals of Law." *New Yorker,* April 19, 1976, 42–97.

Hartmann, Susan M. "Women's Issues and the Johnson Administration," In *The Johnson Years: LBJ at Home and Abroad,* ed. Robert A. Divine. Lawrence: University of Kansas Press, 1994.

Hewitt, Nancy A. "Compounding Differences." *Feminist Studies* 18 (Summer 1992): 313–26.

Higginbotham, Evelyn Brooks. "African-American History and the Metalanguage of Race." *Signs* 17 (Winter 1992): 251–74.

Hoover, Theressa. "Black Women and the Churches: Triple Jeopardy." In *Sexist Religion and Women in the Church: No More Silence!* ed. Alice L. Hageman. New York: Association Press, 1974.

Howe, Harold II. "Sex, Sports, and Discrimination." *Chronicle of Higher Education,* June 18, 1979.

Hoyman, M. "Alternative Models of Policy Compliance by Unions with Civil Rights Legislation." *Law and Policy* 8 (January 1986): 77–103.

Humez, Jean M. "Pauli Murray's Histories of Loyalty and Revolt." *Black American Literature Forum* 24 (Summer 1990): 324–26.

Jenkins, J. Craig. "Nonprofit Organizations and Policy Advocacy." In *The Nonprofit Sector: A Research Handbook,* ed. Walter W. Powell. New Haven: Yale University Press, 1987.

Jenkins, J. Craig. "Resource Mobilization Theory and the Study of Social Movements." *Annual Reviews in Sociology* 9 (1983): 527–53.

Kannenberg, Lisa. "The Impact of the Cold War on Women's Trade Union Activism: The UE Experience." *Labor History* 34 (Summer 1993): 309–23.

Katzenstein, Mary Fainsod. "Discursive Politics and Feminist Activism in the Catholic Church." In *Feminist Organizations: Harvest of the New Women's Movement,* ed. Myra Marx Ferree and Patricia Yancey Martin. Philadelphia: Temple University Press, 1995.

Katzenstein, Mary Fainsod. "Feminism Within American Institutions: Unobtrusive Mobilization in the 1980s." *Signs* 16 (Autumn 1990): 27–54.

King, Deborah K. "Multiple Jeopardy, Multiple Consciousness: The Context of a Black Feminist Ideology." *Signs* 14 (Autumn 1988): 42–72.

Klandermans, Bert. Introduction to "Interorganizational Networks." Part 4 of Bert Klandermans, ed., *International Social Movement Research: A Research Annual* 2 (1989): 301–14.

Klandermans, Bert. "The Social Construction of Protest and Multiorganizational Fields." In *Frontiers in Social Movement Theory*, ed. Aldon D. Morris and Carol McClurg Mueller. New Haven: Yale University Press, 1992.

McCarthy, John D., and Mark Woodson. "Consensus Movements, Conflict Movements, and the Cooptation of Civic and State Infrastructures." In *Frontiers in Social Movement Theory*, ed. Aldon D. Morris and Carol McClurg Mueller. New Haven: Yale University Press, 1992.

McColloch, Mark. "The Shop-Floor Dimension of Union Rivalry: The Case of Westinghouse in the 1950s." In *The CIO's Left-Led Unions*, ed. Steve Rosswurm. New Brunswick, N.J.: Rutgers University Press, 1992.

Mann, Jim. "Hard Times for the ACLU." *New Republic*, April 15, 1978, 14.

Markowitz, Deborah L. "In Pursuit of Equality: One Woman's Work to Change the Law." *Women's Rights Law Reporter* 11 (Summer 1989): 73–97.

Martin, Joan. "Speaking out from a Black Perspective." *Church Woman* 44 (November 1978): 11–13.

Murray, Pauli. "Black Theology and Feminist Theology." In *Black Theology: A Documentary History, 1966–1979*, ed. Gayraud S. Wilmore and James H. Cone. Maryknoll, N.Y.: Orbis, 1979.

Murray, Pauli. "The Liberation of Black Women." In *Voices of the New Feminism*, ed. Mary Lou Thompson. Boston: Beacon, 1970.

Murray, Pauli, and Mary O. Eastwood. "Jane Crow and the Law: Sex Discrimination and Title VII." *George Washington Law Review* 34 (December 1965): 232–56.

Musil, Caryn McTighe, and Ruby Sales. "Funding Women's Studies." In *Transforming the Curriculum: Ethnic Studies and Women's Studies*, ed. Johnella E. Butler and John C. Walter. Albany: State University of New York Press, 1991.

Nelson, Bruce. "Class, Race and Democracy in the CIO: The 'New' Labor History Meets the 'Wages of Whiteness.'" *International Review of Social History* 41 (December 1996): 351–74.

Newman, Winn. "The Policy Issues: Presentation III." *Signs* 1 (Spring 1976): 265–72.

Newman, Winn, and Jeanne M. Vonhof. " 'Separate but Equal'—Job Segregation and Pay Equity in the Wake of *Gunther.*" *University of Illinois Law Review* (1981): 269–331.

Newman, Winn, and Carole W. Wilson. "The Union Role in Affirmative Action." *Labor Law Journal* 32 (June 1981): 323–42.

O'Connor, Karen, and Lee Epstein. "The Importance of Interest Group Involvement in Employment Discrimination Litigation." *Howard Law Journal* 25 (1982): 709–29.

Pilpel, Harriet F. "Birth Control and a New Birth of Freedom." *Ohio State Law Journal* 27 (1966): 679–90.

Pilpel, Harriet F. "The Challenge of Privacy." In *The Price of Liberty,* ed. Alan Reitman. New York: Norton, 1968.

Pilpel, Harriet F. "The Crazy Quilt of Our Birth Control Laws." *Journal of Sex Research* 1 (July 1965): 135–42.

Pilpel, Harriet F., and Dorothy E. Patton. "Abortion, Conscience and the Constitution: An Examination of Federal Institutional Conscience Clauses." *Columbia Human Rights Law Review* 6 (1974–75): 279–305.

Robinson, Donald Allen. "Two Movements in Pursuit of Equal Employment Opportunity." *Signs* 4 (Spring 1979): 413–33.

Rosenberg, Rosalind. "Pauli Murray and the Killing of Jane Crow." In *Forgotten Heroes from America's Past,* ed. Susan Ware. New York: Free Press, 1998.

Russell, Avery. "The Women's Movement and Foundations." *Foundation News* 13 (November–December 1972): 16–22.

"Ruth Bader Ginsburg." In *Particular Passions: Talks with Women Who Have Shaped Our Times,* ed. Lynn Gilbert and Gaylen Moore. New York: Clarkson N. Potter, 1981.

Saario, Terry N., Carol Nagy Jacklin, and Carol Kehr Tittle. "Sex Role Stereotyping in the Public Schools." *Harvard Educational Review* 43 (August 1973): 386–416.

Strauss, Susan R. "Strategy for Failure: Affirmative Action in a Mass Production Context." In *Union Voices: Labor's Responses to Crisis,* ed. Glenn Adler and Doris Suarez. Albany: State University of New York Press, 1993.

Tully, Mary Jean. "Funding the Feminists." *Foundation News* 16 (March–April 1975): 24–33.

Useem, Bert, and Mayer N. Zald. "From Pressure Group to Social Movement: Efforts to Promote Use of Nuclear Power." In *Social Movements in an Organizational Society: Collected Essays,* ed. Mayer N. Zald and John D. McCarthy. New Brunswick, N.J.: Transaction, 1987.

Von Drehle, David. "The Quiet Revolutionary." *Washington Post National Weekly Edition,* July 26–August 1, 1993, 6–9.

Wolfe, Deborah Partridge. "Women in the Church: The Crisis of Changing Identity and New Roles." *Church Woman* 41 (May 1975): 23–26.

Zahavi, Gerald. "Passionate Commitments: Race, Sex, and Communism at Schenectady General Electric, 1932–1954." *Journal of American History* 83 (September 1966): 514–48.

Books

Babcock, Barbara Allen, Ann E. Freedman, Eleanor Holmes Norton, and Susan C. Ross. *Sex Discrimination and the Law: Causes and Remedies.* Boston: Little, Brown, 1975.

Berger, Margaret A. *Litigation on Behalf of Women: A Review for the Ford Foundation.* New York: Ford Foundation, 1980.

Billingsley, K. L. *From Mainline to Sideline: The Social Witness of the National Council of Churches.* Washington, D.C.: Ethics and Public Policy Center, 1990.

Blum, Linda M. *Between Feminism and Labor: The Significance of the Comparable Worth Movement.* Berkeley: University of California Press, 1991.

Boles, Janet K. *The Politics of the Equal Rights Amendment: Conflict and the Decision Process.* New York: Longman, 1979.

Boyd, Lois A., and R. Douglas Brackenridge. *Presbyterian Women in America: Two Centuries of a Quest for Status.* 1983. 2d ed. Westport, Conn.: Greenwood, 1996.

Buechler, Steven M. *Women's Movements in the United States: Woman Suffrage, Equal Rights, and Beyond.* New Brunswick, N.J.: Rutgers University Press, 1990.

Carden, Maren Lockwood. *Feminism in the Mid-1970s: A Report to the Ford Foundation.* New York: Ford Foundation, 1977.

Collins, Patricia Hill. *Black Feminist Thought: Knowledge, Consciousness, and the Politics of Empowerment.* New York: Routledge, 1990.

Copp, Terry. *The IUE in Canada: A History.* Elora, Ont.: Cumnock, 1980.

Costain, Anne N. *Inviting Women's Rebellion: A Political Process Interpretation of the Women's Movement.* Baltimore: Johns Hopkins University Press, 1992.

Created Equal: A Report on Ford Foundation Women's Programs. New York: Ford Foundation, 1986.

Cunningham, Sarah, ed. *We Belong Together: Churches in Solidarity with Women.* New York: Friendship Press, 1992.

Davis, Flora. *Moving the Mountain: The Women's Movement Since 1960.* New York: Simon and Schuster, 1991.

Douglas, Susan. *Where the Girls Are: Growing up Female with the Mass Media.* New York: Random House, 1994.

Echols, Alice. *Daring to Be Bad: Radical Feminism in America, 1967–1975.* Minneapolis: University of Minnesota Press, 1989.

Evans, Sara. *Personal Politics: The Roots of Women's Liberation in the Civil Rights Movement and the New Left.* New York: Vintage, 1979.

Ferree, Myra Marx, and Beth Hess. *Controversy and Coalition: The New Feminist Movement.* Rev. ed. Boston: Twayne, 1994.

Findlay, James F. *Church People in the Struggle: The National Council of Churches and the Black Freedom Movement, 1950–1970.* New York: Oxford University Press, 1993.

Freeman, Jo. *The Politics of Women's Liberation: A Case Study of an Emerging Social Movement and Its Relation to the Policy Process.* New York: David McKay, 1975.

Gabin, Nancy. *Feminism in the Labor Movement: Women Workers and the United Auto Workers, 1935–1975.* Ithaca, N.Y.: Cornell University Press, 1990.

Garrow, David. *Liberty and Sexuality: The Right to Privacy and the Making of Roe v. Wade.* New York: Macmillan, 1994.

Gelb, Joyce, and Marion Lief Palley. *Women and Public Policies.* Princeton, N.J.: Princeton University Press, 1982.

Giddings, Paula. *When and Where I Enter: The Impact of Black Women on Race and Sex in America.* New York: Bantam, 1985.

Gilbert, Lynn, and Gaylen Moore. *Particular Passions: Talks with Women Who Have Shaped Our Times.* New York: Clarkson N. Potter, 1981.

Gilmore, Glenda Elizabeth. *Gender and Jim Crow: Women and the Politics of White Supremacy in North Carolina, 1896–1920.* Chapel Hill: University of North Carolina Press, 1996.

Gould, William B. *Black Workers in White Unions: Job Discrimination in the United States.* Ithaca, N.Y.: Cornell University Press, 1977.

Graham, Hugh Davis. *The Civil Rights Era: Origins and Development of National Policy, 1960–1972.* New York: Oxford University Press, 1990.

Greenberg, Jack. *Crusaders in the Courts: How a Dedicated Band of Lawyers Fought for the Civil Rights Revolution.* New York: Basic, 1994.

Griffith, Elisabeth. *In Her Own Right: The Life of Elizabeth Cady Stanton.* New York: Oxford University Press, 1984.

Halberstam, David. *The Best and the Brightest.* Greenwich, Conn.: Fawcett, 1973.

Hall, Jacquelyn Dowd. *Revolt Against Chivalry: Jessie Daniel Ames and the Women's Campaign Against Lynching.* Rev. ed. New York: Columbia University Press, 1993.

Harrison, Cynthia. *On Account of Sex: The Politics of Women's Issues, 1945–1968.* Berkeley: University of California Press, 1988.

Hedgeman, Anna Arnold. *The Gift of Chaos: Decades of American Discontent.* New York: Oxford University Press, 1977.

Higginbotham, Evelyn Brooks. *Righteous Discontent: The Women's Movement in the Black Baptist Church, 1880–1920.* Cambridge: Harvard University Press, 1993.

hooks, bell. *Talking Back: Thinking Feminist, Thinking Black.* Boston: South End Press, 1989.

Hoover, Theressa. *With Unveiled Face: Centennial Reflections on Women and Men in the Community of the Church.* New York: Women's Division, General Board of Global Ministries, United Methodist Church, 1983.

Hutner, Frances C. *Equal Pay for Comparable Worth: The Working Woman's Issue of the Eighties.* New York: Praeger, 1986.

Kessler-Harris, Alice. *A Woman's Wage: Historical Meanings and Social Consequences.* Lexington: University of Kentucky Press, 1990.

Klein, Ethel. *Gender Politics: From Consciousness to Mass Politics.* Cambridge: Harvard University Press, 1984.

Levy, Peter B. *The New Left and Labor in the 1960s.* Urbana: University of Illinois Press, 1994.

Linden-Ward, Blanche, and Carol Hurd Green. *American Women in the 1960s: Changing the Future.* New York: Twayne, 1993.

Lynn, Susan. *Progressive Women in Conservative Times: Racial Justice, Peace, and Feminism, 1945 to the 1960s*. New Brunswick, N.J.: Rutgers University Press, 1992.

McAdam, Doug. *Political Process and the Development of Black Insurgency, 1930–1970*. Chicago: University of Chicago Press, 1982.

McCann, Michael W. *Rights at Work: Pay Equity Reform and the Politics of Legal Mobilization*. Chicago: University of Chicago Press, 1994.

McKay, Robert B. *Nine for Equality Under Law: Civil Rights Litigation, a Report to the Ford Foundation*. New York: Ford Foundation, 1977.

Magat, Richard. *The Ford Foundation at Work: Philanthropic Choices, Methods, and Styles*. New York: Plenum, 1979.

Maitland, Sara. *A Map of the New Country: Women and Christianity*. London: Routledge and Kegan Paul, 1983.

Maschke, Karen J. *Litigation, Courts, and Women Workers*. New York: Praeger, 1989.

Mathews, Donald G., and Jane Sherron De Hart. *Sex, Gender, and the Politics of ERA: A State and the Nation*. New York: Oxford University Press, 1990.

Mead, Margaret, and Frances Balgley Kaplan. *American Women: The Report of the President's Commission on the Status of Women and Other Publications of the Commission*. New York: Scribner's, 1965.

Milkman, Ruth. *Gender at Work: The Dynamics of Job Segregation by Sex During World War II*. Urbana: University of Illinois Press, 1987.

Morris, Aldon D., and Carol McClurg Mueller, eds. *Frontiers in Social Movement Theory*. New Haven: Yale University Press, 1992.

Morton, Nelle. *The Journey Is Home*. Boston: Beacon, 1985.

Murray, Pauli. *Song in a Weary Throat: An American Pilgrimage*. New York: Harper and Row, 1987.

Nielsen, Waldemar A. *The Big Foundations*. New York: Columbia University Press, 1972.

Nielsen, Waldemar A. *The Golden Donors: A New Anatomy of the Great Foundations*. New York: Dutton, 1985.

O'Connor, Karen. *Women's Organizations' Use of the Courts*. Lexington, Mass.: Heath, 1980.

O'Farrell, Brigid, and Joyce L. Kornbluh. *Rocking the Boat: Women, Unions, and Change, 1915–1975*. New Brunswick, N.J.: Rutgers University Press, 1996.

Painter, Nell Irvin. *Sojourner Truth: A Life, a Symbol.* New York: Norton, 1996.

Paterson, Judith. *Be Somebody: A Biography of Marguerite Rawalt.* Austin, Tex.: Eakin Press, 1986.

Petchesky, Rosalind Pollack. *Abortion and Woman's Choice: The State, Sexuality, and Reproductive Freedom.* Boston: Northeastern University Press, 1985.

Powell, Walter W., ed. *The Nonprofit Sector: A Research Handbook.* New Haven: Yale University Press, 1987.

Pratt, Henry J. *The Liberalization of American Protestantism: A Case Study in Complex Organizations.* Detroit: Wayne State University Press, 1972.

Reichley, A. James. *Religion in American Public Life.* Washington, D.C.: Brookings Institution, 1985.

Reilly, Philip R. *The Surgical Solution: A History of Involuntary Sterilization in the United States.* Baltimore: Johns Hopkins University Press, 1991.

Rupp, Leila, and Verta Taylor. *Survival in the Doldrums: The American Women's Rights Movement, 1945 to the 1960s.* New York: Oxford University Press, 1987.

Russell, Letty M., ed. *The Liberating Word: A Guide to Nonsexist Interpretation of the Bible.* Philadelphia: Westminster, 1976.

Schatz, Ronald W. *The Electrical Workers: A History of Labor at General Electric and Westinghouse, 1923–1960.* Urbana: University of Illinois Press, 1983.

Shannon, Margaret. *Just Because: The Story of the National Movement of Church Women United in the U.S.A., 1941 Through 1975.* Corte Madera, Calif.: Omega, 1977.

Shapiro, Thomas M. *Population Control Politics: Women, Sterilization and Reproductive Choice.* Philadelphia: Temple University Press, 1985.

Spelman, Elizabeth V. *Inessential Woman: Problems of Exclusion in Feminist Thought.* Boston: Beacon, 1988.

Staggenborg, Susan. *The Pro-Choice Movement: Organization and Activism in the Abortion Conflict.* New York: Oxford University Press, 1991.

That 51 Per Cent: Ford Foundation Activities Related to Opportunities for Women. New York: Ford Foundation, 1974.

That 51 Per Cent . . . Plus: A Ford Foundation Report. New York: Ford Foundation, 1979.

Tilly, Charles. *From Mobilization to Revolution.* Reading, Mass.: Addison-Wesley, 1978.

Tinker, Irene, ed. *Women in Washington: Advocates for Public Policy.* Beverly Hills, Calif.: Sage, 1983.

Walker, Samuel. *In Defense of American Liberties: A History of the ACLU.* New York: Oxford University Press, 1990.

Wandersee, Winifred D. *On the Move: American Women in the 1970s.* Boston: Twayne, 1988.

Weaver, Mary Jo. *New Catholic Women: A Contemporary Challenge to Traditional Church Authority.* New York: Harper and Row, 1996.

Wedel, Cynthia. *Employed Women and the Church.* New York: National Council of Churches of Christ in the U.S.A., 1959.

Willard, Frances E. *Glimpses of Fifty Years: The Autobiography of an American Woman.* Chicago: Woman's Temperance Publication Association, 1889.

Women's Role in Contemporary Society: The Report of the New York City Commission on Human Rights, September 21–25, 1970. New York: Avon, 1972.

Zald, Meyer N., and John D. McCarthy, eds. *Social Movements in an Organizational Society: Collected Essays.* New Brunswick, N.J.: Transaction, 1987.

Zieger, Robert. *The CIO, 1935–1955.* Chapel Hill: University of North Carolina Press, 1995.

INDEX

Morrison, Toni, 176
Mothers, single, 149, 167, 168, 188, 200
Ms. (magazine), 135
Murray, Pauli, 12, 33, 68, 89, 119, 138, 163, 178, 197, 202, 235n36; promotes women's legal equality, 5, 53, 54, 61–66, 71–74, 76–82 *passim,* 85, 183, 210; and formal women's movement, 5, 80, 177, 189–90, 191, 192, 204; career, 62, 83, 179–80, 183–84; links women's rights to civil rights, 65, 74, 186, 190, 192, 198–99, 205, 206, 211; interracial connections, 192–95
Myrdal, Alva, 156

National Abortion Rights Action League, 9, 70–71, 89, 211
National Association for the Advancement of Colored People, 45, 137; Legal Defense and Education Fund, 56, 162, 163
National Association of Office Workers, 169
National Association of Women Lawyers, 65
National Black Feminist Organization, 194
National Coalition for Women and Girls in Education, 161
National Committee on Household Employment, 167, 168
National Council of Churches (NCC), 1, 133, 135, 138, 145, 155, 210–15 *passim;* feminist initiatives in, 5, 8, 10, 11, 12, 13, 102–31 *passim;* black women and 6, 95, 103, 115, 119–21, 177, 181, 188, 191, 194, 196, 201, 202–4, 205; Justice for Women program, 11, 113, 115–17, 118, 197, 214; relations with Church Women United, 96, 97, 98–102; women's caucus, 96, 102–5, 106, 108, 109, 112, 115, 123, 178, 182, 213; position of women in, 99, 102, 103–4, 106–9, 202, 213; Commission on Women in Ministry, 113, 115, 117–23, 203, 214; Task Force on Ethnic Women in Ministry, 119, 203; Task Force on Gay Women in Ministry, 121
National Council of Negro Women, 35, 98
National Education Association, 174
National Federation of Business and Professional Women, 65
National Labor Relations Board, 23, 35, 36–37
National Organization for Women (NOW), 1, 15, 34, 56, 58, 120, 133, 139, 144, 148, 211, 212; origins, 2, 3, 4, 16, 54, 63; agenda, 7, 45, 48, 70, 89, 110, 204; membership and resources, 9, 159; Legal Defense and Education Fund, 46, 85, 160–62, 163, 190; members active in ACLU, 55, 75, 76, 78, 82, 90; and African American women, 177, 189–91, 197

DATE DUE

DEC 19			
DEC 18 2001			
Nov. 24, 01			
DEC 22 2001			
GAYLORD			PRINTED IN U.S.A.